FILM AND LITERATURE: CONTRASTS IN MEDIA

FILM AND LITERATURE: CONTRASTS IN MEDIA

Fred H. Marcus, comp. 1921-

CHANDLER PUBLISHING COMPANY
An Intext Publisher • Scranton / London / Toronto

Copyright © 1971 by Chandler Publishing Company.
All rights reserved. Printed in the United States of America.
Library of Congress Catalog Card Number 78-139779
International Standard Book Number 0-8102-0409-6

Previously published and copyrighted materials are reprinted with the permission of authors, publishers, or copyright owners as listed below.

Rudolf Arnheim, *Film As Art,* © 1957 R. Arnheim; originally published by the University of California Press; reprinted by permission of The Regents of the University of California (passage quoted in Robert Richardson, "Verbal and Visual Languages").

Selections from Bela Balázs, *Theory of the Film* (London, Dobson Books Ltd., 1952), reprinted by permission of the publishers.

Martin C. Battestin, "Osborne's *Tom Jones:* Adapting a Classic," from *Man and the Movies,* ed. W. R. Robinson (Baton Rouge: Louisiana State University Press, 1967). Reprinted in paperback by Penguin Books, Ltd.

George Bluestone, "The Grapes of Wrath," from *Novels into Film* (Berkeley and Los Angeles: University of California Press, 1957) Copyright © 1957 The Johns Hopkins Press. Reprinted by permission.

Lee R. Bobker, "The Art of Film Editing," from *Elements of Film* by Lee R. Bobker, © 1969 by Harcourt Brace Jovanovich, Inc. and reprinted with their permission.

Albert R. Cirillo, "The Art of Franco Zeffirelli and Shakespeare's *Romeo and Juliet,*" reprinted by permission of *TriQuarterly,* Northwestern University, Evanston Illinois.

Donald P. Costello, "Pygmalion," from *The Serpent's Eye* (Notre Dame: University of Notre Dame Press, 1965). Reprinted by permission of the publisher.

Raymond Durgnat, "The Mongrel Muse," from *Films and Feeling.* Reprinted by permission of Faber and Faber, Ltd. American edition published by MIT Press.

"Tone and Point of View" in *The Film Experience* by Roy Huss and Norman Silverstein. Copyright © 1968 by Roy Huss and Norman Silverstein. Reprinted by permission of Harper & Row, Publishers.

"The Concealed Art of Carol Reed" from *Going Steady,* by Pauline Kael, by permission of Atlantic-Little, Brown and Co. Copyright © 1968, 1969, 1970 by Pauline Kael.

Notices of copyright in materials included in this book are continued on the page facing this, which is hereby incorporated into this page for the purpose of the Copyright Law (Title 17, U.S.C., § 20).

For Joel Marcus

CONTENTS

ILLUSTRATIONS

PREFACE

We live in the golden age of film. Cinematic art flourishes today much as painting, sculpture, and architecture flowered during the Italian Renaissance. Spurred by a youthful zest for exhilarating movie experiences and an accelerating technology, the decade of the 1960s represented a mighty peak in a superb mountain range of motion pictures.

Film thrives in our culture. The "film generation" (16-24) has been weaned on moving images. Directors like Antonioni, Fellini, Godard, Bergman, Richardson, Schlesinger, Buñuel, Nichols, and Kurosawa are acclaimed nationally and internationally. Film festivals grace cities and campuses. Creative youth no longer seek to write the great American novel; they are out shooting the great American film. Cinema societies sprout; film courses and curricula expand dramatically on both college and high school campuses. Belatedly, an American Film Institute modeled on the prestigious British Film Institute lends its increasing stature to the development of archives and financial aid to experimental filmmakers and those engaged in film-related activities.

Social conversations center on movies—from *La Dolce Vita* to *Bonnie and Clyde,* from *Tom Jones* to *Romeo and Juliet,* from 8½ to *Catch-22,* from *Last Year at Marienbad* to *Midnight Cowboy,* from *The Virgin Spring* to *Blow-Up,* from *2001: A Space Odyssey* to *Easy-Rider.* Movie critics cease to be anonymous. Judith Crist, Bosley Crowther, Pauline Kael, Stanley Kauffmann, and Dwight Macdonald are names eagerly attached to advertising blurbs. University presses and influential journals publish books and articles on film theory, directorial styles and influences as well as critical studies. Experimentation with the film medium ranges across a broad spectrum—animation techniques, cinema verité, low-budget features dealing with sex, drugs, et al. more candidly than ever before, and utilizing techniques that have paced television commercials.

National tendencies in film reveal some interesting differences. References to the "new wave" or the *auteur* theory conjure up young

French directors. Italy's 1940 and 1950 neo-realism emphasized social problems; the leading Italian filmmakers are still realists, but far more they are individualists turning toward the experience of "being" and repressing the feeling of play-acting. The British retain a potent concern for social problems and an awareness of changing—or unchanging —institutions. Their films frequently stem from literary sources; the lusty and vibrant dominance of drama in Elizabethan England, dormant after its magnificent maturity, showed signs of re-emerging in the "school of anger" in the mid-1950s. But it is film that sparks much English creativity today.

Since *Rashomon* burst upon the Western world, the Japanese have had success exploring sources in their earlier culture; from these sources, universal themes have emerged. More and more, however, the zenith of film development is attributable to the creative directors now dominating the industry. Most of them transcend parochial national limitations. Bergman and Buñuel dramatically illustrate this point. Changes are occurring in Russia as their contemporary directors aspire to the reputation of an earlier age when Sergei Eisenstein was shaking the film world. A number of modern American directors have outgrown the studio provinciality that was a Hollywood trademark. The search for realism and the decline of censorship are significant contributors to the contemporary film scene.

In this anthology, the two separate sections seem to suggest a dichotomy. But readers will quickly discover that the writers on "the art of film" support many of their perceptions and generalizations with copious reference to specific motion pictures. The critics' individual insights add up to a mosaic of film theory. The opening section serves two other major purposes. Embedded within the articles and book extracts, one encounters much of "the language of film," in contexts that clarify that language. Secondly, the section aims at historical perspective. The first two authors are among the most august names in the entire history of film criticism, and their insights remain substantive. The next group of theorists writes from the perspective of the late 1960s. Their articles and books recur in serious film bibliographies; they are anthologized; they write well and knowledgeably. The last two writers complement each other. Both have written extensively and both are astute observers of the film world. Father Schillaci's essay, which appeared in the *Saturday Review*, draws upon films that are still part of the social discussions focusing on movies. In logical historical sequence, Kauffmann examines the "new American cinema," the avant-garde whose experimental film efforts may color the decade of the 1970s.

Alternatively, the reader who begins with the second section may well find the inductive method closer to his taste. Beginning with "contrasts in media" written by movie critics, film-oriented professors, and theorists of cinematic art, the analyses in part two contain a substantial body of current film theory. Moving to the first section after reading section two, the reader may find "the art of film" more fully comprehensible, since he now brings an additional dimension to his reading.

While the major emphasis of part two centers on contrasts between movies and the literary sources from which they were adapted, three of the selections could easily have been placed in the opening section. Richardson, Linden, and Nicoll have written excellent books in which the film medium and literary medium are contrasted. Moreover, their theoretical observations are buttressed by detailed examples from motion pictures. Richardson's chapter was chosen deliberately so that a reader starting with the second section will encounter a brilliant general account of the differences and similarities in the verbal and visual arts. Linden's book probes deeply into the subject of film aesthetics. Moreover, he uses the able teacher's device of examining a failure in media transformation for illustrative purposes. Allardyce Nicoll's chapter, from a book published in 1936 (light-years away in the history of film), is one of the most illuminating chapters ever written on film and drama.

Among the "contrasts in media" explications, the novel receives and merits the most attention, since the novel is the literary form most commonly adapted to film. Dramatic literature follows, while short stories have not served, numerically, as the original impetus for many feature length films. Since many excellent movies have been transformed from literary sources, it becomes an excellent focal point for the anthology. Anyone plunging into any part of this book should be dissuaded very quickly from a much too common tendency, a tendency to assume that a literal "following the book" is useful for assessing movies. Many people seem to feel that books are automatically superior to films. Therefore, they expect directors simply to detach book details and attach them to movies. In Elizabethan England, Shakespeare's plays for the groundlings received the same disdainful response from the Latinists of his day.

While it is easy to assert that a book is verbal and a film primarily visual, such assertions may mean very little in practice to a reader not well-versed in the implications of the truism. For example, many friends I have asked seem to think that film has more in common with a play than with a novel. Yet, the judgment is completely inaccurate. A playgoer watching a dramatic performance has a fixed point of vision; he cannot observe tiny details, whatever symbolic significance such details might have. The film director, in contrast, has an arsenal of technical versatility available. He may use angle shots to create desired effects; he may use close-ups for his purposes; he can cut from character to

character; he can eliminate whatever will not serve his intent. Structurally, the play builds in scenes and acts; these are large building blocks.
The movie director uses hundreds of shots with a wide latitude for
juxtaposing them. He builds a mosaic with gaps to which he can return
at will. The novelist comes much closer to the filmmaker on these points.
The reader of a novel proceeds at his own choice of pace; he can return
to re-examine particulars. Moreover, he can put the novel down and
return. The film viewer does not control the speed of the unreeling
film. Film pace is pre-determined by the film director.

The novelist may write a narrative or a descriptive sentence, but
because words are arranged in fixed linear sequence, he cannot do both
simultaneously. The filmmaker *can* communicate narrative and descriptive elements simultaneously; he would, however, find it very difficult
to communicate some abstract ideas, since film shots are concrete. One
example may suffice. A filmmaker turning to the opening line of Hawthorne's novel, *The Scarlet Letter,* finds:

> A throng of bearded men, in sad-colored garments, and gray,
> steeple-crowned hats, intermixed with women, some wearing
> hoods and others bare-headed, was assembled in front of a wooden
> edifice, the door of which was heavily timbered with oak, and
> studded with iron spikes.

The filmmaker encountering this statement would have a vast
array of alternatives available to him. If, however, he read the next
sentence, he would find:

> The founders of a new colony, whatever Utopia of human virtue
> and happiness they might originally project, have invariable recog-
> nized it among their earliest practical necessities to allot a portion
> of the virgin soil as a cemetery, and another portion as the site of
> a prison.

While Hawthorne uses verbal irony to conjoin Utopia and prison, it
would be rather more difficult for the film director to find visual equivalents. Thus, verbal abstraction can not always find a visual equivalent.

The sheer bulk of many novels—and Shakespearean plays—de-
crees that films adapted from such sources must necessarily condense,
delete, and alter the sources to fit the Procrustean bed of film length.
Excellent directors expect to add invented visuals with an immediacy
of impact. Illustrations of such invention by gifted directors fill the
"contrasts in media" section.

What films come to mind that have weathered the processes of transformation and adaptation? In the decade of the 1960s, *Romeo and Juliet, Goodbye, Columbus, Ulysses, Tom Jones, Sons and Lovers, The Loneliness of the Long Distance Runner, The Graduate, Z, Zorba the Greek, In Cold Blood, Becket, A Man for All Seasons, Midnight Cowboy,* and *Catch-22* are surely representative of quality movies. An earlier time period would augment these with *All Quiet on the Western Front, Hamlet* (Olivier's), *The Grapes of Wrath, All the King's Men, Henry V, Rashomon,* and *The Informer.* Given the filmmaker's proclivity for utilizing literary sources, and given the great significance and power of modern films, the dual focus of this anthology becomes apparent.

THE ART OF FILM

1

Bela Balázs

from *THEORY OF THE FILM*

Balázs, an eminent early theorist on film art, recognized the significance of motion pictures as a communication force. In these short segments from his *Theory of the Film,* he anticipates current cinema criticism. *Der Sichtbare Mensch (The Visible Man),* written in 1923, welcomed the silent visual film, contrasting it even then with a print-oriented culture.

IN PRAISE OF THEORY

Dangers of Ignorance

We all know and admit that film art has a greater influence on the minds of the general public than any other art. The official guardians of culture note the fact with a certain amount of regret and uneasiness. But too few of us are sufficiently alive to the dangers that are an inevitable consequence of this fact. Nor do we realize clearly enough that we must be better connoisseurs of the film if we are not to be as much at the mercy of perhaps the greatest intellectual and spiritual influence of our age as to some blind and irresistible elemental force. And unless we study its laws and possibilities very carefully, we shall not be able to control and

From Bela Balázs, *Theory of the Film* (London: Dobson Books Ltd., 1952)

direct this potentially greatest instrument of mass influence ever devised in the whole course of human cultural history. One might think
that the theory of this art would naturally be regarded as the most important field for present-day art theory. No one would deny today that
the art of the motion picture is *the* popular art of our century — unfortunately not in the sense that it is the product of the popular spirit but the
other way round, in the sense that the mentality of the people, and particularly of the urban population, is to a great extent the product of this
art, an art that is at the same time a vast industry. Thus the question of
educating the public to a better, more critical appreciation of the films
is a question of the mental health of the nations. Nevertheless, too few
of us have yet realized how dangerously and irresponsibly we have
failed to promote such a better understanding of film art.

Why Are People Not Taught To Appreciate Films?

Nowadays social considerations are taken into account in the cultural
sphere no less than in others. Nevertheless, the aesthetics of the film
are nowhere included in the official teaching of art appreciation. Our
academies have sections for literature and every established art, but
none for the new art of our day — the film. It was not until 1947 that the
first film maker was elected to the French *Académie*. At our universities
there are chairs for literature and all arts except that of the film. The
first art academy which included the theory of film art in its curriculum
was opened in Prague in 1947. The textbooks used in our secondary
schools discuss the other arts but say nothing of the film. Millions hear
about the aesthetics of literature and painting who will never make use
of such knowledge because they read no books and look at no pictures.
But the millions who frequent the movies are left without guidance —
no one teaches them to appreciate film art.

Need for General Culture

There are numerous film schools in the world and no one denies that
there may be need of a theory of the film — for specialists. In Paris, in
London, and elsewhere, film institutes and scientific film societies have
been formed to study the "science" of the film. But what is needed is
not specialized knowledge; it is a general level of culture. No one who
had not the faintest conception of literature or music would be considered well educated. A man who had never heard of Beethoven or
Michelangelo would be out of place among people of culture. But if he
has not the faintest idea of the rudiments of film art and had never heard
of Asta Nielsen or David Wark Griffith, he might still pass for a well-
educated, cultured person, even on the highest level. The most important
art of our time is that about which one need know nothing whatever. And

yet it is an urgent need that we should cultivate enough discrimination to influence the art which shapes the popular taste in the highest degree. Until there is a chapter on film art in every textbook on the history of art and on aesthetics; until the art of the film has a chair in our universities and a place in the curriculum of our secondary schools, we shall not have firmly established in the consciousness of our generation this most important artistic development of our century.

DER SICHTBARE MENSCH*

The invention of printing gradually rendered illegible the faces of men. So much could be read from paper that the method of conveying meaning by facial expression fell into desuetude.

Victor Hugo wrote once that the printed book took over the part played by the cathedral in the Middle Ages and became the carrier of the spirit of the people. But the thousands of books tore the *one* spirit, embodied in the cathedral, into thousands of opinions. The word broke the stone into a thousand fragments, tore the church into a thousand books.

The visual spirit was thus turned into a legible spirit and visual culture into a culture of concepts. This of course had its social and economic causes, which changed the general face of life. But we paid little attention to the fact that, in conformity with this, the faces of individual men, their foreheads, their eyes, their mouths, had also of necessity and quite concretely to suffer a change.

At present a new discovery, a new machine is at work to turn the attention of men back to a visual culture and give them new faces. This machine is the cinematographic camera. Like the printing press, it is a technical device for the multiplication and distribution of products of the human spirit; its effect on human·culture will not be less than that of the printing press.

For not to speak does not mean that one has nothing to say. Those who do not speak may be brimming over with emotions which can be expressed only in forms and pictures, in gesture and play of feature. . . . The gestures of visual man are not intended to convey concepts which can be expressed in words, but such inner experiences, such nonrational emotions as would still remain unexpressed when everything that can be told has been told. Such emotions lie in the deepest levels of the soul and cannot be approached by words that are mere reflections of concepts; just as our musical experiences cannot be expressed in rationalized

*This excerpt is taken from Balázs' book, *Der Sichtbare Mensch* (The Visible Man), written in 1923.

concepts. What appears on the face and in facial expression is a spiritual experience which is rendered immediately visible without the intermediary of words.

In the golden age of the old visual arts, the painter and sculptor did not merely fill empty space with abstract shapes and forms, and man was not merely a formal problem for the artist. . . . The artist could present in its primary form of manifestation the soul's bodily incarnation in gesture or feature. But since then the printing press has grown to be the main bridge over which the more remote inter-human spiritual exchanges take place and the soul has been concentrated and crystallized chiefly in the word. There was no longer any need for the subtler means of expression provided by the body. For this reason our bodies grew soulless and empty — what is not in use deteriorates.

The expressive surface of our body was thus reduced to the face alone and this not merely because the rest of the body was hidden by clothes. For the poor remnants of bodily expression that remained to us the little surface of the face sufficed, sticking up like a clumsy semaphore of the soul and signaling as best it could. Sometimes a gesture of the hand was added, recalling the melancholy of a mutilated torso. In the epoch of word culture the soul learned to speak but had grown almost invisible. Such was the effect of the printing press.

Now the film is about to inaugurate a new direction in our culture. Many million people sit in the picture houses every evening and purely through vision, experience happenings, characters, emotions, moods, even thoughts, without the need for many words. For words do not touch the spiritual content of the pictures and are merely passing instruments of as yet undeveloped forms of art. Humanity is already learning the rich and colorful language of gesture, movement and facial expression. . . . Man has again become visible.

. . . The now developing art of facial expression and gesture will bring just as many submerged contents to the surface. Although these human experiences are not rational, conceptual contents, they are nevertheless neither vague nor blurred, but as clear and unequivocal as is music. Thus the inner man, too, will become visible.

But the old visible man no longer exists today and the new visible man is not yet in existence. As I have said before, it is the law of nature that unused organs degenerate and disappear, leaving only rudiments behind. The animals that do not chew lose their teeth. In the epoch of word culture we made little use of the expressive powers of our body and have therefore partly lost that power. The gesturing of primitive peoples is frequently more varied and expressive than that of the educated European whose vocabulary is infinitely richer. A few more years of film art and our scholars will discover that cinematography enables them to compile encyclopedias of facial expression, movement and gesture, such as have long existed for words in the shape of dictionaries. The public, however, need not wait for the gesture encyclopedia and grammars of future academies; it can go to the pictures and learn it there.

We had, however, when we neglected the body as a means of expression, lost more than mere corporal power of expression. That which was to have been expressed was also narrowed down by this neglect. For it is not the same spirit, not the same soul that is expressed once in words and once in gestures. Music does not express the same thing as

Great Expectations (1947) ". . . the language of gestures is far more individual and personal than the language of words . . ." Gluttony, disapproval, excessiveness: all are conveyed by gesture within a single frame. (Still by courtesy of The Rank Organization, Ltd.)

poetry in a different way—it expresses something quite different. When we dip the bucket of words in the depths, we bring up other things than when we do the same with gestures. But let no one think that I want to bring back the culture of movement and gesture in place of the culture of words, for neither can be a substitute for the other. Without a rational, conceptual culture and the scientific development that goes with it there can be no social and hence no human progress. The connecting tissue of modern society is the word spoken and written, without which all organization and planning would be impossible. . . .

But the language of the gestures is far more individual and personal than the language of words, although facial expression, too, has its habitual forms and conventionally accepted interpretations, to such an extent that one might—and should—write a comparative "gesturology" on the model of comparative linguistics. Nevertheless this language of facial expression and gesture, although it has a certain generally accepted tradition, lacks the severe rules that govern grammar and by the grace of our academies are compulsory for us all. No school prescribes that you must express your cheerfulness by this sort of smile and your bad humor with that sort of wrinkled brow. There are no punishable errors in this or that facial expression, although children doubtless do observe and imitate such conventional grimaces and gestures. On the other hand, these are more immediately induced by inner impulses than are words. Yet it will probably be the art of the film after all which may bring together the peoples and nations, make them accustomed to each other, and lead them to mutual understanding. The silent film is free of the isolating walls of language differences. If we look at and understand each other's faces and gestures, we not only understand, we also learn to feel each other's emotions. . . .

THE CLOSE-UP

. . . the basis of the new form-language is the moving cinematographic camera with its constantly changing viewpoint. The distance from the object and with it the size and number of objects in the frame, the angle and the perspective all change incessantly. This movement breaks up the object before the camera into *sectional pictures,* or "shots," irrespective of whether that object is moving or motionless. Sectional pictures are not details of a whole film. For what is being done is not to break up into its constituent parts a picture already taken or already envisaged. The result of this would be detail; in this case one would have to show every group and every individual in a crowd scene from the same angle as the one from which they are seen in the total picture; none of the people or things could move — if they did, they would no longer be details of the same total. What is done is not to break up into detail an already existent, already formed total picture, but to show a living, moving scene or landscape as a synthesis of sectional pictures, which merge in our consciousness into a total *scene* although they are not the parts of an existent immutable mosaic and could never be made into a total single *picture*.

What Holds the Sectional Picture Together?

The answer to this question is: the montage or cutting, the mobile composition of the film, an architecture in time, not space, of which much more is to be said later. For the time being we are interested in the psychological question of why a scene broken up into sectional pictures does not fall apart but remains a coherent whole, remains in the consciousness of the spectator a consistent unity in both space and time. How do we know that things are happening simultaneously and in the same place, even though the pictures pass before our eyes in temporal sequence and show a real passing of time?

This unity and the simultaneity of pictures proceeding in time is not produced automatically. The spectator must contribute an association of ideas, a synthesis of consciousness and imagination to which the film-going public had first to be educated. This is that visual culture of which we have spoken in previous chapters.

But the sectional picture (or "shot") must be correctly ordered and composed. There may be shots which slip out of the whole and in respect of which we no longer feel that we are in the same place and see the same scene as in the preceding shots. This is a matter for the director, who can, if he chooses, make the spectator feel the continuity of the scene, its unity in time and space even if he has never once shown him a total picture of the whole scene for his orientation.

This is done by including in every shot a movement, a gesture, a form, a something which refers the eye to the preceding and following shots, something that protrudes into the next shot like the branch of a tree or a fence, like a ball that rolls from one frame to the other, a bird that flies across, cigar smoke that curls in both, a look or gesture to which there is an answer in the next shot. But the director must be on his guard not to change the angle together with the direction of movement — if he does, the change in the picture is so great as to break its unity. The sound film has simplified this job of remaining in step. For sound can always be heard in the whole space, in each shot. If a scene is enacted, say, in a night club, and we hear the same music we will know that we are in the same night club even if in the shot itself we see nothing but a hand holding a flower or something of the sort. But if we suddenly hear different sounds in this same shot of a hand we will assume, even if we don't see it, that the hand holding the flower is now in a quite different place. For instance, to continue the picture of the hand holding the rose — if instead of dance music we now hear the twittering of birds, we will not be surprised if, when the picture widens into a long shot, we see a garden and the owner of the hand picking roses. This sort of change-over offers opportunities for good effects.

Sound Is Indivisible
This totally different nature of sound has a considerable influence on the composition, montage and dramaturgy of the sound film. The sound camera cannot break up sound into sections or shots as the cinematographic camera can break up objects. In space, sound is always heard indivisibly and homogeneously; that is, it has the same character in one part of space as in any other; it can only be louder or softer, closer or more distant and mixed with other sounds in differing ways. In the night club, for instance, we may first hear only dance music and then the loud talking and laughter of a noisy company at one of the tables may almost drown it.

Sound In Space
All sound has an identifiable place in space. By its timbre we can tell whether it is in a room, or a cellar, in a large hall or in the open air. This possibility of placing sound also helps to hold together shots the action of which takes place in the same space. The sound film has educated our ear — or might and should have educated it — to recognize the timbre of sound. But we have made less progress in our aural than in our visual education. In any case, the sound film which could use sound as its artistic material in a similar way as the silent film had used the visual impression was soon superseded by the talkie, which was in a sense a step backward toward the photographed theater.

The Face of Things
The first new world discovered by the film camera in the days of the silent film was the world of very small things visible only from very short distances, the hidden life of little things. By this the camera showed us not only hitherto unknown objects and events: the adventures of beetles in a wilderness of blades of grass, the tragedies of day-old chicks in a corner of the poultry-run, the erotic battles of flowers and the poetry of miniature landscapes. It brought us not only new themes.

By means of the close-up the camera in the days of the silent film revealed also the hidden mainsprings of a life which we had thought we
already knew so well. Blurred outlines are mostly the result of our in-
sensitive shortsightedness and superficiality. We skim over the teeming
substance of life. The camera has uncovered that cell-life of the vital
issues in which all great events are ultimately conceived; for the greatest
landslide is only the aggregate of the movements of single particles. A
multitude of close-ups can show us the very instant in which the general
is transformed into the particular. The close-up has not only widened
our vision of life, it has also deepened it. In the days of the silent film
it not only revealed new things, but showed us the meaning of the old.

Visual Life

The close-up can show us a quality in a gesture of the hand we never
noticed before when we saw that hand stroke or strike something, a
quality which is often more expressive than any play of the features.
The close-up shows your shadow on the wall with which you have lived
all your life and which you scarcely knew; it shows the speechless face
and fate of the dumb objects that live with you in your room and whose
fate is bound up with your own. Before this you looked at your life as a
concertgoer ignorant of music listens to an orchestra playing a sym-
phony. All he hears is the leading melody; all the rest is blurred into a
general murmur. Only those can really understand and enjoy the music
who can hear the contrapuntal architecture of each part in the score.
This is how we see life: only its leading melody meets the eye. But a
good film with its close-ups reveals the most hidden parts in our polyph-
onous life, and teaches us to see the intricate visual details of life as one
reads an orchestral score.

Lyrical Charm of the Close-Up

The close-up may sometimes give the impression of a mere naturalist
preoccupation with detail. But good close-ups radiate a tender human
attitude in the contemplation of hidden things, a delicate solicitude, a
gentle bending over the intimacies of life-in-the-miniature, a warm sensibility. Good close-ups are lyrical; it is the heart, not the eye, that has
perceived them.

Close-ups are often dramatic revelations of what is really happening
under the surface of appearances. You may see a medium shot of someone sitting and conducting a conversation with icy calm. The close-up
will show trembling fingers nervously fumbling a small object — sign of
an internal storm. Among pictures of a comfortable house breathing a
sunny security, we suddenly see the evil grin of a vicious head on the

carved mantelpiece or the menacing grimace of a door opening into darkness. Like the leitmotiv of impending fate in an opera, the shadow of some impending disaster falls across the cheerful scene.

Close-ups are the pictures expressing the poetic sensibility of the director. They show the faces of things and those expressions on them which are significant because they are reflected expressions of our own subconscious feeling. Herein lies the art of the true cameraman.

THE FACE OF MAN

The basis and possibility of an art of the film is that everyone and everything looks what it is

. . . When we see the face of things, we do what the ancients did in creating *gods* in man's image and breathing a human soul into them. The close-ups of the film are the creative instruments of this mighty visual anthropomorphism.

What was more important, however, than the discovery of the physiognomy of things was the discovery of the human face. Facial expression is the most subjective manifestation of man, more subjective even than speech. This most subjective and individual of human manifestations is rendered objective in the close-up.

2

V. I. Pudovkin

from *FILM TECHNIQUE AND FILM ACTING*

Writing in Russian during the twenties, Pudovkin reads like a basic primer for modern cinematographers, particularly in the crucial area of film editing. A fine filmmaker himself, he illustrates perceptive observations with concrete examples. In the annals of film criticism and theory, he towers above most movie critics.

METHODS OF TREATMENT OF THE MATERIAL

Structural Editing

A cinematograph film, and consequently also a scenario, is always divided into a great number of separate pieces (more correctly, it is built out of these pieces). The sum of the shooting script is divided into sequences, each sequence into scenes, and, finally, the scenes themselves are constructed from a whole series of pieces (script scenes) shot from various angles. An actual scenario, ready for use in shooting, must take

From V. I. Pudovkin, *Film Technique and Film Acting,* trans. Ivor Montagu (London: Vision Press Ltd., 1958)

13

into account this basic property of the film. The scenarist must be able to write his material on paper exactly as it will appear upon the screen, thus giving exactly the content of each shot as well as its position in sequence. The construction of a scene from pieces, a sequence from scenes, and reel from sequences, and so forth, is called *editing*. Editing is one of the most significant instruments of effect possessed by the film technician and, therefore, by the scenarist also. Let us now become acquainted with its methods one by one.

EDITING OF THE SCENE

Everyone familiar with a film is familiar with the expression "close-up." The alternating representation of the faces of the characters during a dialogue; the representation of hands, or feet, filling the whole screen — all this is familiar to everyone. But in order to know how properly to use the close-up, one must understand its significance, which is as follows: The close-up directs the attention of the spectator to that detail which is, at the moment, important to the course of the action. For instance, three persons are taking part in a scene. Suppose the significance of this scene consists in the *general* course of the action (if, for example, all three are lifting some heavy object); then they are taken simultaneously in a *general* view, the so-called long shot. But suppose any one of them changes to an independent action having significance in the scenario (for example, separating himself from the others, he draws a revolver cautiously from his pocket); then the camera is directed on him alone. His action is recorded separately.

What is said above applies not only to persons, but also to separate parts of a person, and objects. Let us suppose a man is to be taken apparently listening calmly to the conversation of someone else, but actually restraining his anger with difficulty. The man crushes the cigarette he holds in his hand, a gesture unnoticed by the other. This hand will always be shown on the screen separately, in close-up, otherwise the spectator will not notice it and a characteristic detail will be missed. The view formerly obtained (and is still held by some) that the close-up is an "interruption" of the long shot. This idea is entirely false. It is no sort of interruption. It represents a proper form of construction.

In order to make clear to oneself the nature of the process of editing a scene, one may draw the following analogy. Imagine yourself observing a scene unfolded in front of you, thus: A man stands near the wall of a house and turns his head to the left; there appears another man slinking cautiously through the gate. The two are fairly widely distant from one another — they stop. The first takes some object and shows it to the other, mocking him. The latter clenches his fists in a rage and throws himself at the former. At this moment a woman looks out of a window on the third floor and calls, "Police!" The antagonists run off in opposite directions. Now, how would this have been observed?

1. The observer looks at the first man. He turns his head.

2. What is he looking at? The observer turns his glance in the same direction and sees the man entering the gate. The latter stops.

3. How does the first react to the appearance on the scene of the second? A new turn by the observer; the first takes out an object and mocks the second.

4. How does the second react? Another turn; he clenches his fists and throws himself on his opponent.

5. The observer draws aside to watch how both opponents roll about fighting.

6. A shout from above. The observer raises his head and sees the woman at the window shouting.

7. The observer lowers his head and sees the result of the warning — the antagonists running off in opposite directions.

The observer happened to be standing near and saw every detail, saw it clearly, but to do so he had to turn his head, first left, then right, then upward, whithersoever his attention was attracted by the interest of observation and the sequence of the developing scene. Suppose he had been standing farther away from the action, taking in the two persons and the window on the third floor simultaneously, he would have received only a general impression, without being able to look separately at the first, the second, or the woman. Here we have approached closely the basic significance of editing. Its object is the showing of the development of the scene in relief, as it were, by guiding the attention of the spectator now to one, now to the other separate element. The lens of the camera replaces the eye of the observer, and the changes of angle of the camera—directed now on one person, now on another, now on one detail, now on another—must be subject to the same conditions as those of the eyes of the observer. The film technician, in order to secure the greatest clarity, emphasis, and vividness, shoots the scene in separate pieces and, joining them and showing them, directs the attention of the spectator to the separate elements, compelling him to see as the attentive observer saw. From the above the manner in which editing can even work upon the emotions is clear. Imagine to yourself the excited observer of some rapidly developing scene. His agitated glance is thrown rapidly from one spot to another. If we imitate this glance with the camera we get a series of pictures, rapidly alternating pieces, creating a *stirring scenario editing construction*. The reverse would be long pieces changing by mixes, conditioning a calm and slow editing construction (as one may shoot, for example, a herd of cattle wandering along a road, taken from the viewpoint of a pedestrian on the same road).

We have established, by these instances, the basic significance of the constructive editing of scenes. It builds the scenes from separate pieces, of which each concentrates the attention of the spectator only on that element important to the action. The sequence of these pieces must not be uncontrolled, but must correspond to the natural transference of attention of an imaginary observer (who, in the end, is represented by the spectator). In this sequence must be expressed a special logic that will be apparent only if each shot contains an impulse toward transference of the attention to the next. For example, (1) a man turns his head and looks; (2) what he looks at is shown.

EDITING OF THE SEQUENCE

The guidance of the attention of the spectator to different elements of the developing action in succession is, in general, characteristic of the film. It is its basic method. We have seen that the separate scene, and often even the movement of one man, is built up upon the screen from separate pieces. Now, the film is not simply a collection of different scenes. Just as the pieces are built up into scenes endowed, as it were, with a connected action, so the separate scenes are assembled into groups forming whole sequences. The sequence is constructed (edited) from scenes. Let us suppose ourselves faced with the task of constructing the following sequence: Two spies are creeping forward to blow up a powder magazine; on the way one of them loses a letter with instructions. Someone else finds the letter and warns the guard, who appears in time to arrest the spies and save the magazine. Here the scenarist has to deal with simultaneity of various actions in several different places. While the spies are crawling toward the magazine, someone else finds the letter and hastens to warn the guard. The spies have nearly reached their objective; the guards are warned and rushing toward the magazine. The spies have completed their preparations; the guard arrives in time. If we pursue the previous analogy between the camera and an observer, we now not only have to turn it from side to side, but also to move it from place to place. The observer (the camera) is now on the road shadowing the spies, now in the guardroom recording the confusion, now back at the magazine showing the spies at work, and so forth. But, in combination of the separate scenes (editing), the former law of sequence succession remains in force. A consecutive sequence will appear upon the screen only if the attention of the spectator be transferred correctly from scene to scene. And this correctness is conditioned as follows: The spectator sees the creeping spies, the loss of the letter, and finally the person who finds the letter. The person with the letter rushes for help. The spectator is seized with inevitable excitement — Will the man who found the letter be able to forestall the explosion? The scenarist immediately answers by showing the spies nearing the magazine — his answer has the effect of a warning, "Time is short." The excitement of the spectator — Will they be in time? — continues; the scenarist shows the guard turning out. Time is very short — the spies are shown beginning their work. Thus, transferring attention now to the rescuers, now to the spies, the scenarist answers with actual impulses to increase the spectator's interest, and the construction (editing) of the sequence is correctly achieved. . . .

One must learn to understand that editing is in actual fact a compulsory and deliberate guidance of the thoughts and associations of the spectator. If the editing be merely an uncontrolled combination of the various pieces, the spectator will understand (apprehend) nothing from it; but if it be co-ordinated according to a definitely selected course of events or conceptual line, either agitated or calm, it will either excite or soothe the spectator.

EDITING OF THE SCENARIO

. . . The scenario is composed of a series of sequences. In discussing the construction (editing) of the scenario from sequences, we introduce a new element into the scenarist's work — the element of so-called dramatic continuity of action. . . . The continuity of the separate sequences when joined together depends not merely upon the simple transference of attention from one place to another, but is conditioned by the development of the action forming the foundation of the scenario. It is important, however, to remind the scenarist of the following point: A scenario has always in its development a moment of greatest tension, found nearly always at the end of the film. To prepare the spectator, or, more correctly, preserve him, for this final tension, it is especially important to see that he is not affected by unnecessary exhaustion during the course of the film. . . .

Thus, first the action of the scenario is worked out, the action is then worked out into sequences, the sequences into scenes, and these constructed by editing from the pieces, each corresponding to a camera angle.

EDITING AS AN INSTRUMENT OF IMPRESSION

Relational Editing

We have already mentioned, in the section on editing of sequences, that editing is not merely a method of the junction of separate scenes or pieces, but is a method that controls the "psychological guidance" of the spectator. We should now acquaint ourselves with the main special editing methods having as their aim the impression of the spectator.

Contrast. — Suppose it be our task to tell of the miserable situation of a starving man; the story will impress more vividly if associated with mention of the senseless gluttony of a well-to-do man.

On just such a simple contrast relation is based the corresponding editing method. On the screen the impression of this contrast is yet increased, for it is possible not only to relate the starving sequence to the gluttony sequence, but also to relate separate scenes and even separate shots of the scenes to one another, thus, as it were, forcing the spectator to compare the two actions all the time, one strengthening the other. The editing of contrast is one of the most effective, but also one of the commonest and most standardized, of methods, and so care should be taken not to overdo it.

Parallelism. — This method resembles contrast but is considerably wider. Its substance can be explained more clearly by an example. In a scenario as yet unproduced a section occurs as follows: A workingman, one of the leaders of a strike, is condemned to death; the execution is fixed for 5 A.M. The sequence is edited thus: A factory owner, employer of the condemned man, is leaving a restaurant drunk; he looks at his wrist watch: four o'clock. The accused is shown — he is being made ready to be led out. Again the manufacturer; he rings a doorbell to ask the time: four-thirty. The prison wagon drives along the street under heavy guard. The maid who opens the door — the wife of the condemned — is subjected to a sudden senseless assault. The drunken factory owner snores on a bed, his leg with trouser end upturned, his hand hanging down with wrist watch visible; the hands of the watch crawl slowly to five o'clock. The workman is being hanged. In this instance two thematically unconnected incidents develop in parallel by means of the watch that tells of the approaching execution. The watch on the wrist of the callous brute, as it were, connects him with the chief protagonist of the approaching tragic denouement, thus ever present in the consciousness of the spectator. This is undoubtedly an interesting method, capable of considerable development.

Symbolism. — In the final scenes of the film *Strike,* the shooting of workmen is punctuated by shots of the slaughter of a bull in a stockyard.

The scenarist, as it were, desires to say: Just as a butcher fells a bull with the swing of a pole-axe, so, cruelly and in cold blood, were the workers shot down. This method is especially interesting because, by means of editing, it introduces an abstract concept into the consciousness of the spectator without use of a title.

Simultaneity. — In American films the final section is constructed from the simultaneous rapid development of two actions, in which the outcome of one depends on the outcome of the other. . . . The whole aim of this method is to create in the spectator a maximum tension of excitement by the constant forcing of a question such as, in this case, Will they be in time? Will they be in time?

This method is a purely emotional one, and nowadays overdone almost to the point of boredom, but it cannot be denied that of all the methods of constructing the end hitherto devised it is the most effective.

Leitmotiv (reiteration of theme). — Often it is interesting for the scenarist especially to emphasize the basic theme of the scenario. For this purpose the method of reiteration exists. Its nature can easily be demonstrated by an example. In an antireligious scenario that aimed at exposing the cruelty and hypocrisy of the Church in the employ of the Tsarist regime the same shot was several times repeated: a church bell slowly ringing and, superimposed on it, the title, "The sound of bells sends into the world a message of patience and love." This piece appeared whenever the scenarist desired to emphasize the stupidity of patience, or the hypocrisy of the love thus preached.

The little that has been said above of relational editing naturally by no means exhausts the whole abundance of its methods. It has merely been important to show that constructional editing, a method specifically and peculiarly filmic, is, in the hands of the scenarist, an important instrument of impression. Careful study of its use in pictures, combined with talent, will undoubtedly lead to the discovery of new possibilities and, in conjunction with them, to the creation of new forms.

THE ENVIRONMENT OF THE FILM

All the action of any scenario is immersed in some environment that provides, as it were, the general color of the film. This environment may, for example, be a special mode of life. By more detailed examination, one may even regard as the environment some separate peculiarity, some special essential trait of the given mode of life selected. This environment, this color, cannot, and must not be rendered by one explanatory scene or a title; it must constantly pervade the whole film, or its appropriate part, from beginning to end. As I have said, the action must be immersed in this background. A whole series of the best films

of recent times has shown that this emphasis by means of an environment in which the action is immersed is quite easily effected in cinematography. . . .

A wonderful example, affording unquestionably an achievement of
this kind, are the pictures of the misty dawn rising over the corpse of
the murdered sailor in *The Battleship Potemkin.* The solution of these
problems — the depiction of the environment — is an undoubted and important part of the work on the scenario. And this work naturally cannot be carried out without direct participation by the director. Even a
simple landscape — a piece of nature so often encountered in films — must,
by some inner guiding line, be bound up with the developing action.

I repeat that the film is exceptionally economical and precise in
its work. There is, and must be, in it no superfluous element. There is
no such thing as a neutral background, and every factor must be col-
lected and directed upon the single aim of solving the given problems.
For every action, insofar as it takes place in the real world, is always
involved in general conditions — that is, the nature of the environment.

The action of the scenes may take place by day or by night. Film
directors have long been familiar with this point, and the effort to render
night effects is to this day an interesting problem for film directors. One
can go further. The American, Griffith, succeeded in the film *America*
in obtaining, with marvelous tenderness and justness, gradations of
twilight and morning. The director has a mass of material at his disposal
for this kind of work. The film is interesting, as said before, not only in
that it is able to concentrate on details, but also in its ability to weld
to a unity numerous materials, deriving from widely embraced sources.

As example, this same morning light: To gain this effect, the director can use not only the growing light of sunrise, but also numerous
correctly selected, characteristic processes that infallibly relate themselves with approaching dawn in the apprehension of the spectator. The
light of lampposts growing paler against the lightening sky, the silhouettes of scarcely visible buildings, the tops of trees tenderly touched with
the light of the not yet ascended sun, awakening birds, crowing cocks,
the early morning mist, the dew — all this can be employed by the director, shot, and in editing built to a harmonious whole.

In one film an interesting method was used of representing the
filmic image of a dawn. In order to embrace in the editing construction
the feeling of growing and ever wider expanding light, the separate
shots follow one another in such wise that at the beginning, when it is
still dark, only details can be seen upon the screen. The camera took only
close-ups, as if, like the eye of man in the surrounding dark, it saw only
what was near to it. With the increase of the light the camera became
ever more and more distant from the object shot. Simultaneously with
the broadening of the light, broader and broader became the view field

embraced by the lens. From the close-ups in darkness the director changed to ever more distant long shots, as if he sought directly to render the increasing light, pervading everything widely and more widely. It is notable that here is employed a pure technical possibility, peculiar only to the film, of communicating a very subtle feeling.

It is clear that work on the solution of problems of this kind is bound up so closely with the knowledge of film technique, so organically with the pure directorial work of analysis, selection of the material, and its unification in creative editing, that such problems cannot, independently of the director, be resolved for him by the scenarist alone. At the same time, it is, as already mentioned, absolutely essential to give the expression of this environment in which the action of every film is immersed, and accordingly, in the creation of the scenario, it is indispensable for the director to collaborate in the work.

THE CHARACTERS IN THE ENVIRONMENT

I should like to note that in the work of one of the strongest directors of the present day, David Griffith, in almost every one of his films, and indeed especially in those in which he has reached the maximum expression and power, it is almost invariably the case that the action of the scenario develops among characters blended directly with that which takes place in the surrounding world.

The stormy finale of the Griffith film is so constructed as to strengthen for the spectator the conflict and the struggle of the heroes to an unimagined degree, thanks to the fact that the director introduces into the action gale, storm, breaking ice, rivers in spate, a gigantic roaring waterfall. When Lillian Gish, in *Way Down East,* runs broken from the house, her happiness in ruins, and the faithful Barthelmess rushes after her to bring her back to life, the whole pursuit of love behind despair, developing in the furious tempo of the action, takes place in a fearful snowstorm; and at the final climax, Griffith forces the spectator himself to feel despair, when a rotating block of ice, on it cowering the figure of a woman, approaches the precipice of a gigantic waterfall, itself conveying the impression of inescapable and hopeless ruin.

First the snowstorm, then the foaming, swirling river in thaw, packed with ice blocks that rage yet wilder than the storm, and finally the mighty waterfall, conveying the impression of death itself. In this sequence of events is repeated, on a large scale, as it were, the same line of that increasing despair — despair striving to make an end, for death, that has irresistibly gripped the chief character. This harmony — the storm in the human heart and the storm in the frenzy of nature — is one of the most powerful achievements of the American genius. This example shows particularly clearly how far-reaching and deep must be that connection, between the content of the scenario and the director's general treatment, that adds strength and unity to his work. The director not only transfers the separate scenes suggested by the scenarist each into movement and form, he has also to absorb the scenario in its entirety, from the theme to the final form of the action, and perceive and feel each scene as an irremovable, component part of the unified structure. And this can be the case only if he be organically involved in the work on the scenario from beginning to end.

When the work on the general construction has been finished, the theme molded to a subject, the separate scenes in which the action is realized laid down, then only do we come to the period of the hardest work on the treatment of the scenario, that stage of work when, already concrete and perceptible, that filmic form of the picture that will result can be foreseen; do we come to the period of the planning out of the editing scheme for the shots, of the discovery of those component parts from which the separate images will later be assembled.

To bring a waterfall into the action does not necessarily mean to create it on the screen. Let us remember what we said regarding the creation of a filmic image that becomes vivid and effective only when the necessary details are correctly found. We come to the stage of utilizing the pieces of real space and real time for the future creation of filmic space and filmic time. If it may be said at the beginning of the process that the scenarist guides the work — and that the director has only to pay attention so properly to apprehend it organically, and so as, not only to keep contact with it at every given moment, but to be constantly welded to it — now comes a change. The guide of the work is now the director, equipped with that knowledge of technique and that specific talent that enables him to find the correct and vivid images expressing the quintessential element of each given idea. The director organizes each separate incident, analyzing it, disintegrating it into elements, and simultaneously thinking of the connection of these elements in editing. It is here of special interest to note that the scenarist at this later stage, just as the director in the early stages, must not be divorced from the work. His task it is to supervise the resolution to editable shape of every separate problem, thinking at every instant of the basic theme — sometimes completely abstract, yet current in every separate problem.

Only by means of a close collaboration can a correct and valuable result be attained. Naturally one might postulate as the ideal arrangement the incarnation of scenarist and director in one person. But I have already spoken of the unusual scope and complexity of film creation that prevents any possibility of its mastery by one person. Collectivism is indispensable in the film, but the collaborators must be blended with one another to an exceptionally close degree.

3

Ralph Stephenson
and Jean R. Debrix

from *THE CINEMA AS ART*

Ralph Stephenson brings a broad background of film experience to *The Cinema
As Art*. He has worked for the British
Film Institute, written a book on film
animation (*Animation in the Cinema*,
A. S. Barnes, 1967), published five novels,
and lectured widely on film. J. R. Debrix
heads the film section at the French Ministry of Cooperation; he has written an
earlier book on film and also *Argile*, a
prize-winning novel. His theory is rooted
in practice since he has also directed
films.

DRAMATIC TIME

For thousands of years the tragedies and dramas of the real world have
been re-enacted for the edification or entertainment of an audience. In
the most primitive of these representations, dramatic time was very little
different from the time which the events themselves would have taken
in actuality. The interminable length of medieval mysteries indicates
the difficulty which writers of the period had in altering the time scale.
A drama which did not take virtually as long as the events it depicted
would not have commanded the spectator's belief or attention.

In more sophisticated drama, some *condensation* of the time of actual events became permissible. According to one of the three dramatic unities, laid down in classical times and respected by classical dramatists of the seventeenth and eighteenth centuries (but not by Shakespeare), twenty-four hours was the maximum period which could be compressed into the three or four hours which a play lasted. Nowadays, the dramatist is entirely free and we have plays depicting different generations, or the life of a man from the cradle to the grave shown in a series of episodes.

The cinema has descended from modern, not medieval, drama and only a handful of films have tried to keep exactly the same time scale as reality: Hitchcock's *Rope,* Wise's *The Set-Up,* Zinnemann's *High Noon,* and recently Agnès Varda's *Cléo de 5 à 7. Rope* is a curiosity—a film using camera movement exclusively and without a single cut from beginning to end. In fact it cheats and there are breaks caused by the camera moving to a dark surface and the screen blacking-out. In *The Set-Up* and *High Noon,* the fact that the events of the film take just an hour and a half is indicated by including shots of clocks which show the time. But these films cheat too and include a mass of incident occurring *in different places to different people* during this time which (if laid end to end) would in reality take far longer. In other words, space has been substituted for time. But these films remain an exception, and most films either condense or expand the time of everyday life.

Yet although the film director has freedom to deal with time as he likes, an attempt to distil too great a time period into a film can cause a loss of dramatic power. In Griffith's film *Intolerance* for instance, which ranges over the whole of history from the Babylonian empire to the present day, the various episodes never really form a single unity and the film is not as dramatically effective as the same director's *Birth of a Nation,* which covers the few years of the American Civil War. Preminger's *Exodus* would have been a better film if it had not tried to combine two entirely separate sections—one in Cyprus, the other in Israel.

In the case of a film whose story is in two widely separated parts, unity of time (and place) can to some extent be preserved by means of a flash-back. Instead of showing the beginning and then the end ten or twenty years later, the film can start with the second period, flash back to the first period, then return and finish in the second period. Thus the main containing action forms a unity based on the present, which covers only a short time span, the structure is more symmetrical, and the flashback to past time is relegated to a subordinate role. There are innumerable examples—*Le Jour se lève, Le Diable au corps, The Lost Weekend, Citizen Kane, Hiroshima mon amour,* and so on. In some cases the present is limited to a few minutes at the beginning and end of the film, the whole of the story being set in the past, for example *Variety,* or *Le Crime de*

Monsieur Lange. In this case, it is perhaps preferable to regard the open-ing and closing sequences as forming a prologue and epilogue to the main part of the film (a structure similar to Shakespeare's *The Taming of the Shrew*) rather than to regard the body of the film as a flash-back. Similar are films in which a series of short episodes is held together by some unifying device: men in a club swapping (Somerset Maugham's) yarns as in *Quartet*, stories from books in an old book-shop (Allessandro Blasetti's *Altri tempi*); a woman visiting the men she danced with at her first ball (*Un Carnet de bal*).

Cutting from shot to shot may be a means of shortening time and leaving out the inessential. Because a film is composed of hundreds of bits of time joined together, it can effect this condensation of time con-tinuously from beginning to the end of the film. The theatre has steadily grown more flexible in this respect by abandoning elaborate stage set-tings, and allowing changes of place or time to be represented by mov-ing a spotlight from one side of the stage to another, or by changing a cardboard tree for a cardboard street-lamp, and so making it possible to have far more changes of scene. But the threatre is still not so flexible as the cinema.

How much can be left out, how quickly the narrative can proceed, is something which the director must have continually in mind. If too much is left out, the sequence of events may be difficult to follow. As in the case of space, more can be left out between sequences than within the same sequence, and the various transition devices which have al-ready been discussed just as they carry the spectator over a change of place, will carry him over a change of time.

Two unorthodox time transitions in John Schlesinger's first feature film *A Kind of Loving* are fitting examples. There is a long sequence in which the young man persuades his girl to make love to him. It ends on a quiet, a curiously quiet, note, both of them inwardly still. . . . Then suddenly by a straight cut we go with a bang into a raucous, violent dance scene — the band playing as loudly as possible, the girl being man-handled by a clumsy oaf of a partner. It is about a month later and the girl is worried that she is going to have a baby. The transition is very successful, no doubt because of the strong contrast in tone from *pianis-simo* to *fortissimo*. Later in the film we see the same couple on their honeymoon. The camera (long-shot) is looking out from the hotel bed-room at them on the beach at dusk, as they turn to come to the hotel. Before this shot quite ends *we hear their voices in the hotel bedroom* in low intimate tones, and only then does the camera pull back and pan over to the couple lying in bed. This transition, achieved in a single shot, is a striking illustration of the cinema's ability to telescope time. Again, in Terence Young's *Dr No*, time is neatly telescoped in the following

An Occurrence at Owl Creek Bridge
(1962) "A man is being hung under martial law during the American Civil War.
. . . The main part of the film occurs
during the fraction of a second of his
fall—a flash of wish-fulfilling thought."

sequence. A beautiful spy plans to decoy James Bond by asking him up
to her bungalow in the hills. She rings him up and as she gives him directions over the telephone we dissolve to Bond actually in his car
driving and obviously following the directions which her voice goes on
giving. . . .

Instead of condensation from real time to dramatic time there
will sometimes be expansion. This can take two forms: either the film
concentrates on a particular occurrence, repeats it, gives different aspects of it, stretches it out; or else there may be inserted a sequence
which in thought takes place in a flash but in the film takes many minutes.
An example of the first occurs in Michael Curtis's film *The Charge of the
Light Brigade,* in which the famous charge lasts more than ten minutes,
although in reality the horses had to gallop only two kilometers.

An example of the second from *Death of a Salesman* has already
been quoted. In the fraction of a second between Willy asking his wife

a question and her answering it, he thinks of an affair with another woman; in the film the time is expanded to allow the love scene with the other woman to be played out. There is an experimental film *The Last Moment* by Paul Fejos which opens with a figure struggling in the water and a hand reaching up. The film follows the chief character's boyhood, youth, first love-affair, war service, unhappy love-affair, decision to commit suicide. Then the opening sequence is repeated, the hand gradually sinks into the water and the film ends. Two films of this kind have been made from an identical Ambrose Bierce story: *The Spy* by Charles Vidor (1932) and *Incident at Owl Creek* by Robert Enrico (1962). A man is being hung under martial law during the American Civil War. The hanging takes place on a bridge and, as he drops, the rope breaks, he plunges into the stream, and by swimming under water, escapes. There is a long sequence of him making his way through the forest to his wife and home — then suddenly we are back at the bridge, the body dangling at the end of the rope. The main part of the film has occurred during the fraction of a second of his fall — a flash of wish-fulfilling thought.

This is a suitable point to consider the length of films. Bela Balázs held that films in practice could not last longer than an hour and a half because for physiological reasons the viewer could not watch for longer than this. 'This predetermined length,' he wrote, 'is itself a style which the artist must master.' If ten thousand feet was the limit of length when Balázs wrote, it is certainly not so now, and the number of long films, two hours, two and a half hours and more, is sufficient to show that the spectator's physiology is no bar. Tyranny of length arises rather from commercial considerations and films are still cut down or stretched out to fit into programmes. Buñuel's son said of his father's latest film, *The Exterminating Angel,* that it was slightly too short for commercial exhibition, so he simply repeated a sequence at the beginning! The guests come into the hall of the house, mill around for a moment or two looking for the servants (who have gone) and then go up the grand staircase. Then the whole thing is repeated. Certainly it is an odd repetition without any clear symbolic meaning (as there is in other parts of the film) so the explanation given may be correct. Balázs is right in counting length as part of the style. It should be part of the total conception of the film and will largely depend on the content — what the artist has to say. Because of the pattern of commercial exhibition the most neglected form in the cinema is the short-story film and many short-story ideas are padded out to feature length. Short documentary films are not much seen in cinemas, either, but at least they flourish in other spheres — it is for the short fiction film that there is least place. Perhaps television will provide a medium, as it already has provided a medium for a great many documentary and cartoon films.

4

Lee R. Bobker

The Art of Film Editing

Lee R. Bobker has garnered over 200 awards at film competitions including prizes at the Cannes, Edinburgh, San Francisco, and Venice film festivals. Besides directing movies, he has taught courses in cinema at major universities in the U.S. and abroad.

Film editing begins when the editor is given a script to read and analyze. As mentioned above, each day on set the director chooses several takes of each scene and orders a print made of these takes. Editor and director then view the selected takes, called *rushes* or *dailies,* and determine how the finished film should look and sound. During this screening, the editor gets his first glimpse of the film. As he looks over all the elements that the director has given him, he considers the following points:

(1) *Variety of coverage.* From how many angles and viewpoints has the director photographed the scene?
(2) *Quality of performance.* From which angle or in which take or section of the scene is performance most effective?
(3) *Number of supportive elements available.* How many silent "detail"

From Lee R. Bobker, *Elements of Film* (New York: Harcourt Brace Jovanovich, Inc. 1969).

shots are included? What additional "atmosphere" sound is available? What else in the way of image and sound has the director provided in support of the scene?

As the editor views the footage, he forms his own ideas as to the most effective way to assemble the material. He eliminates those scenes, angles and sections of film that are obviously substandard and works with the best (in his own judgment) of what was shot and recorded. Some directors maintain an authoritarian control of the editing process; most often, however, the editor is left on his own during this stage. As he works with the material, running the film back and forth in the moviola, he imposes his own esthetic judgments on the film. In this process, he functions as a creative artist.

The film editor's role is distinct from that of the director or cameraman. The director deals with structure and performance, with mood and philosophical ideas; the cameraman deals with composition and light, with images that move and change. The editor, however, is concerned with the following elements: (1) time, (2) rhythm and pace, and (3) visual and aural relationships.

TIME

As we view a motion picture, we are, for the time spent in the darkened theater, totally under the influence of the film we are watching. In two hours, one film may cover a lifetime; another, only ten minutes. *Goodbye Mr. Chips,* a popular British film of the 1930's, spans sixty years in the life of a British schoolteacher, and while the film is in progress, we feel sixty years are going by. The award-winning French short subject based on Ambrose Bierce's *Incident at Owl Creek Bridge* expands the action of a split second (the moment a man is hanged) into a thirty-minute motion picture.

Time is the single major factor in the art of editing. The editor, in effect, controls time. He can so extend a scene that action supposedly taking place in one minute will feel like an hour; and he can, by means of fragmented flash-cutting, compress an hour's action into a minute.

An early example of the ability of the film editor to manipulate time is the famous sequence on the steps of St. Petersburg in Eisenstein's *Potemkin.* This sequence has been much studied and copied by other filmmakers. The action itself, the people of St. Petersburg running up the steps into the guns of the Czarist soldiers, actually takes place in a few minutes. But because of the many "detail shots" cut into the action — feet, faces, guns, and falling bodies — the sequence seems to go on for a much longer period of time.

An excellent example of the film editor's total control of time is the editorial architecture of the final sequence of *Bonnie and Clyde*. The ambush is prepared. Bonnie and Clyde agree to assist the old man with his car. The action seems to proceed at a snail's pace because of the many detail shots edited into the sequence. The basic action, if allowed to run without interruption, would happen briefly and quickly. The editor, however, continually intercuts other shots: the bushes behind which the police hide, trees, and faces. Finally, just before the dénouement, there is a superb extension of time—the exchange of looks between Bonnie and Clyde, held just a beat or two too long and suspending the audience for what seems to be forever. This is followed by a fusillade of gunfire that also goes on and on. Nothing in the sequence takes place in a realistic time duration. Everything is done for effect. Throughout the sequence, the film editor controls time on an absolute scale, accelerating or retarding it to achieve a desired end.

The film editor controls time in two ways: (1) by expanding or contracting the normal time of an action through the use of intercuts, and (2) by using optical effects to link scenes and sequences.

The Use of Intercuts

By using a single intercut, the editor can eliminate large segments of time from the action. For example, at a key moment in a fast-moving dialogue scene, the leading character gets up and walks across the room to get a glass of water. If the editor feels that this pause slows down the pace, he simply adds a close-up of someone watching the walker. The intercut of the face can be shown on screen for a split second, followed by a shot of the leading character already at the water cooler (thereby eliminating the entire walk). We accept this artificial tampering with time because we are "involved" in the action. The shift of attention produced by the intercut distracts us momentarily, and we are no longer able to judge how much time the walk should take. We accept the unreal acceleration of time simply because it is done. The man is already at the water cooler—our eyes do not lie.

Conversely, if the editor wishes to retard the pace of the action, he can insert a sequence of intercuts that actually uses up more screen time than the offscreen walk to the water cooler could possibly take. Again, because we are momentarily distracted by the intercuts, we do not question this manipulation of time.

This type of artistic manipulation is like a cinematic "shell game." We see only what the editor wishes us to see, whatever he chooses to put on screen. Since we cannot judge offscreen action in terms of elapsed time, the editor becomes the sole arbiter of the time of such action. Thus the editor is in complete control of the time of a scene or sequence.

When his selection of intercuts is skillful and well handled, the audience is completely in his hands.

From our own experience we know how long it usually takes a person to mount a flight of stairs. If we view this action through a single shot, the time element is totally within our own experience. The scene is simply a shot of a man mounting steps. Once the film editor begins to manipulate such a scene, however, we become subject to an artificially created time segment. For example, if the editor fragments the scene by adding carefully selected shots that are slowly and languidly paced, the normal time sequence will begin to expand. Presented [below in sequence A, B] are two ways to edit this scene. Each creates a totally different sense of elapsed time.

In example A, the normal flow of time is retarded. The action is constantly interrupted—we are taken away from the main action and presented with shots that are in themselves static in character. Each time we return to the main action, the man has not advanced sufficiently to account for the time that our attention was diverted. Thus time is expanded.

A

Long shot: Man ascending stairs
Close-up: Feet mounting stairs
Close-up: Clock
Close-up: Candles burning
Medium shot: Face
Close-up: Hand gripping banister
Long shot: Man continuing to climb
Reverse angle shot: Man viewed from above
Close-up: Feet
Medium shot: Face
Close-up: Clock
Close-up: Candles flickering
Slow dolly shot following the man

B

Close-up: Feet mounting stairs
Close-up: Hand sliding up banister
Close-up: Face
Long shot: Man halfway up
Close-up: Feet
Askew angle shot: Man coming at camera
Long shot: Man at top of stairs

In example B, fewer intercuts are used, and they simply cover gaps in the main action. When we return to the main action, the man has advanced much farther than he possibly could have during the short time of the intercuts. In addition, the sharp angle of the intercuts heightens the pace of the central action. Thus time is compressed.

There are few general rules concerning the way time can be manipulated. Editing is largely an intuitive process. The editor simply cuts a scene until it "feels" right. He is bound by no rules other than the very pragmatic one, *Does it work?*

The film editor should also recognize that every image has its own "feeling" as to time, and he should select his intercuts with careful attention to the desired effect. In the above sequence, the editor's selection of a clock or candle shot is based on his own feeling about the effect of such a shot on the audience. A clock without a second hand shows no movement at all — time seems to be standing still. A flickering candle is also normally a "still" shot. By inserting such shots within a sequence, the editor can retard time, and the "feeling" of the inserted shots will carry over into subsequent shots of the main action.

The editor's control of time has an important effect on the entire film. For example, if the central dramatic unit of a film is a long and difficult journey, as in David Lean's film *Bridge on the River Kwai,* the editor must convey a sense of the hardship of that journey. It does not matter whether the audience is told, via dialogue, how long the trip will take. The audience must still *feel* the length of the journey in viewing the film. Thus the film editor's sense of time must be perfect. If the audience feels that the journey is too short to be really difficult, the central dramatic structure of the film will fail. If the journey is so drawn out that the audience cannot accept the attrition, again the film will fail. The editor must decide how many days and nights should be shown on screen and how long each day should seem.

In *Bridge on the River Kwai,* the long, difficult trek into the jungle is shown through a series of long shots freely mixed with close-ups. Some days are covered in two or three shots; others are covered in fifty shots. The audience does not question this uneven distribution of time. The days following the injury to the leader's foot are extended by the repeated use of shots of the bandages and bleeding leg, of the sun glinting through the trees, and of the faces of the crew. As the journey nears its end, time is drawn out and extended — just as it must have seemed drawn out to the participants in the journey.

To achieve the opposite effect, the compression of time, the editor often utilizes *flash-cutting,* the insertion of split-second fragments of scenes between direct cuts from scene to scene. Excellent examples of this type of compression occur in the work of Richard Lester. In *The*

Knack, the comic sequence in which a bed is moved across London consists of so many extraneous fragments that time is almost forgotten. A normal four-hour task is compressed into a few minutes by means of constant interruptions that divert our attention from the central action. This technique of interrupting the prime action with bits and pieces of film speeds up the passage of time in much the same manner as an animated cartoon. The fragments appear and disappear so rapidly that the bed seems to be racing around London.

The Use of Optical Effects

Optical effects can be used to link scenes and sequences. These effects include (1) *flip frames,* the "flipping" of frames to reveal a new scene, (2) *wipes,* the horizontal or vertical crossing on screen of an outgoing and incoming scene, and (3) *supers,* the imposition of one scene over another. These effects create changes from scene to scene within seconds and propel the audience into another place in time. It is the film editor who selects and designs these optical effects and who must decide how each pair of scenes will be altered by the optical effect that joins them.

Every optical has its own effect on the pace of the film, an effect related directly to the audience's conception of time. Long, slow dissolves usually retard time. Good examples of this are the long dissolves joining a series of sequences in George Steven's *A Place in the Sun* and the dissolves joining the "reunion" scenes of Lara and Zhivago in *Doctor Zhivago.* Flips and wipes usually speed up time, linking scenes that occur weeks or even months apart by means of an abrupt optical trick that erases the missing time segment from the consciousness of the audience. The audience becomes involved in the incoming scene while the outgoing scene is still on screen and thus has no chance to consider the time gap.

RHYTHM

Every film contains unique internal and external cadences. Indeed, these cadences — or rhythms — impart to the film much of its quality and character. The control of internal and external cadences lies largely in the province of the film editor.

Internal Rhythm

In addition to mood and impact of performance, every scene has an inherent quality of movement, an *internal rhythm.* In viewing a film, we are often aware of individual scenes that seem especially slow or

fast. As obvious examples, a scene photographed from a speeding motorcycle imparts a feeling of fast movement; a scene photographed from a
gondola in Venice imparts a sense of languor and slow movement.

The editor, relying chiefly on his intuitive sense, must recognize
the particular rhythm of each scene. This rhythm is determined by everything happening within the scene — the movement of the camera, the
pace of the action, the speed of the dialogue, the number of events
occurring at the same time. Once the film editor understands the rhythmic quality of a scene (for example, "dreary," "interminable," or "fre-
netic"), he can determine where to place the scene, how long it should
run, and which scenes it should follow or precede. The editor must select
scenes that both in themselves and in relation to preceding and following
scenes will achieve the desired effect.

Consider the "health spa" sequence in the early part of Fellini's
$8\frac{1}{2}$. This sequence was edited to a fast-moving Rossini overture. The
scenes themselves, however, contain slow and languid rhythms that
transmit a sense of idle purposelessness — a mood that gives this sequence its brilliant satiric quality. Thus, even though the music moves
swiftly, filled with mercurial configurations typical of Rossini, the
scenes convey a feeling of torpor — figures float by, the camera pans
lazily past the guests, hands reach slowly for mineral water, and the
camera dollies at an almost artificially retarded pace. In all, it is the
internal rhythm of each scene that carries the mood and pace of the
sequence. Despite the frantic pace of the music, the entire sequence
transmits a mood of somnolence and death.

The opposite effect — rapid pace — is achieved in *Bonnie and Clyde*
in one of the most violent sequences ever created by an American film-
maker. As the sequence begins, Bonnie and Clyde, Clyde's brother and
sister-in-law, and C. J. are enjoying one of their many "just folks" recre-
ational respites from the law. Suddenly, they are surrounded by the
police. From the moment they break out of the motel room until the
brother dies in the field, the sequence has an incredibly frantic pace.
The cinematic elements that give this sequence its power were created
in the film editing. There is little of the flash-cutting so common in
contemporary films; rather, the editor has selected scenes that contain
in themselves a high degree of rapid physical movement: the escape
from the motel, the leap into the cars, the overturned car bursting into
flame, the race through the night, the spin of the cars into the open field,
the bodies falling and twisting, and finally, the camera circling around the
dying man. The editor keeps each scene in high movement, rarely paus-
ing for a static close-up.

Another example of the effect of internal rhythm on the editing of a sequence is the "island search" sequence in *L'Avventura.* The aimless wandering over the rocky island is heightened by the choice of shots. Each scene contains a minimum amount of movement, and the rhythm of the sea smashing purposelessly over the rocks seems to be the key to all the other scenes. The actors glide in and out of the haze; the camera pans tortuously from place to place. These rhythms convey a mood of isolation and pointlessness that communicates the central purpose of the sequence. The transitions from scene to scene are also slow and empty (for example, dissolves within contemporaneous action).

The mood of each sequence — so essential to the film — is created largely by the editing, by the *use* of the material. The editor determines the length of each scene, the transitions from scene to scene, the order of the scenes, and all supporting elements (sound, music, voices) that will be used. These creative decisions make the sequence work.

External Rhythm

The *external* rhythm of a film depends largely on the length of time that each scene runs. The easiest and most obvious way to heighten the pace of a sequence is to successively shorten a series of scenes. Richard Lester's films (*The Knack, Help!, Hard Day's Night*) are excellent ex amples of rapid external cadence. The action within each scene is frantic; in addition, the action is interrupted constantly at unusual and strange moments. In traditional editing practice, the editor does not interrupt camera movement (pan or dolly) until it has been completed. But in modern cutting techniques, the editor often deliberately interrupts movement when the audience is least prepared for it.

The external rhythm of a film is also strongly affected by the editorial choice of *how* to interrupt movement. In other words, *What do we cut to?* Again, in traditional practice, the editor cuts to elements that are contained within the scene or cued by the sound track. Modern film editors, however, frequently utilize the totally *unrelated cut* to heighten impact and greatly increase pace. For example, in a scene from *Hiroshima Mon Amour,* the camera follows a baby carriage through the park. Suddenly, the camera cuts to a peace demonstration in Tokyo. We, as audience, are totally unprepared for the scene and are barely able to catch our breath when the scene is over and we are back in the park. Our disorientation is so great that the action seems to be greatly accelerated.

In every motion picture of artistic merit, careful attention is given to the cadences, or "pulse," of the film. We remember a film as being "fast moving" or "poetic," as having "tremendous punch," or as conveying "a sense of peace and beauty." These phrases are the articulated descriptions of the cadences created by the film editor.

VISUAL AND AURAL RELATIONSHIPS

In the editing of a motion picture, there are three important relationships to be considered: (1) image to image, (2) sound to sound, and (3) image to sound.

Image To Image

Every scene is affected by the scenes that precede and follow it. To demonstrate the effect of scene upon scene, consider the following:

> *Scene 1:* Close-up of a man smiling
> *Scene 2:* Close-up of a gun going off
> *Scene 3:* A body falling
> *Scene 4:* Close-up of a sad face

If these scenes are edited in the order 1 2 3 4, they tell the story of a happy man shooting someone who is then mourned by a third person. If the scenes are edited in the order 4 2 3 1, they tell the story of someone regretfully shooting someone else to the joy of a third party. Thus the ordering of the scenes determines the audience's reaction to the shooting.

In a well-edited film, we are never aware of the cuts themselves; we sense only the continuity of the film as a whole. Thus we are often unaware that our emotional response to a scene is carefully conditioned by a preceding scene. As each shot leads inevitably to the next, it imparts emotional and intellectual "memories" that often change the values in the following scene.

The film editor has the power to change the character and purpose of a scene. Since there are no immutable laws governing his choices, the film editor can transcend the boundaries of time and space to achieve a desired effect. A party can be given somber overtones by a cut to a funeral shot—a casket being lowered into a grave. It is not necessary for the audience to know whose funeral or whose casket it is. The shot is simply an *effect shot;* it makes a comment and achieves a desired result. If the funeral shot is used with a realistic script (for example, while the party is going on, miles away the hero's mother dies), the shot will change the character of the party scenes. We become angry or ashamed at the participants, and the very gaiety of the party becomes depressing. If the editor chooses to run an entire party sequence before proceeding to the funeral sequence, the party scenes will retain their inherent gaiety until the funeral. If, however, the funeral and the party are *intercut*—a shot of laughter followed by a shot of gloom—the party shots will be destroyed by the funeral shots. . . .

Image To Sound

The third major relationship that the film editor works with is the relationship of image to sound. Every sound affects the audience's reaction
to what is seen, and every image conditions the audience's response to
what is heard. The audience's reaction to a given scene is determined
by the type of sound used to support that scene. A simple scene of a
man walking down a city street can become a tense, nerve-wracking
experience by the addition of confused traffic noises. The same scene
can become an exercise in isolation and loneliness if all realistic sound
is removed and we hear only the wind. In the opening scene of Fellini's
$8\frac{1}{2}$, the hero, Guido, is caught in a car in a traffic jam. By using silence,
Fellini presents the scene as a nightmare. In David Lean's *Lawrence of
Arabia,* the sense of loneliness and alienation conveyed by the desert
images is immeasurably heightened by the soft, monotonous sounds
of the wind in almost every scene. In turn, the desert images impart to
the sounds a vividness that makes the audience aware of even the most
subtle noises originating from both onscreen and offscreen sources. An
imaginative editor does not rely exclusively on sounds that are already
a part of the sync track; rather, he adds sounds that have no direct visual
cues but that serve to enrich the scene.

Current editing techniques have made exciting use of the *overlap
sound cut,* in which the sound accompanying one scene overlaps into a
preceding or following scene. The editor uses this technique to alter or
enrich unrelated visual images, to link action from scene to scene, and
to heighten the pace of the film.

Excellent use of the overlap sound cut appears in the film *The
Graduate.* The middle section of the film, from Benjamin's seduction by
Mrs. Robinson to his meeting with Elaine, consists of a time-flow segment. Benjamin's meetings with Mrs. Robinson are juxtaposed against
his idle, almost paralytic life by the swimming pool at home. The images
flow into one another without traditional optical connecting devices.
Thus Benjamin, lying by the pool, gets up and walks into the cabana;
as he crosses the doorway, he is walking into Mrs. Robinson's hotel
room. In another scene, Benjamin hoists himself out of the pool onto a
rubber raft; as he makes this move, a cut is made and he is rolling over
on top of Mrs. Robinson in bed.

In traditional editing practice, each picture cut is generally accompanied by a sound cut. In *The Graduate,* however, the editor permits the
sound of the outgoing scene to extend briefly into the incoming scene, or
the sound of the incoming scene to overlap the final seconds of the
outgoing scene. In some instances, a sentence is cut in half and joined
with part of a sentence from the new scene. The sound affects the new

scene by sustaining the intellectual and emotional overtones of the scene to which it belongs. This deliberate mismatching of sound unifies, in impact and idea, a sequence that would otherwise consist of disparate elements. The imaginative use of sound-to-image relationships successfully contrasts Benjamin's comatose existence at home with his emotional affair with Mrs. Robinson.

In the films of 1930's and 1940's, the relationships between picture and sound were relatively unimaginative and mechanical. Since that time, film editing has undergone a number of changes. Today, the creative film editor, through the skillful and imaginative employment of image and sound relationships, adds richness to the finished film.

As the director becomes more freewheeling in his execution, and as film becomes less tied down to the studio, the film editor will continue to experiment. One major weapon in the editor's arsenal is the *montage,* a series of images and sounds joined only by internal relationships and capable of transporting the viewer just about anywhere.

MONTAGE

Over the past two decades, no term in cinema has been more distorted or abused than "montage." Every time a film editor puts two or more scenes together in a series of short cuts, he claims to have created a montage. Nonetheless, montage can be a key creative term in the filmmaker's lexicon. Practically speaking, cinematic montage is *the use of a succession of visual images and/or sounds to create emotional impact.* Generally, the montage is used to compress or expand time or space and to create special moods. Several basic types of montage are discussed below.

The Time-Transition Montage
The pool game between Paul Newman and Jackie Gleason in *The Hustler* (directed by Robert Rossen) is a good example of the time-transition montage. The audience watches a series of fragmented scenes of two men playing a tense game of pool. The screen shows only bits and pieces of scenes linked by long, lingering dissolves. Each scene is superimposed on the next. But from this succession of images we feel that we have been through the entire game.

The Mood Montage
The opening scenes of Fred Zinnemann's historical drama *A Man for All Seasons* illustrate the effect of mood montage. The departure of Sir Thomas More (Paul Scofield) to London is shown through a series of images of the Thames in early morning. These images create a mood of

time and place. This opening montage permeates the entire film and helps to expand this chamber play into an exciting motion picture.

The Impact Montage

Lindsay Anderson's film of the early 1960's, *This Sporting Life*, deals with the life of a professional rugby football player. To delineate the effect of this vicious body-contact sport on the hero, Anderson uses several impact montages of the game. These montages consist of fragmented long-lens shots of the body-contact aspects of the sport, coupled with the sounds of the game—thuds, groans, and bone-crunching noises. The audience is thus propelled *into* the game.

There are, of course, an endless variety of uses for the montage. Indeed, it is one of the real refinements of the editor's art. The montage involves crucial picture-to-picture relationships. Every scene chosen must be exactly right in position and length. The sound too—whether dialogue, effects, or music—must be carefully chosen. The flow of images propels the audience to a desired destination. One wrong scene and the entire "visual train" will be derailed. There are no restrictions in the art of cinematic montage. The film editor edits viscerally—instinctively—and makes decisions based on what he feels will do the job.

EFFECTIVE EDITING

As the film editor organizes the finished film, he achieves many of the writer's and/or the director's goals. In effective film editing, control of the audience's attention must be absolute. The editor must carefully manipulate each element—time, rhythm, and visual and aural relationships—and must structure these elements to convey the meaning and emotional content of the film.

Alain Resnais' film *Hiroshima Mon Amour* is a good example of effective editing. The film contains, in both script design and execution, some of the most complex elements ever attempted on screen. Although the action takes place in a single day, the film spans several years (the history of a complex and profound woman) and examines timeless themes—the effect of war on man, the nature of the relationship between two people in love.

As the film begins, the two lovers are in bed conversing about Hiroshima. The editor leaves this scene, permitting the dialogue to continue, and creates a montage—a flow of images giving a memorable view of the bomb in action. These images are edited in brilliant counterpoint to the continuing dialogue. The editor moves freely between past and present. The woman looks from the terrace at her sleeping lover, and the camera cuts to a jolting fragment from another time and place: the hand of her dead German lover, followed by a swift pan to his head. Suddenly, there is another cut, and we are back in the present.

The film is designed like a fantastic jigsaw puzzle. The editor selects key episodes from the heroine's past and pieces fragments of these episodes into the onscreen action. In effect, the editor is duplicating the very process that is going on in the heroine's mind. Her past is thrusting itself into her present, building up a pressure that even she is not aware of. The film editor makes this process the very substance of his cutting. The fragmented scenes become meaningful as the heroine begins to remember things she had sought to repress. The past forces its way to the surface. As the action continues, the editor permits us to see entire sequences, still moving freely between past and present. He is in complete control of every element. Images and dialogue overlap; music provides clues and pace. The editorial choices are so appropriate that we are hardly aware of them. We know and understand. The film communicates to us because the editor has used each element perfectly — the first flashback cut (the hand of the German), the overlapping dialogue during the museum scenes, the steady extension of the flashback scenes (as both audience and heroine become aware of the forces that now move her), and the precise moment that the music is heard beginning the walk through the city.

In playing his cinematic "shell game," the film editor must be in complete control. He must carefully manipulate his shells, hiding the pea under one while the audience is watching the other two. The film editor moves his images in succession, keeping the eye of the audience totally in his control. He uses a variety of elements — all relating to visual and aural impressions — to reinforce this control. The film editor is an artist capable of intuitively recognizing visual impact — a musician, a dramatist, a poet. At the same time, he is a highly skilled technician capable of moving a dozen tracks and a picture through a multiheaded monster called a moviola. Like the writer, the director, and the cameraman, the editor is a basic creator of the finished work of art — the film.

5
Michael Roemer

THE SURFACES
OF REALITY

Michael Roemer experimented with
silent film fantasy while a student at
Harvard. After reviewing films for *The
Reporter* magazine, he directed *Nothing
But A Man,* a brilliant study of a black
man seeking identification. Roemer was
invited to show his film at the 1964
Venice Film Festival, the only American
so honored.

As Siegfried Kracauer effectively demonstrates, the camera photographs
the skin; it cannot function like an X-ray machine and show us what is
underneath. This does not mean, however, that the film-maker has no
control over the surfaces rendered by his camera. On the contrary, he
chooses his surfaces for their content, and through their careful selection
and juxtaposition builds a structure of feeling and meaning that are the
core of his work.

There are times in the history of the medium when story, treatment
and performance drift so far into a studio never-never land that we
cannot help but make a virtue of "pure" reality, as free from interference

Michael Roemer, "The Surfaces of Reality," *Film Quarterly,* Vol. XVIII, No. 1,
Fall 1964, pp. 15-22.

on the part of the film-maker as possible — even at the risk of creating something shapeless. This should not, however, obscure the fact that a film, like a poem or painting, is basically an artifact.

The assertion that film is nothing more than a documentary recording of reality undoubtedly stems from the fact that the medium must render all meaning in physical terms. This affinity for real surfaces, combined with great freedom of movement both in time and space, brings film closer than any other medium to our own random experience of life. Even the realistic playwright, who — until the advent of the camera — came closest to rendering the appearance of reality, is often forced in his structure to violate the very sense of life he is trying to create. But the film-maker can use the flexible resources at his command to approximate the actual fabric of reality. Moreover, he need not heighten his effects in order to communicate, for he can call on the same sensibilities in his audience that we use in life itself.

All of us bring to every situation, whether it be a business meeting or a love affair, a social and psychological awareness which helps us understand complex motivations and relationships. This kind of perception, much of it nonverbal and based on apparently insignificant clues, is not limited to the educated or gifted. We all depend on it for our understanding of other people and have become extremely proficient in the interpretation of subtle signs — a shading in the voice, an averted glance. This nuanced awareness, however, is not easily called upon by the arts, for it is predicated upon a far more immediate and total experience than can be provided by literature and the theatre, with their dependence on the word, or by the visual arts — with their dependence on the image. Only film renders experience with enough immediacy and totality to call into play the perceptual processes we employ in life itself.

The fact that film exercises this sort of perceptual capacity is, I believe, one of its chief appeals to us. It gives us practice in the delicate and always somewhat uncertain skill of finding out what is going on. As an extreme example, take these lines from *Marty*. They are spoken in a dance hall during the first encounter between a lonely man and a lonely girl. She says: "I'm twenty-nine years old. How old are you?" And he answers: "Thirty-six."

On the stage or the printed page these lines would fall ludicrously flat. But on the screen, when spoken by performers who can make every detail yield a wealth of meaning, they instantly convey — as they would in life itself — a complex web of feeling: the girl's fear that she might be too old for the man, her need to come right to the point, her relief when he turns out to be older, and finally a mutual delight that their relationship has crossed its first hurdle.

Film thrives on this kind of intimate detail, for the camera reports it so closely that nothing essential is lost to the eye or ear. The camera makes it possible to use the stuff of life itself, without amplification or overstatement and without any loss in dramatic value. What is achieved in a large action or an explicit moment on the stage can be rendered just as dramatically on the screen in small and *implicit* terms, for it is not the magnitude of a gesture that makes it dramatic but its meaning and intention.

This is *not* to say that the medium is most aptly used on the kind of everyday story told in *Marty,* or that low-key dialogue without conflict or strong feeling is always effective on the screen. I quote the scene merely as an example of the medium's capacity for finding meaning in the detail of everyday life and would like to suggest that out of such detail, out of the ordinary surfaces of life, the film-maker can structure *any* kind of situation and story — lyrical or dramatic, historical or contemporary.

Like so many films that deal with the past, Dreyer's *Passion de Jeanne d' Arc* might well have been filled with violent action and theatrical confrontations. Instead the story is told in terms of mundane detail. Thus Jeanne is betrayed at a critical moment by a priest who averts his eyes when she turns to him for help. There is no call for anything more explicit. The betrayal is what matters, and the camera renders it far more credibly and forcefully in a mundane detail than it would be in a highly dramatized gesture.

In *Rashomon* and *The Seven Samurai* Kurosawa deals with events of the thirteenth and sixteenth centuries in the most everyday terms. He knows that our basic daily experience of reality has not changed much over the centuries: a war between bandits and samurai in a feudal Japanese village was as full of mud and rain, as gritty and as grotesque as a twentieth-century skirmish. Film at its best uses the language of ordinary experience — but uses it subtly and artfully.

In a contemporary setting, Bresson's *A Man Escaped* chronicles the efforts of a French resistance fighter to break out of a German prison. Much of the film takes place within the confines of a cell, and the camera records how he painstakingly prepares his escape by fashioning tools out of spoons and rope out of blankets. It is all very ordinary and physical, but out of the grimy detail emerges a devout and heroic assertion of life and human freedom and of the need to preserve them in the face of all odds. In the hands of a sensitive film-maker the ordinary moment becomes a channel for deep feeling and a sequence of apparently insignificant scenes is structured into a world of great complexity.

This use of ordinary surfaces requires great skill and discipline since the audience can sense every false move and movement, every false note in the dialogue, every unsubstantiated relationship. The very thing that works *for* the film-maker if he can master it—reality—can quickly turn against him, so that the most ordinary moment becomes utterly unreal. Not surprisingly most directors avoid the challenge and set their stories in unfamiliar parts, among unusual people and in unusual circumstances.

Because most good films use the language of the commonplace, they tend to have an unassuming appearance, whereas films that make a large claim—that speak nobly and poetically about life, love and death —almost invariably prove to be hollow. A good film is concrete: it creates a sequence of objective situations, actual relationships between people, between people and their circumstances. Thus each moment becomes an objective correlative; that is, feeling (or meaning) rendered in actual, physical terms: objectified.

By contrast, most movies are a series of conventional communicative gestures, dialogues, and actions. Most movie-makers *play* on the feelings of their audience by setting up a sequence of incidents that have a proven effect. The events are not rendered; they are merely *cited.* The films do not use the vocabulary of actuality but rather a second-hand language that has proven effective in other films—a language that is changed only when the audience no longer responds.

This language of conventions gives most pictures the appearance of ludicrous unreality fifteen or twenty years after they have been acclaimed as masterpieces. The dramatic conventions of the 1940's are recognized as a system of hollow clichés by the sixties. When *The Best Years of Our Lives* was first shown, references to the war were enough to make an audience feel strongly about a situation or character without any substantiation whatever; there were feelings abroad which, when touched, produced the desired effect. By 1964 this is no longer true and the tissue of the film disintegrates.

Audiences can be "played" by a skillful movie-maker with a fair amount of predictability, so that even discriminating audiences are easily taken in. At the beginning of Bergman's *Wild Strawberries* Professor Borg dreams that he is on a deserted street with all its doors and windows shuttered tight. He looks up at a clock that has no hands and pulls out his own watch only to find that its hands are missing also. A man appears on the corner with his head averted; when he turns, he has no face and his body dissolves into a pool on the sidewalk. A glass hearse comes down the street and spills a coffin that opens. Borg approaches and discovers his own body in the coffin. The corpse comes to life and tries to pull him in.

The nightmare quality in this sequence is derivative. The deserted, shuttered street, the clock and watch without hands, the glass hearse, the faceless man are all conventions familiar to surrealist painting and literature. Bergman uses them skillfully and with conviction to produce an effect in the audience, but they are not true film images, derived from life and rendered in concrete, physical terms.

There is a similar nightmare in Dreyer's *Vampire*. A young man dreams that he has entered a room with an open coffin in it. He approaches and discovers that he himself is the corpse. The camera now assumes the point-of-view of the dead man: we look up at the ceiling. Voices approach and two carpenters appear in our field of vision. They close the coffin with a lid but we continue to look out through a small glass window. Talking indistinctly, they nail down the lid and plane the edges of the wood. The shavings fall onto the window. One of them has put a candle down on the glass and wax drips onto it. Then the coffin is lifted up and we pass close under the ceiling, through the doorway, beneath the sunlit roofs and the church steeple of a small town—out into the open sky.

Here the detail is concrete: an experience is rendered, not cited; the situation is objective and out of it emerges, very powerfully, the feeling that Dreyer is after: a farewell to life, a last confined look at the earth before the coffin is lowered into the grave. Once again we note that the unassuming detail can render a complex feeling (or meaning) which eludes the more obviously ambitious but abstract statement.

Good film dialogue, too, has this concrete quality. Like the speech of everyday life, it does not tell you *directly* what is felt or meant. One might call it symptomatic dialogue: symptomatic because it is a surface manifestation of what is going on inside the person. The dialogue in most films is, of course, the opposite: a direct statement of feeling or meaning: "I love you"; "I am so happy"; "You are this"; "I am that." But just as the action should be a physical or surface correlative that permits the audience to discover for itself the implicit meaning, so the dialogue should be a *surface* that renders its content by implication—not directly. The two lines quoted from *Marty* are good film dialogue. In contrast, here is an incident from Bergman's *The Seventh Seal.*

Shortly before his death the knight Antonius Block shares a meal with a young couple in front of their covered wagon. "I shall always remember this moment," he says. "The silence, the twilight, the bowls of strawberries and milk, your faces in the evening light. Mikhael sleeping, Jof with his lyre. I'll try to remember what we have talked about. I'll carry this moment between my hands as carefully as if it were a bowl filled to the brim with fresh milk. And it will be an adequate sign—it will be enough for me."

Without this lengthy and explicit verbalization, one would have little insight into the feelings of Antonius Block. The situation itself does not communicate them and Bergman uses dialogue as a way of getting us to understand and feel something the film itself does not render. In Kurosawa's *Ikiru*, a petty official who is dying of cancer and trying desperately to give meaning to his life by pushing a playground project through the sterile bureaucracy, stops on his way home from work to look at the evening sky. "It's beautiful," he says to his companion, "but I have no time." Here the dialogue is part of the objective situation. No direct statement is needed since the man and his feelings are clear.

What is true for dialogue is equally true for performance. A good film performance is a carefully integrated sequence of concrete actions and reactions that render the feelings and thoughts of a character. It is not a system of hollow gestures that, like bad dialogue, *tell* the audience what is going on. Most film performances are drawn from the vast repertory of acting conventions. Conversely, the good film actor — whether trained in the Method or not — tries to render feelings through the use of surface correlatives. He is not concerned with the demonstration of feeling but with the symptom of feeling.

Chaplin's best work is continuously physical and concrete. If his performance in *The Gold Rush* had been generalized (or conventionalized) the scene in which he boils and eats his shoe would have become preposterous. He executes it, however, in the most careful physical detail. While the shoe is cooking, he pours water over it as if he were basting a bird. He carves and serves it with meticulous care, separating the uppers from the sole as though boning a fish. Then he winds the limp laces around his fork like spaghetti and sucks each nail as if it were a delicate chicken bone. Thus a totally incongruous moment is given an absolute, detailed physicality; the extraordinary is made ordinary, credible — and therefore funny.

It must be noted again that while the screen exceeds all other media in verisimilitude, its reality is nevertheless a *mode*. We appear to be looking at reality but are actually looking at a representation of it that may be as carefully structured as a still-life by Cézanne. The film-maker uses the surfaces of life itself — literal photographic images and accurately reproduced sounds. But the arrangement of these images and sounds is totally controlled. Each moment, each detail is carefully coordinated into the structure of the whole — just like the details in a painting or poem. By artfully controlling his images, the film-maker presents an unbroken realistic surface; he preserves the appearance of reality.

This means that he should at no time interpose himself between audience and action. He must be absent from the scene. An example of this is the use of the camera. In the standard film the camera is often editorial; the director uses it to *point out* to the audience what he wants them to see. Imagine a scene between husband and wife: we see them in a medium-shot, talking; then we cut to a close-up of the woman's hand and discover that she is slipping her wedding ring off and on. The director has made his point: we now know that she is unhappily married. But by artifically lifting the detail out of context and bringing it to our attention, the autonomous reality of the scene is violated and the audience becomes aware of the film-maker. Of course a good director may also be said to use the camera editorially—to point out what he wants us to see. But he never seems to be doing so; he preserves the appearance of an autonomous reality on the screen. The moment with the ring would have been incidental to the scene—for the camera must follow the action, not lead it.

Since the process of editing is an obvious and continued intrusion by the film-maker on the material, an editor tries to make most of his cuts in such a way that the cut itself will be obscured. In order to cut from a medium-shot to a close-up of a man, he will probably use a moment when the man rises from a chair or turns rapidly. At such a time the audience is watching the action and is unaware of the jump; once again, the effort is to preserve an apparently autonomous reality.

At the end of *Notti di Cabiria* the girl and the man she has just married are sitting in a restaurant. We see her from the back, talking. Then Fellini cuts to a shot from the front and we see that she has taken out a large wad of bank notes—her savings. We immediately realize, with something of a shock, that the man is after her money. If Fellini had actually *shown* us Cabiria taking the money out of her pocketbook, the moment would have become self-conscious and overloaded with meaning; we would have had too much time to get the point. By jumping the moment and confronting us suddenly with the money, Fellini renders the meaning *and* preserves the apparent autonomy of the situation.

Spontaneity, the sense that what is happening on the screen is happening for the first time and without plan or direction, is an essential factor in establishing a reality. It is also extremely difficult to achieve, since a huge industry has sprung up around the medium, putting enormous financial and technical pressure on the moment before the camera. Years of routine and a high degree of established skill in every department of film-making all conspire against it. From writing and casting to the angles of the camera a monstrous if unintended predictability crushes all life. Even a strong director is often helpless against the machinery; and even location shooting, which should be a liberating force, turns into a dead-end when a huge crew descends on the place, seals it off hermetically and effectively turns it into a studio. The channels have been set up too long and too well; all vision is trapped into standardized imagery and the living moment cannot survive.

For this reason an almost improvised film — like *Shadows* or *Breathless*, made without great skill or art by relatively inexperienced people — can carry far greater conviction than the standard theatrical product. In spite of obvious flaws there is a spontaneity to the action that endows it with life. Of course the experienced director, working in freedom and under good conditions, can achieve spontaneity without relying on improvisation. Kurosawa shot parts of *The Seven Samurai* with several cameras; this made it unnecessary for the actors to repeat, and so deaden, the action with every shift in camera position. Chaplin, on the other hand, used to rehearse and shoot endlessly to achieve a perfect but seemingly effortless result. Both men were after the same thing: spontaneity — and with it, reality.

Our sense of reality is so delicately attuned that certain moments are better left off the screen or the situation is destroyed. This is especially true for violence and death. When someone's head is cut off in a fiction film we know perfectly well that a trick is employed and unless a scene of this kind is handled with great care, it ends up being incredible or even funny. Similarly, when someone dies on the screen and remains in full view, many of us cannot resist watching for the slightest sign of life in the supposed corpse. We are pitting our own sense of reality against the movie-maker's; needless to say, *we* come out on top and the scene is destroyed.

In Dreyer's unproduced script on the life of Christ he describes the crucifixion by showing us the back of the cross, with the points of the nails splintering through the wood. On the screen these would be undeniably real nails going through real wood, and the authenticity of the moment would not be challenged. If, however, Dreyer had chosen to show us the cross from the front we would know absolutely that the nails going through the *flesh* are a deception — and the suffering figure would turn into a performer.

The nail splintering through the wood forces us to use our imagination — forces us to visualize what is happening on the other side of the cross. This involves us in a far deeper participation than could be achieved by the spurious horror of a nail going through the flesh of an actor.

There is something to be learned here about the entire process of perception in film. If we are explicitly told something, as we are in most pictures, we remain passive and essentially outsiders. If, however, we have to draw our *own* conclusions on the basis of evidence presented, as we do in life itself, we cannot help but participate. We become actively involved. When we are told something explicitly, we are in a sense deprived of the experience. It has been digested for us and we are merely informed of the results, or the meaning. But it is *experience* we are after, even if it remains vicarious experience.

This brings us to another characteristic of the medium—one that is profoundly related to our previous discussion. Although the experience of the motion-picture audience remains essentially vicarious, film comes closer than any other medium to giving us the illusion of a *primary* experience. This has been studied by psychologists who have found that the dark theatre, the bright hypnotic screen, the continuous flow of images and sounds, and the large anonymous audience in which we are submerged all contribute to a suspension of self-awareness and a total immersion in the events on the screen.

Beyond this, however, the medium itself encourages the illusion of a primary participation. The camera can induce an almost physical response—so that when Chaplin sits on a hypodermic needle in the lair of a dope fiend, or when Dreyer's Jeanne d'Arc has her head shaved and some of the hair falls onto her lip, the sensation produced in us is almost physical. Moreover, this physical participation is not limited to sharp sensory detail; it extends to the realm of movement.

Most directors think of the screen as of a *picture frame* within which each shot is carefully composed. They emphasize the *pictorial* quality of film. But while the medium is visual, it is not pictorial in the conventional sense. A sequence of beautifully composed shots tends to leave the audience outside the frame—spectators who are continually aware of the director's fine eye for composition. A good director tries to eliminate this distance between audience and action, to destroy the screen as a picture frame, and to drag the audience *through* it into the reality of the scene. That is the function of the running shots in *Rashomon* and of the extraordinarily emphatic camerawork of Fellini, who leans subtly into every movement and propels us into the action kinesthetically. By contrast, we have the autonomous camera motion and stiff pictorial composition of most films.

Images of movement rather than beautifully composed shots are at the heart of the medium, and significantly some of the most haunting moments in film derive their effect from motion. In Vigo's *L'Atalante,* a bride on her wedding night, still dressed in her white gown, walks along the deck of a moving barge. The barge moves forward, she is walking toward the stern, and the camera is set on the edge of the canal, so that there is a dark stationary line in the foreground. The combination of the silent forward gliding of the barge with the backward motion of the girl, whose gown and veil are streaming in the wind, has a profound emotional impact; it renders perfectly both her feelings and our own.

At the end of *Ikiru* the dying bureaucrat has succeeded in building the playground. It is a winter night; the camera moves slowly past a jungle-gym; beyond it we see the old man, swaying to and fro on a child's swing and singing to himself under the falling snow. The various components of this scene are hard to separate: the hoarse, cracked voice of the dying man; his happiness; the song itself. But the motion of the camera, the falling snow, and the low movement of the swing certainly

Hamlet (1948) Hamlet sees the ghost, but Gertrude does not. Unlike the realistic theatre, the screen can reach out and envelop us in the subjective vision of the characters. (Still courtesy of The Rank Organization, Ltd.)

contribute to the extraordinary sense of peace and reconciliation that is communicated by the image.

A last example: in Dreyer's *Day of Wrath,* a witch is burned in a seventeenth-century town. We see her bound to the top rungs of a tall ladder. Then Dreyer cuts to a long-shot and side view: on the left a huge pile of faggots is burning; to the right soldiers are raising the ladder toward the fire by means of long poles. When it stands perpendicular, they topple it forward so that the woman falls screaming across the entire frame toward the flames. The falling arc described by the victim is rendered in coldly objective terms, from far away—but it transmits her terror completely and draws us relentlessly into the action.

Kurosawa has developed a way of staging that makes it hard for an audience to remain detached. On the theory that no one should be seen entirely from the back, many directors stage their scenes in a three-quarter view. As a result, no one is seen full-face: *we* look at the actors, but they look away. In *Rashomon* and *The Seven Samurai,* however, the actors either have their backs to camera or face us frontally. When they face us, they are all but looking at us—with only their eyes turned slightly left or right of lens to indicate that they are addressing each other and not us. Of course, a face seen frontally is much more exposed than a three-quarter view, and far less likely to leave us detached.

Film can further strengthen the illusion of a primary experience by using a subjective point-of-view. In the ancient and Elizabethan theatres, while we remain in objective possession of the entire stage, the poetry and particularly the soliloquy can focus our attention on one person and shift it to his point-of-view. At any given moment the world can be seen through his eyes, subjectively. In the realistic theatre, with its fidelity to the surfaces of everyday life, this has become difficult if not impossible. We *know* how Ibsen's Nora sees the world but except for rare moments do not *experience* it from her point-of-view. She cannot, as it were, reach out and envelop us in her vision—as Hamlet and Lear can.

On the screen it again becomes possible to shift from an objective vision of a person to a vision of what *he* sees. This is done continually, often with little understanding or control. We see a girl enter a room in an objective shot. Then the camera renders what *she* sees: there is a party and her husband is talking to another woman. The next moment might be objective again, or it might be seen from the husband's point-of-view. Montage makes it possible to shift from objective to subjective, or from one subjective point-of-view to another. Film can render a place, a person, or a situation not just as they are but in the context of the protagonist's experience—*as* his experience. A point-of-view can be so carefully articulated that we comprehend every object, every passing figure, every gesture and mood in terms of the protagonist. The medium thus extends the meaning of realistic surfaces beyond their objective value; it renders them in their subjective context as well.

This brings us to an apparent paradox, for we have insisted throughout that film is at its best when rendering an objective situation. It is true, of course, that a moment can be rendered subjectively on the screen and still retain its objective reality. When the girl sees her husband talking to another woman, we see them through her eyes and so become privy to a subjective state. But the husband and the other woman are *in themselves* rendered objectively: they look no different; they are not affected by the point-of-view. The basic language of the medium, the realistic surface, has not been violated. The same may be said of most flash-backs: a subjective recollection is rendered — but in objective, undistorted terms.

There are, however, moments on the screen in which the realistic surface is in fact destroyed and a purely subjective state is created. The processional at the end of Vigo's *Zero de Conduite* is shot in slow-motion, with the boys in their white gowns gliding through a snow of pillow feathers to the accompaniment of a totally distorted but oddly ecstatic song. In such scenes, and it must be noted that while they are often attempted they do not often succeed, the reality of the feeling is so compelling that an audience accepts and assimilates a totally subjective image. The participation is so intensive that instead of rejecting an image we know to be "unreal," we enter into it eagerly.

When successful, scenes of this kind are deeply moving for they are predicated on a rare and free flow of feeling between audience and material. But they are moments of grace and cannot be counted on — like those rare moments in a performance when pure feeling breaks out of the actor and is communicated directly, without the mediation of a physical correlative.

By and large the language of the medium remains the surface of reality, and there seem to be few experiences that cannot be rendered in this language. Moreover, there is a great challenge in making the commonplaces of life, that have so long eluded art, yield up their meaning and take their rightful place in the larger patterns of existence. Film is indeed, as Kracauer put it, the redemption of physical reality. For we are finally able to use the much-despised and ephemeral detail of everyday life, the common physical dross, and work it into the gold of art.

6

**Roy Huss and
Norman Silverstein**

TONE AND POINT
OF VIEW

The title of this chapter from *The Film Experience* indicates a language common to film and literary criticism. Both Roy Huss and Norman Silverstein are professors at Queens College. Huss has written widely on film and taught film courses. Silverstein recently spent a year in Poland lecturing on film. Their book is a natural choice for studying contrasts in media.

Although cinematography is regarded as the most objective of the arts, because it most directly records reality, it conveys, like other arts, the artist's attitude and feeling. Even when the film maker is trying to be totally objective, as is the case of the newsreel photographer or the documentarist, he can never avoid coloring the film with his own temperament and personality. He may offer the viewer pictures of actual events, hard visual facts, such as a battle, a parade, or an inverview; he may show objects, such as the Eiffel Tower, the S.S. *United States,* or a Picasso mural. Yet, however much he considers these materials to be "unmalleable" or presented in a straightforward manner, no filmed object or event is, strictly speaking, unmalleable. Although an object has its naked existence, it also has enormous potential for larger significance. It can be clothed, as it were, in broader meanings, which can be

53

conveyed by the way the object is lighted, or by the angle from which it is seen, or through the context of its presentation. The film maker chooses his lighting, angle, and frame, and even the length of time he will shoot the object. In so doing, he evokes an atmosphere and expresses a style.

Art, no matter what the form or medium or how realistic it attempts to be, works through conventions that are meant to encourage credibility. Perspective and chiaroscuro are devices which establish illusion through convention, so that even the painter who pursues realism must deal with his subject obliquely. In so doing, he is bound to express something of himself. In like manner, the film maker, even when he is filming a true-to-life story, not only provides the authentic setting in which the life was lived but conveys a feeling about that life. Whatever degree of realism is intended, there will be in such a film a complex of attitudes, as embodied in the various characters and in the over-all atmosphere that represents the point of view of the film maker. Thus the film maker not only shows us what he wants us to see but also forces us to react to what he is showing us in the manner that he desires.

The writer of fiction immediately assumes a stance from which to see and judge the persons and events of his story. He may allow both himself and the reader the "aesthetic distance" afforded by third person narration — that is, the point of view of the omniscient author; or he may try to get the reader to identify more closely with what is going on by using the first-person narration — that is, having a character recount the events.

Some definitions are in order. The attitudes expressed in film may be objective, as in newsreels; subjective, as when the audience sees the world from the point of view of a character; or objective-subjective, as when the director intermixes objective and subjective shots in order to impose his own attitude on the film the audience is seeing. *Point of view,* therefore, refers to whether the filmed material purports to be unmalleable reality (objective) or reality as seen by a character (subjective). *Attitude* is the film maker's manipulation of objective and subjective shots in order to reveal his meaning. *Tone* is the attitude of the film maker both toward his filmed material and toward the audience with which he is communicating. Tone involves the film maker's and the audience's feelings of pleasure and pain, or their mixed feelings; their belief in the truth of what is on the screen; their awareness of whether the mixture of objective and subjective shots creates a style that is straightforward or ironical.

Because the movie camera can move and "see" the way a character in a film would, it allows film makers to use a first-person point of view. The camera "walks" by dollying; it raises or lowers its "head" by tilting;

it surveys a scene by panning or climbs and descends by "craning"; it gets dizzy by swish-panning and faints by going out of focus. When such effects as these are consciously exploited throughout the film we get an effect known as "subjective camera." In films containing hospital scenes, the world is often seen from the point of view of the patient as he is rushed to or from the operating room. Often we see only the lights of the ceiling rushing by, or the faces of those walking by seen from a "subjective," upward angle. And usually when the patient awakens from an operation the camera lens is made gradually to change the face of the attending doctor or nurse from a soft blur to a sharp focus. In fact, such use of the subjective camera has become a convention for scenes in which a person regains consciousness. On a more vigorous plane, when lovers are shown in a swoon of passion, the camera loses focus and the pictures fade out. (The ego is often made identifiable by clarity of registration while the forces of "unreason" are suggested by the camera's being off focus.) When it seems that the audience can be induced to identify most completely with the character undergoing stress, as when losing consciousness, the film director will shift to this kind of subjective point of view.

Also conventional is the trick of placing the camera on fast-moving vehicles upon which characters are supposedly traveling in order to "subjectify" their kinesthetic sensations. In *Entr'acte* (1924) René Clair, in anticipation of Cinerama, placed the camera on a moving roller coaster. He frightens and dizzies the spectator even more by keeping the camera upside down. E. A. Dupont made the audience share the kinesthetic sensations of the acrobats of *Variety* (1926): for the death-defying trapeze act, he placed a camera on one of the swinging trapezes and intercut that perspective of the action with objective shots of the performers doing their routine. A similar effect was achieved during the fox hunt in *Tom Jones* when a camera was mounted on a running horse to approximate Tom's experience more closely.

The very rate at which movement is photographed can be used artistically to suggest moods and the workings of a character's mind. If the camera's rate is slowed as it photographs a moving object, the projection of the film at normal speed will make the action seem accelerated; for the contrary effect, if the camera's rate is speeded up, the movement of the projected image appears as slowed down. Very frequently this second phenomenon (slow motion) is used to suggest a surrealistic dream or an entire emotion-laden memory going on in a character's mind. One of the most effective of these occurs in the boy's dream in Buñuel's *Los Olvidados (The Young and the Damned)* (1950). The sight of the mother coming to give her son a piece of raw meat and bestow her affection upon him is made peculiarly nightmarish by her approach in slow motion. Another instance is the vision experienced by the protagonist in Lindsay Anderson's *This Sporting Life* (1963) as his team slowly and unrelentingly scrimmages in the mud. Here the gruesome tone is enhanced by complete silence on the sound track and a twilight effect in the lighting. In both these cases the antigravitational effect of the slow motion seems particularly appropriate to the uninhibited nature of the memory or dream.

Other cinematic methods of pictorially rendering a subjective dream or memory consist of the photographic superimposition of images—involving double printing—or a flash-back shot. Usually the subjective sequences are recapitulations of a character's previous experiences rather than surrealistic distortions of them. In *The Birth of a Nation* (1915) Margaret Cameron "sees in her imagination the death of her second brother, *Wade* . . . killed during the battle of Atlanta."[1] A balloon vignette of Wade appears. He lies prostrate on the earth near a fence, refugees streaming past him, and he closes his eyes in death.

The superimpositions we are speaking about show the memory and the rememberer simultaneously and therefore convey a subjective tone—the attitude of the rememberer being activated by the pictures printed with him, as when a man huddling in the cold "dreams" of a warm hearth and his wife and children surrounding him. Griffith often had the reminiscing character stare off into space and then showed in the same shot the remembered person or object or event framed in an iris, perhaps against a solid background. Strictly speaking, the flash back is also a storytelling device in which events are presented out of a time sequence, but with the pictures of past experiences interrupting pictures of the present. Thus in *The Girl Who Stayed at Home* (1918), Robert Herron, portraying a civilian weakling nicknamed "Slouchy," is provoked to action by a memory picture from his past. When Trüberein, a bully in the small town, sees Slouchy with a girl, the bully beats him off, embarrassing him. During World War I, after the army has made a man of him, Slouchy recognizes Trüberein as the enemy German approaching him for single combat. In order to show what Slouchy is thinking, Griffith cuts to the scene in the park where Slouchy was beaten up (a flash back) and cuts back to the revenge of Slouchy, who now knocks out Trüberein.

Other interesting photographing and editing principles have been used to pictorialize characters' mental states or imaginings. The "flash shot," almost subliminal in its effect since it consists of only a few frames, has been used by avant-gardist Gregory Markopoulas in *Twice a Man* (1963), by Alain Resnais in *Last Year at Marienbad* (1962), and by Joseph

---

[1] Seymour Stern, "The Birth of a Nation: Part I," Special Griffith Issue, *Film Culture*, No. 36 (Spring-Summer, 1965), p. 86.

Strick in *Ulysses* (1967) to represent flashes of memory. In *Marienbad* an increased lens aperture in one of these shots causes an intensification of light, underlining the climax of the man's memory of running toward the woman. Jan Kadar in *The Shop on Main Street* (1965) uses intensified light along with distorted motion for two "dream" sequences — the man and woman at one point seeming to glide, at another moving with exaggerated slowness. Again, after the protagonist has killed the Jewish woman, the camera at first behaves subjectively, that is, simulates his eye movements by "looking around" the shop, and then seems to become his antagonist as it presses in on him accusingly. In the latter case the camera is endowed with the moods of the participant.

Another frequently used method of shifting to subjective camera is that of exaggerating camera angles. Films featuring children as principal figures may abound in low-angle shots of adults because the director may wish to remind the audience frequently of the perspective of a child's reality. In Carol Reed's *The Fallen Idol* (1949) we are often reminded that adult experiences are affecting the sensibilities of a small boy. This is accomplished through low-angle shots of their behavior as he observes them. Likewise, in a sequence from Laughton's *The Night of the Hunter,* a low-angle shot of Robert Mitchum looming up over the children as he pursues them into the water combines a realistic presentation of their low angle of vision with a more expressionistic indication of their nightmarish awareness of his overpowering force. A similar device was used by David Lean in *Great Expectations:* the angle enables Magwitch to appear suddenly hovering over the frightened Pip. In Nicholas Ray's *Bigger Than Life* (1955), a man made megalomaniac by excessive use of cortisone says, "I feel ten feet tall," and the camera shoots him from a low angle.

Very rarely does a film maker seek to sustain throughout the entire film a subjective tone from the point of view of one of the characters. *Lady in the Lake* (1947) is an exceptional instance in which this is attempted. In this film the detective-hero is not photographed but is "experienced" only through the flexible moving eye of the camera. Occasionally we see his hands or arms reach up into the bottom of the frame, and several times we even see his reflection in a mirror. But these are not really violations of the subjective camera or first-person point of view because a person is always capable of seeing "objectively" parts of his own body or his own mirror image.

In the theater, the principal means — perhaps the *only* means — open to the playwright who wants to achieve considerable subjectivity in the viewpoint of a character is expressionism. Thus in Elmer Rice's *The Adding Machine* the set designer must plaster the walls with huge numerals in order to project the state of mind of the accountant-protagonist.

It is interesting to compare such an effort on the stage with a similar highly reputed one on the screen — *The Cabinet of Dr. Caligari.* At the end of the film the audience discovers that the wild distortions in the design of the painted sets represent projections of an insane mind. Film historians have often observed that *Caligari,* despite its effectiveness, is both the alpha and omega of expressionism in films, but few have said precisely why. The answer is probably that the film's expressionistic devices were theatrical and not cinematic. The camera itself, through such functions as angle, movement, and focus, could have more effectively created the mad doctor's subjective view of the world which in the theater is almost the sole province of the set designer.

Not all shifts to the subjective camera are as dramatic as those accomplished by moving the camera in exceptional ways or placing it in exceptional positions, blurring or sharpening its focus, placing it on fast-moving vehicles, or varying its rate of speed or light intensity as it photographs.

Frequently the switch from an omniscient "third-person" point of view to a "first-person" one is so unobtrusive that the audience is not conscious of it. This is partly because no unorthodox camera techniques are used but, even more likely, it is because the change is mandatory for continuity. A shot framing a character looking at something off screen naturally arouses an expectation in the audience that the succeeding shot will show what the character is looking at. The first of these, what Vorkapich calls the "look of outward regard," indicates that a character is looking at something. The second, called an "eye-line shot," is what he sees. Even though the latter may not involve an impressionistic visualization (as shown, say, by the blurred focus or low camera angle) and though it therefore may seem to be merely fulfilling the objective requirement of continuity, it is subjective in that it stands for what the character sees.

If the director forgets that a shot containing a "look of outward regard" almost inevitably requires that the next shot will be a subjective view of what is seen, he runs the risk of creating a confusion or absurdity. For instance, Vorkapich holds that in *L'Avventura,* when Antonioni follows a shot of Monica Vitti looking up to a bedroom window with a supposedly objective shot of a couple making love inside, we momentarily feel that the second scene represents her voyeuristic observance of the pair — an impression not intended. If the "objective" shot is from Antonioni's point of view, the first has falsely prepared the spectator for a subjective, eye-line shot. Or when Flaherty, in *Man of Aran* (1934), photographs a woman gazing through a window (she remarks that her husband is seven days out at sea) and then follows this with a middle shot of fishermen sitting in boats, the audience for a moment has the mistaken notion that the second shot dramatizes some incredible power in the woman to see many miles out to sea. But, like Antonioni, Flaherty ignores the rule, and entertains poetic, or cinematic, license by abruptly shifting from the point of view of the character to his own, imposing his own feelings on the sequence. Antonioni willfully uses cinematic license because he is astonished by the free sensuality of the couple who make love knowing that Monica Vitti is waiting for them; Flaherty is willing to confuse the audience momentarily in order to regale the movie-goer with the power of the cinema to take the journey from the woman to the men at sea, a journey that the woman cannot take. Both Antonioni and Flaherty intermix objective and subjective shots in order to convey their own attitudes.

As we have seen, a shift to the subjective camera seems both reasonable and desirable when a character gets caught up in an intense or exciting experience or when his "eye line" is directed off camera. Like first-person narration in fiction, the subjective shot not only dramatizes a character's or film maker's attitude or point of view but involves the spectator more intimately in the action. In other words, even though the moviegoer remains aware that he is observing the emotional reaction of a separate character, the subjective camera at the same time impels him into the shock or delight of an immediate experience.

Frequently the subjective camera technique may secure the spectator's participation in an event without there being any portrayal of a character to share the emotional involvement. Cinerama, which employs such tricks as placing a camera on a roller coaster, is an obvious contemporary example of this, for here the camera does not represent a character who is part of a fiction but attempts to substitute for the filmgoer himself. In the same way, camera angles, besides expressing the point of view of a particular character, as in *The Fallen Idol*, may be a direct invitation from the film maker to the audience to share in his own attitude or feeling. When Murnau in *The Last Laugh* has his camera "look up" at the old doorman's good fortune by means of low-angle shots, and later makes it "look down" at his misery with high-angle ones, he is not only enhancing the tragic reversal, but is imposing upon us — perhaps without our awareness or conscious consent — attitudes of reverence, condescension, and social judgment of a sort. When Ozu, often called the most Japanese of Japan's film directors, insists on shooting almost all his scenes with the camera elevated only three feet from the floor, he is supposedly forcing all of us to maintain a Japanese outlook, for according to film critic Iwasaki Akira,

Ozu's reasoning . . . is as follows: the Japanese people spend their lives seated on "tatami" mattings spread over the floor;

to attempt to view such a life through a camera high up on a tripod
is irrational; the eye-level of the Japanese squatting on the "tatami"
becomes, of necessity, the level for all who are to view what goes
on around them; therefore the eye of the camera must also be at
this level.[2]

There are of course other less subtle types of "audience participation" films involving the subjective camera. In *Tom Jones* the characters
occasionally wink at or address the camera (i.e., the audience). Tom at
one point virtually accuses it of pruriently peeking at Mrs. Waters' semi-
nudity by clapping his hat over the lens; at another point he brands it
phlegmatic when in jubilation at Allworthy's recovery he tears down
the black drapes to "cover first the pious ones [Blifil, Thwackum, Square,
and Dowling], then the screen."[3] The detached, comical tone achieved
by Richardson springs from intermixed objective and subjective shots.
However, a director may have no purpose in shifting from one camera
angle to another. He may be achieving nothing more than cinematic
coherence, as when Cukor in *Rhapsody* (1954) achieves a visual balance
by shooting all sequences of a violinist from below and all those of a
pianist from above.

The film maker may withdraw from the material by allowing the
actors to perform or events to occur as if he were not manipulating them,
or even present, or he may introduce himself by self-conscious technique
—variable camera distance, space play, or masking—with a great degree
of involvement. Through his style, he intrudes himself and therefore his
attitude, unwilling to allow the actors and the story to "roll" by without
his "comment."

Within the third-person, objective point of view, there are degrees
of self-consciousness. To some of the early readers of novels the device
of the omniscient narrator itself must have seemed strange, since it is
unreal for a reporter of events to know what every character is thinking
or doing. Homer and Virgil overcame this potential awkwardness by
pretending that their knowledge and inspiration came directly from an
all-knowing, all-seeing muse. However, some of the early English novelists like Fielding did not seek to make the "unreality" of the convention unobtrusive, but on the contrary capitalized for comic effect on
their readers' awareness of the narrator's omniscience and omnipresence.
Fielding's tone was that of a creator delighted to present and control
his puppets but frequently lapsing into mock horror and disavowal of
responsibility as their immoral behavior led them to take on a life of their
own. Thus the comedy was partly achieved by the author's reminding

2"Yasujito Ozu," *Film*, No. 36 (Summer, 1963), p. 9.
3John Osborne, *Tom Jones: a Filmscript* (New York: Grove Press, 1964), p. 67.

us of his role and insisting upon a tone of detachment and of moral and aesthetic distance.

By what special cinematic devices can a film maker establish this same tone of comic detachment through a third-person narrator? Tony Richardson's film version of *Tom Jones* provides some interesting insights into the more palpable uses of the camera as self-conscious narrator.

Although Richardson used the voice of a narrator (a surrogate of Fielding) on the sound track, a total reliance on this device would obviously have been verbal and literary rather than cinematic. Fortunately Richardson did not attempt a literal transcription of the novel, but found suitable movie substitutes, principally in order to equalize in cinema the humorous tone which we recognize as mock-heroic. Many of these consisted of revivals of archaic artifices, such as the wipe (in every possible variation),* stop photography, photoanimation, and accelerated action. The continual intrusion of these almost forgotten techniques (particularly the fancy wipes) is a constant reminder of the "author's" presence, control, detachment, and bemusement.

Part of our delight in comedy is the sight of someone caught in a mechanistic order of existence. The art of the cinema, dependent as it is upon a complex and ingenious machine, is aptly suited for the creation of such a tone. In *Tom Jones* Richardson accomplishes this kind of farcical effect several times. In the bedroom farce at the inn, involving Mrs. Waters, for example, people are reduced to frantic, scurrying insects because the action is greatly accelerated—a standard comic technique going back to the earliest days of film making. Strangely enough, speeded action seems more rigidly confined to expressing a farcical tone than is slow motion in expressing serious feelings. Accelerated motion resists being used for tones other than farcical. In *Nosferatu* (1922) Murnau shot the journey of the vampire's carriage and later the loading of the coffins into the wagon in fast motion in order to indicate the villain's supernatural powers, but succeeded only in making these amusing rather than frightening.

Another incident in *Tom Jones* involves an entirely different technique for achieving a mechanical mode of comic behavior while emphasizing the mock-heroic tone of the film maker. While Tom is recovering from a broken arm, he engages in donkey riding. By means of "stop photography" Richardson is able to make it appear as if Tom follows

---

*When Richardson editorializes in the manner of Henry Fielding, his intrusive wipes underline his attitude. As Tom and Molly Seagram are about to make love in the woods, he censors the scene with a wipe which resembles the closing of sliding doors, and when he returns to the censored scene, he uses its opposite. A discreet amount of time is presumed to have passed.

Richardson uses the spiral wipe to show Tom ecstatic in his new London clothes and a bar wipe to introduce the actual bars of the prison in which Tom is confined.

himself in a procession. The effect is that of a merry-go-round composed of several Joneses on donkeys.

Most of the self-conscious techniques used by Richardson for aesthetic distance in *Tom Jones* had first been revived from films of three or four decades ago by Truffaut in his *Jules and Jim,* which contained additional intrusive elements like an intentional graininess in texture to suggest tintype photographs. These conventions are becoming so widespread in television commercials that they are losing their quaintness and with it their suggestion of a critical distance between the artist and his creation.

Sometimes a startling tone is created by accident, whether due to lighting or to interruption. A news photographer may begin to film objectively but discover that the product is enlivened by accidental circumstances. When the camera finds itself reacting impulsively, as it were, to an unpredictable situation, newsreels and *cinema vérité* may reach their epitome of dramatic effectiveness. In the frequently shown footage of the moments immediately following the assassination of President Kennedy in Dallas the camera swings confusedly, searching about for the source of the trouble, passing over the fearful bystanders throwing themselves to the ground, then to a policeman drawing his gun, then to the speeded-up motorcade — the street all the while seeming to tilt at crazy angles as the photographer seeks to aim the camera. In retrospect the cameraman, originally interested only in making a newsreel of the procession, probably regretted his lack of aplomb and professional control over his machine. But the excited quality of the filming, despite its amateurishness, caught the emotional impact of the incident in a way that might have been impossible under the conditions of cool professionalism.

In the "News on the March" sequence in *Citizen Kane,* Orson Welles at one point anticipates *cinema vérité* technique in order to emphasize the rarity of a glimpse of Kane's seclusion in his later years. The camera which captures the inaccessible tycoon being wheeled about in the garden of a private sanitarium seems to move surreptitiously from behind a tree and to record with some haste and difficulty. (The rest of the "News on the March" sequence, a parody of the "March of Time" series, is done in traditional newsreel style: highly mannered in its spoken commentary and well planned in its camera arrangements.) In this instance we have a highly conscious camera technique masquerading as an impulsive, unplanned style, as if it were on the spot like the camera that filmed Kennedy's assassination.

In George Landow's "loop film" entitled *This Film Will Be Interrupted After Eleven Minutes for a Commercial* the ultimate in self-consciousness is achieved, although not by camera techniques but by a special process of photographic printing and projection. Landow calls attention to all the mechanical aspects of film projection of which the audience is not supposed to be aware, or becomes aware of only during a faulty projection, and seeks to transform them into a meaningful aesthetic experience. This is comparable to a cultivated self-consciousness in other art forms — in the theater, for instance, when Pirandello, Wilder, or Genêt has characters directly address the audience to remind them that they are in a theater, or in architecture when the architect allows the skeleton of his structure to protrude in order to become an integral part of the effect. In Landow's loop the self-consciousness of technique seems designed to direct our attention away from subject matter and into a kinesthetic involvement with the film's rhythm and movement.

Supposedly the diametric opposite of using camera and projector for aesthetic self-consciousness is *cinema vérité,* or direct cinema, which aims at recording the completely spontaneous, or only partly improvised, "happening." This is made possible by the light and mobile hand-held camera, which the operator can easily thrust into intimate situations and hope for the "gift" or accident of something spontaneously beautiful or inherently exciting. The following is a description of one of the more successful pioneering efforts in this movement:

> *Desistfilm* [by Stan Brakhage] employs all the techniques of a spontaneous cinema. It describes a wild party held by a young group of youths, with all their youthful exhibitionisms, adolescent games and adolescent love images, and was shot in one evening at a real improvised party with a 16mm camera, most of the time hand-held, following every movement wildly, without any premeditated plan. This technique of the freed camera enabled him to recreate the mood and tempo of the party, with all its little details of foolish, silly, marginal actions, its outbursts of adolescent emotions. The camera, freed from its tripod, gets everywhere, never intruding, never interfering; it moves into close-ups, or follows the restless youths in fast, jerky tilts and pans. There seems to be a perfect unity here of subject matter, camera movement, and the temperament of the film maker himself. The free flight of life has been caught, and the film has vitality, rhythm, and also the temperament of a poem by Rimbaud, of a naked confession — all improvisation, with no artist's hand visible.[4]

While the director can make us conscious of his technique in order to retain "editorial" control of what his audience feels, he also can more

---

[4]Jonas Mekas, "Cinema of the New Generation," *Film Culture,* No. 21 (Summer, 1960), p. 15.

subtly manipulate audience reaction by his choice of camera distances. Close shots, which peer at objects, create intensity; long shots, by their distance, imply detachment. During a television interview in 1964, French film maker Jean-Luc Godard made the rather startling statement that "tragedy is close-up and comedy is long shot,"[5] but that he often took pleasure in reversing these in his own films. The resultant tone reflects Godard's tragicomic view of life.

What does the first part — the traditional part — of this statement amount to essentially? If we think of a Chaplin film like *City Lights,* we remember that most of the farcical scenes are shot roughly within the range of middle to long shot. Since Chaplin's comic art is mainly one of bodily movement (including acrobatics and the dance), we can understand why this is necessary. In contrast, when we recall scenes of strong pathos in *City Lights,* as when the previously blind girl recognizes the tramp as her benefactor, the close-up shot of Chaplin's face seems necessary to convey the heartfelt emotions registered there.

Since it is generally true that film comedy consists mainly of people interacting in a physical way with objects or each other and that the principal physiological movement at times of grief is facial, Godard's assumption about traditional cinema seems true. However, in the examples mentioned above the camera functioned more as a recorder of the emotion than as a creator of it. Many film makers, including Godard himself, are not content merely to use variable focal lengths as an optical convenience but rather insist on using it to signal a tone.

In reminiscing about two of his films — *Long Day's Journey into Night* (1962) and *A View from the Bridge* (1961) — Sidney Lumet remarked that close-ups were a predominant feature of the first film whereas some extremely long shots had been used with particular purpose in the latter film. Since both are tragedies and both are adaptations from stage plays, the contrasts in camera distance are noteworthy. Lumet felt that the many close-ups he used in *Long Day's Journey* helped to convey the sense of confinement and entrapment the protagonist suffers in the heart of his family. But perhaps more importantly his use of close-ups allowed him to make Katharine Hepburn's face the real playing area in the film. To the extent that tragic emotions, being movements of the *psyche,* are most clearly registered in the face, this seems entirely appropriate. In *A View from the Bridge,* close-ups are also helpful in establishing the crowded conditions in the tiny Brooklyn apartment, especially after the arrival of the immigrants Marco and Rodolfo. But these scenes are not climactic in that they are not part of Eddie s tragic ordeal of personal loneliness and eventual alienation from the commu-

[5]"Camera Three," CBS television program, Sunday, September 19, 1964.

nity. The actual intensity of Eddie's plight is emphasized in at least three memorable long shots.

The first of these occurs when Eddie, jealous of the two lovers Rodolfo and Catherine, follows them on their first visit to Manhattan. Eddie's painful separation from the shared intimacy of the young pair as they enjoy the bright lights of Times Square and the Automat is enhanced by his and our long-shot views of them. (Greater lateral distances are also made possible by the wide screen.)

During this sequence Lumet sometimes achieves a tragicomic effect because the use of a deep-focus lens allows both a close-up and long-shot within the same shot. In one of these, in which we see Eddie in the foreground observing the happy cavorting couple in the background, the long shot of the pair allows us detached amusement, while the close-up of Eddie's pained face forces us into compassion for his suffering.

The second significant long shot is an overhead crane shot of Marco and Eddie fighting in the street. Here it is important that we see the broad area of pavement which separates the contenders from the circle of neighbors who are willing to watch but not become involved. While the overhead position of the camera intensifies the tragedy of Eddie's isolation, the distance of the camera and the encompassing view it affords invite us to view the struggle as a kind of "human comedy."

One of the final long shots of the film is done in deep focus to establish even another significant facet of the tragic tone of the film. In the distant background we clearly see the crowd now huddled around Eddie's dead body. A great expanse of empty street (its vastness intensified by the camera's low angle) connects the background group with a phone booth in the foreground. During this shot, Alfiere, Eddie's lawyer-friend and a kind of Greek chorus in the film, detaches himself from the crowd and comes forward across the pavement to the phone booth to report the death to the police (and to us). Here the mood is almost identical with a Greek tragedian's discretion in keeping violent death at a distance and sending a messenger forward to report it.

Although in general the dictum that close-ups are suitable for tragedy and long shots are likely to be used in comedy is sound, we have already demonstrated that it is not universally true, any more than is the use of slow motion solely for seriousness. Whereas tragedy frequently demands of an audience the kind of personal involvement afforded by close-ups and comedy demands the kind of detachment conveyed by long shots, the distant shots of Eddie in the last scene of *A View from the Bridge* were nevertheless tragic.

In like manner, a close-up for comic rather than tragic effect might be illustrated in a scene from *The Idle Class* (1921). We are first given a middle-close-up of the back of Chaplin's head and shoulders heaving in great agitation. Since the audience has just been shown his wife's telegram stating that she has left him in protest against his drinking, it assumes that the movement is caused by weeping. But when he turns toward the camera Chaplin is shaking a cocktail. The middle-close-up of the blankness of his expression—where moviegoers expected to see his face as a "playing area" alive with the emotions of grief—becomes a delightful comic surprise.

But what special tone does Godard achieve by a willful inversion of the usual formula? If we examine the camera distance in certain shots of *A Woman Is a Woman* (1961) and *My Life to Live* (1962) we notice that he achieves the special complexity of tragicomedy or dark comedy. In the latter film, the opening shots of the couple sitting at the coffee bar are "tragic" in that the man and woman are discussing the break-up of a serious marriage, but as close-ups the shots are at the same time "humorous" because the camera keeps panning the totally unrevealing backs of their heads.

A Woman Is a Woman is on the surface a musical comedy but re-verberates with undertones of the pain of serious emotional commitments. One of the most noticeable oddities of the film is that the musical "production" numbers, traditionally (as in Fred Astaire musicals) shot in medium-long shots, are frequently done in close-up. Here it would seem that Godard is not so much inverting the use of close-ups for comic incongruity as he is leading us through them from the obvious farcical tone to a sense of what Sarris calls "the exquisite agony of heterosexual love."[6] The intimacy of the woman's sexual wiles, as she tries to maneuver her lover to give her a child; the subtlety and ambivalence of her feelings of moral indiscretion in getting her lover's friend to seduce her; the signs of her contrition and her lover's forgiveness; and the wink with which she asserts the irresistible urge of a woman to procreate must all be conveyed through close-ups.

Facial close-ups frequently stress the intimacy and eroticism of a love scene. This tradition extends all the way from Edison's close-up of John Rice and May Irwin in *The Kiss* (1896) to Warhol's tight shots of Naomi Levine with various males in *Kiss* (1964). Avant-garde film makers Willard Maas and Stan Brakhage have perhaps pushed the close-up technique to its ultimate limits for eliciting erotic overtones. In his *Geography of the Body* (1954) Maas achieves half-erotic, half-humorous effects by photographing in close-up some of the sexually neutral parts of the body, like the ear, in such minute detail that our loss of the usual perspective makes them appear as a genital organ, breast, or anus. In *Loving*

---

[6]Andrew Sarris in the *Village Voice,* November 12, 1964.

(1956), Brakhage, by moving the camera so rapidly and in such myopic close-up over parts of arms, faces, and shoulders of the two lovers, prevents us from achieving a proper "gestalt" of what we are seeing and thus stimulates us to imagine that we might be observing some "forbidden" body area or movement.

The tonality that the film maker achieves through variable camera distances may be reinforced by the way he composes a shot. By varying camera distance he in fact reorganizes the lines and masses within the frame. For instance, a dark tree on a plain photographed in long shot against a bright sky would blot out less than one percent of the light mass. When registered in middle shot it might occupy one-third of the area; when moved to close-up, perhaps 90 percent. Furthermore, if the camera lens "zooms" the tree from long range to close range, the tree appears to grow because the vertical line of the tree lengthens while the horizontal line caused by the meeting of sky and plain and already extending the full length of the screen remains constant. Thus the film maker creates certain subtle feelings of exhilaration, heaviness, flight, despair, excitement, and so on, not only by the change in distance but by the shift or "play" in the proportion and balance of masses, planes, and lines.

In producing atmosphere and mood by such means film makers are merely giving a more dynamic quality to principles of composition long exercised in painting and still photography. Masses with a predominance of strong horizontal lines, especially if shot from a low angle, establish a feeling of heaviness, quietness, and confinement. The wide flight of the Odessa Steps shot from below in *Potemkin,* or the filming of the "fat man" (Sidney Greenstreet) in black clothes and from a low angle in *The Maltese Falcon,* achieves effects of awesome massiveness. In contrast, the accentuation of vertical lines tends to produce feelings of festivity, freedom, and perhaps soaring inspiration. Church spires, Gothic vaults, trees, and flagpoles, whether symbolically significant or not, may give these impressions, especially when surrounded by large lighted areas.

When diagonal lines stretch across the screen they frequently bring an effect of liveliness and an expansion of movement, especially if they join foreground to background. Waves washing onto a shore will easily produce these effects if the beachline is made to run diagonally across the screen. Circular lines and scattered dots tend to produce a sparkling, happy, fluttering impression (freedom from inhibition because free of structural cohesion or centrality). A memorable overhead shot of the Beatles cavorting on a football field in *A Hard Day's Night* is a case in point. Aerial shots of a terrain dotted by bombardments from an aircraft are joyous regardless of what one's attitudes toward war are supposed to be, as is the shot of Parisians in *Le Joli Mai* (1963) pictured from above at a great distance and separated by great patches of light.

Naturally the structural lines and volumes of masses rarely work alone to produce tonal effects. Balances and imbalances of light and darkness, as just noted, harmonies and disharmonies of planes, dynamism of movement within and between shots are usually crucial as visual complements. Witness, for instance, the following description of how the heavy mood in *The Late Mattia Pascal* (1924) is brought about:

> Cavalcanti, who conceived the settings for Marcel l'Herbier's psychological fantasy after Pirandello, *The Late Mattia Pascal,* has not only set the prevailing mood, but has foreshadowed the entire action of the piece by his emphasis on line and plane, his architectural and decorative distortions. By using heavy shadows and dizzying designs, by distortions of plane and surface, he has underscored the rhythms of this strange, distorted tale of Pirandello's imagining. The long lines of the windows, the abrupt and jagged geometric pattern of the carpet, the heaviness of the Gothic arches, the very artificiality of the studio lighting, are all used to exaggerate the note of morbid unreality of the drama.[7]

In *Sweet and Sour* (1963) lightheartedness and joyful movement are suggested not only by tall thin trees and the waving diagonal line of the shore, but also by the preponderance of white over black, the smooth texture of the ice, the spotted effect of the leaves above, the softness of the focus, and presumably by the dynamic movement of the figures themselves.

A superior film maker will recognize the types of undertones arising from the play of spaces, lines, and volumes on the screen and compose his shots in such a way that they reinforce rather than conflict with his theme, attitude, and intended mood. And since he is not a still photographer or a painter, the play of spaces in his composition must be dynamic rather than static.

One director who succeeded brilliantly in exploiting this kind of compositional movement for achieving unique tonal effects was Ernst Lubitsch. The famous "Lubitsch touch"—characterized by a light, witty, sophisticated approach to a comedy of manners—depended in large part on Lubitsch's insistence on clearing his sets of bric-a-brac so that his camera could glide through space to give a sense of smoothness and ease. Often he welded gracefulness to lightness and airiness by having

---

[7]Evelyn Gerstein, *Theatre Arts Monthly,* XI (April, 1927), pp. 296-97.

both character and camera etch out a line that was both vertical and circular: movement in a wide curve through a great volume of space (a tracking shot of Herbert Marshall's stand-in gliding up and down the wide arc of the stairs in *Trouble in Paradise,* 1932) or movement up into a spiral (craning the camera to pursue a department store employee moving up a spiral stairway in *Bluebeard's Eighth Wife*).

A few directors have been intensely conscious of the limits of size and shape of the screen itself in relation to volume and space to render tonal effects. As Arthur Knight points out, even in the early days of film making directors felt that "the wealth of visual imagery that they were able to project made [the screen's] fixed and static dimensions seem quite inadequate," and eventually some of the more imaginative film makers, led by Griffith, "began to improvise ways of relating the shape of their screen to the mood, the action, the atmosphere of a shot, a sequence, or a scene."[8] Griffith himself achieved this by masking the lighted areas of the screen in various ways, either at top or bottom, and varied its size and shape to intensify the effect. As Knight notes, both limits to the spectrum of possibilities of this device are explored by Griffith in *Intolerance* within a matter of seconds:

> To accentuate the far-flung hordes of Syrian warriors riding toward Babylon, for instance, he blacked out the top and bottom of the frame, producing a narrow, elongated frieze effect—strikingly similar to today's Cinemascope screen. But a moment later, when he wanted to emphasize the height of the walls of Babylon, he masked off the sides of the frame and showed the body of a single soldier hurtling down from the top of the ramparts in a vertical shaft of light.[9]

Cinema-Scope, together with all the other wide-screen variants, of course merely increased the possibilities for space play in a horizontal direction while ignoring any proportional requirements for vertical distance. As far back as the thirties Eisenstein protested against this "mechanical" and "passive" lateral extension of space without any thought to the dramatic and mood requirements for a strong vertical line, and he argued that if a practical means could not be devised for fluctuating the size and shape of the screen during projection, the best compromise was a square screen, since only this would allow comparable dramatic effects from the vertical and horizontal lines. Today directors of wide-screen productions are often forced to regard the increased lateral space in the same way that Victorian theatrical directors regarded their mammoth

[8] Arthur Knight, *The Liveliest Art* (New York: New American Library, 1957), p. 303.
[9] *Ibid.,* p. 304.

stages: not as space to be used dramatically and dynamically, but as a static space to be filled and cluttered with more objects and decor.

Obviously the best use that can be made of a disproportionate increase of width is in the historical epic, the travelogue with panoramic views, and the musical spectacular. But even these occasionally require a varying mood of intimacy or dramatic stress of detail, which can be conveyed only within a smaller space or by emphasis of vertical line or mass. At best one can recall only *parts* of wide-screen productions in which tone or mood is made more effective by the increased lateral vision. This occurs, of course, either when a strong horizontal line is needed for dramatic purposes, or when huge lateral spaces are needed to set off the minuteness or isolation of an object. A powerful illustration of the former is the almost unending line of savages rising over the top of a hill in *Zulu* (1964). A good example of a sense of isolation achieved by lateral space would be the shot of the small town in the middle of the desert in *Bad Day at Black Rock* (1954). In *Lawrence of Arabia* (1962) the way in which a black speck develops into a rider approaching on horseback is made more mystifying by the large surrounding areas of desert.

In achieving and maintaining continuity, the film maker adjusts settings and actors, or even photographic reality itself, in order to convey either his own attitude or that of his characters. His means are moving cameras, chemical processes, shifting camera angles, shot beginnings and endings, slow or accelerated motion, focal lengths, and space play. Using film he can be direct or ironical, simple or subtle, bitter about life or opportunistic (giving the public what it wants). He can win our admiration or our scorn. He cannot, however, hide what he is. As an artist good or bad, he tells us how he feels and what he thinks by the photographic reality he shows us and by the ways he manipulates it.

7 Raymond Durgnat

THE MONGREL MUSE

In this opening chapter from *Films and Feelings*, Durgnat notes the relationship of film to a broad spectrum of the arts. He also examines the perennial question of defining "style" and "content." Chapters from this excellent volume were originally published in such diverse journals as *Films and Filming* and *The Architectural Review*.

The great difficulty in talking about cinema style is that the cinema is a *potpourri* of art forms, sharing elements in common with each, but weaving them into a pattern of its own.

In that it centres on actors, on the human form, it comes closest to the theatre. In its origin, too, it is associated with theatrical forms (the 'music hall' act). But it is 'deficient' theatre, for the show lacks the actor's presence. Instead of one person physically, constantly, present here and nowhere else in the world, we have only a Polyfoto presence, a pack of images, changing in shape and size — half-way to abstraction.

The cinema can compensate in other ways for its shortcomings in this. It can call on all the resources of photography. It can dispense with the human person altogether (the documentary) or merge him with the landscape (the Western). Its sense of place, in flexibility and realism far beyond theatrical possibility, confers on it something of the novel's narrative fluidity.

But compared with the novel its way with words, and therefore with ideas, is clumsy. The talkie's words take second place to the visual presentation of reality. Film visuals can show a 'lame old black cat sitting on a worn grey mat'. Or a 'playful tabby stretched out on a mat with a pattern of roses on it'. But they can't say, simple, 'the cat sat on the mat.' They can show a beautiful statue in sun, then in rain, then in snow, but they can't say simply, 'A thing of beauty is a joy for ever.' Their powers of abstraction are limited. They can't match the writer's swift, deft way with metaphors. Film is a reasonably good medium for persuading, but it's a very clumsy one for arguing. And by means of words, which present objective reality through ideas, the novelist can mix visual reality and ideas in a rich, intimate way. Here the cinema is infinitely poorer.

Yet its literary poverty is compensated by its visual richness. It is a visual art, like painting. In the words of Marcel Carné, 'One must compose images as the old masters did their canvases, with the same preoccupation with effect and expression. Cinema images have the same needs.' The film critic will often need to use the vocabulary of the visual arts rather than of literary criticism.

In sensitivity of line, tone, form and other plastic qualities the ciné-camera is, however, vastly inferior to the painter's brush. The very best cartoons, like Hector Hoppin's and Anthony Gross's *Joie de Vivre* (1934) may have something of the artist's freedom of line, but the cartoon isn't after all the mainstream of cinema.

The photographic cinema can compensate for its deficiences here by its theatrical-narrative interest. And by the visual possibilities opened to it by its being a *succession* of images, in *movement*. Here it has its own possibilities of plastic, formal nuance and organization.

Indeed, it relates here to music and the visual arts at the same time. The visual art of architecture has been described as 'frozen music'— meaning that just as architecture is shapes and structures and tensions standing static in space, music is musical shapes and structures and tensions in time. It's true that there is a certain *time* element in architecture (you walk past a façade, or through an arch), just as there is a 'space' element moving in music (you are conscious of things happening 'simultaneously', in counterpoint). But these are secondary—'time' in architecture is reversible (few buildings are based, like symphonies, on a beginning, a middle and an end). And 'space' in music is a result, rather than a determinant, of form. Only the film is shapes and structures and tensions both in space (the image) *and* in time. Only the film synchronizes, interweaves, visual and musical shapes (picture and soundtrack). Norman MacLaren's *Begone Dull Care* (1949) represents the 'missing link' between painting and music. It shows us visual colours and patterns flashing, dancing, quivering in counterpoint to the Oscar Peterson Quartet.

Thus the cinema combines elements from the various arts into its own synthesis. It can also co-opt the various forms as a whole. The film adds words to pictures to music. As Resnais's camera roams over the surface of Picasso's *Guernica,* 1949 (breaking it down into a *sequence* of smaller images, that is, converting space into time), the commentator intones, first, statistics, then, a poem of Paul Eluard's — thus making a new synthesis of two art forms. Of course, the film will not have the emotional impact of painting *added to* the poem — for so long as the spectator is attending to both, he cannot pay full attention, or respond with his full power, to either.

Elements from different media may be blended in many different ways. One of the most moving moments of Jean Renoir's *Partie de Campagne* (1936) has the camera tracking along a river stippled by raindrops, while a girl sings a wordless song. In Resnais's *Hiroshima Mon Amour* (1959) the camera tracks down streets and corridors while Riva's voice overlaid summarizes her thoughts — and Resnais experimented, matching different reading speeds to different tracking speeds, before finding the combination of speeds which was emotionally just 'right'.

The cinema is not the only 'art of mixed arts'. The opera is notoriously a *beau monstre,* a (sometimes rather absurd) blend of music and theatre. The theatre itself is a mixture of acting, lighting and text. 'Total theatre' is a blend of absolutely everything, taking even cinematic sequences under its wing. The cinema is another such synthesis of the arts.

Ever since the cinema began, aestheticians have sought to define 'pure' cinema, the 'essence' of cinema. In vain. The cinema's only 'purity' is the way in which it combines diverse elements into its own 'impure' whole. Its 'essence' is that it makes them interact, that it integrates other art forms, that it exists 'between' and 'across' their boundaries. It is cruder and inferior to every other art form on that art form's 'home ground'. But it repairs its deficiencies, and acquires its own dignity, by being a mixture.

The film medium depends on a blend of different media, and various films blend them in different proportions. A few films depend principally on criteria analogous to those one would bring to a short story or a novel. Thus for example Joseph L. Mankiewicz's *A Letter to Three Wives* (1948) is to a great extent a 'text' film. The films of Eisenstein require more 'painterly' critical descriptions than those of, say, Howard Hawks. Many films — Garbo's — can only be considered as 'star' performances, and one responds as one would to a 'star' performance in the theatre. The eloquence of Marcel Marceau, of Charles Chaplin, and less obviously Emil Jannings, lies in acting so stylized, so rhythmic, as to be nearer 'mime' than 'realistic' acting. Is Luis Buñuel's and Salvador Dali's *Un Chien Andalou* (1928) a Surrealist 'poem' (because of its 'symbolic meanings') or is it a Surrealist 'painting' (because it is a set of pictures)? An 'abstract' film like Norman MacLaren's *Begone Dull Care* accepts only those criteria that apply to abstract painting, linked with others that apply to music.

Yet each of these films is a mixture of the arts. Each of these films is 'pure' film.

Because there are so many varieties of film it is easy for the best-intentioned spectator to mistake a film's language. In *Strike* (1923) Eisenstein shows the Tsarist cavalry cutting down strikers with drawn sabres. To enhance the effect he intersperses the sequence with shots of a bull being slaughtered and hacked up in an abattoir. Some spectators find that the shots of the bull intensify the horror, while others, on the contrary, find that they distract from it. The difference seems to lie in the way the spectators' minds work. Some spectators get passionately concerned with the strikers and the cavalry. This action is completely distinct in their mind from the bull, which only interrupts, and so de-creases, the tension. Others, presumably those who look at film *style* as such rather than identifying with the people *in* the film, are quicker to make the 'intellectual' connection: the bull=the crowd, the proletariat= cattle, people=lumps of meat. Many filmgoers today find that such meta-phors in Russian silent films weaken rather than strengthen, especially when, unused to the thought and conventions of the time, we mistake a metaphor for a change of scene. Pudovkin means us to understand that 'the prisoner's joy is expressed by the breaking of the ice'. Instead we may assume a change of scene and get completely confused as to who's where. 'He was in his cell, now he seems to be standing by the riverside, has he been let out? or is this a dream? or are we with someone else altogether? By the time we work it out, the film's gone as cold as a fish on the slab.

Similarly a spectator used to looking for detailed psychology, realistic acting, location settings, and so on, may be quite at sea with films whose subtleties are entirely visual ones. Most film critics (outside Italy) have a literary background, and the fact that films, like novels, tell stories, reinforces their tendency to consider the 'core' of film as being somehow 'literary'. Their indebtedness to a (waning) fashion *in* literary criticism usually leads to the further assumption that the 'core' of litera-ture is 'psychological insights' — exact definition and motives, and so on. To these displaced persons a film's visual qualities are only 'style'. The documentarists' influence on film criticism completes the long-dominant emphasis on literary qualities, psychological realism, and social con-sciousness.

On the other hand, it was also apparent that the dominating cre-ative 'charge' of many films was the director's, rather than the writer's or the actor's. So here was a paradox: the *quality* of a film depended less on the writers and actors, who one might have expected to contribute the literary-psychological interest, than on a man whose province was that of 'visuals' and 'style'. 'Visual' directors like Eisenstein, Murnau and Dreyer retained their prestige as 'geniuses' less, one feels, because these critics really understood or thrilled to their films, than before they were protected by an aura of 'prestige'. The critics of, for example, *Sight and Sound* whom, for all their individual differences, it is reasonable to consider as a team with a common attitude, typify a fading English critical orthodoxy, with all its confusions and contradictions—summarizable as: 'literary content' and 'style' are either indistinguishable or the same thing but the first is emphatically more important than the second.

This part attempts to offer some new ideas, to revive some very old ones which fell into disuse when the 'literary content' school acquired their stranglehold on film criticism, and to revitalize principles to which it consents in theory but obscures in practice. Space, unfortunately, forbids us from examining each point from as many angles as one would like to. It offers only a series of signposts, rather than a map.

Let us first look at the implications of the antithesis of 'content' and 'style'. Among film critics 'content' is equated with 'literary content', that is, anything in a film which a novelist could fairly easily put into words if he were writing 'the book of the film'. And 'style' becomes, virtually, anything which isn't 'content'.

In the other arts the uses of the word 'style' are rather different. In painting 'literary content' is obviously of minor importance, while much great music is absolutely devoid of all 'literary content' whatsoever. By this definition abstract paintings and symphonies would be 'pure' style, altogether devoid of meaning—and importance? Clearly then there must be a sense in which 'style=content'.

The opening definition of 'style' in *The Concise O.E.D.* is: 'Manner of writing, speaking or doing . . . as opposed to the matter to be expressed or thing done.' In other words, an artist's 'style' is his answer to the problems with which he is faced in the course of creating his work of art. On the one hand, he has a certain intention, a certain 'vision' or 'drive', an experience to communicate (even if he isn't himself too sure in his conscious mind of exactly what it is). Similarly, the film director has a scene in a script, or a certain plot point to make. This scene is built around this point, so he thinks of it, for a while, as what the scene 'contains', his 'content'. But his sense of craftsmanship, certain practical exigencies, the need for a slick, easy flow of ideas across the screen, etc., confront him with various practical problems. Should he make the actor walk into shot? or should he pan the camera to pick up the actor? There may be no particular reason for his choice, except, in the case of a dull director, habit or convention, or, in the case of an original director, some

intuitive, inexplicable preference. It just feels right to him—more
smooth, more elegant, more lively than other possibilities. That choice
is his 'personal' style. The writer, the actor, the cameraman, the director,
will each have such a personal style of his own—favourite, intuitive, un-
examined ways of doing things. Often he will be quite unaware that
other solutions would have been possible. The director, as *integrator* of
everybody's work, has more 'stylistic' problems than anyone else; hence
his 'style' usually flavours the film.

Now let us look at 'style' in a medium other than the cinema. Two
actors will declaim Shakespeare's words ('content') in altogether different
ways ('style'). One makes Hamlet a warrior-hero who can't make up
his mind. The other makes him a neurotic intellectual who can't steel
himself to action. The 'literary content' is exactly the same but the
'theatrical content' (gesture, voice) is altogether different. So different
that it transforms the meaning of the text. Here, the style is just as much
a part of the content as the 'content'. In fact much of what film critics
call 'literary content' is in fact 'theatrical content', depending less on
the text than on acting and staging, and, to this extent, the ordinary fiction
film is nearer the theatre than literature.

Of course, not all features of 'style' make much difference to the
'content'. It may make no difference whatsoever whether an actor lifts
his left eyebrow before or after he waggles his right finger-tip. This is a
change of 'content' too, but only a minor one.

From this definition, the question whether style is more important
than content is a misleading one. Style is simply those pieces of content
which arise out of the way the artist makes his basic points. These may
(as often in painting and poetry) be only a pretext, a wire on which to
'thread the beads'. If style is 'manner of doing', then we can say that the
way a thing is done is often a way of doing a different thing. To say 'sorry'
superciliously is doing a different thing from saying 'sorry' courteously
or servilely, etc. Certain tones of voice make 'sorry' mean: 'Look where
you're going, you clumsy imbecile.' 'It ain't what you do it's the way
that you do it.' 'Le style, c'est l'homme.' . . .

Suppose a director has filmed four takes of the same scene which
shows an argument between two equally sympathetic characters. Take
(1) shows the scene as a series of 'reverse angles' (alternating full-face
close-ups). Take (2) is a continuous two-shot of two profiles. Take (3)
shows B's full face, but the back of A's head prominent on the screen.
Take (4) is an 'over-shoulder' of A, with B's head not very obtrusively
present over to one side of the screen. In (1) we will feel each person's
responses intensely during *his* close-up, and the other's responses will
be temporarily soft-pedalled, even forgotten; until we return to him with
a little 'shock'. Our identifications alternate. In (2) we see and feel both

responses simultaneously. Our reaction to A's words is continuously modified by B's reaction, which may be sceptical or pitying. We feel a smoother, softer, mixture of feelings. In (3) with the back of A's head, almost in the middle of the frame, we will be very conscious of his constant 'obstruction'; he is a real force, but an enigmatic one. In (4) we may almost be unaware of him and be aware mainly of A's feelings — although the vague presence of B makes for a more complicated composition and 'feel' than a mere close-up.

Are these differences of style, or of content? Both. And the differences are not a matter of *information provided* about the characters so much as of *the spectator's participation* in their feelings.

The distinction between '*literary* content' and 'visual style' is particularly misguided because even in the work of literature much of the 'content' comes from the 'style'. Suppose we call someone 'slow but thorough' we feel this is, on the whole, a compliment. His slowness is a trifling disadvantage, the last word acts as a summing-up, and assertion of his value. But if we call him 'thorough but slow' there is an implication of criticism. The ideas and the words are exactly the same — but to change their order is like inserting some invisible words. One order says: 'We can rely on him.' The other: 'He should pull his socks up.' More often, literary 'style' is a matter of choosing different words — different ideas, different content. My friends are 'unfaltering', my enemies are 'obstinate'. I show 'intensity of purpose', you are a 'fanatic'. Our friends are 'original', our rivals 'eccentric'. Writers show such concern over points of 'style' (e.g. *le mot juste*) because of their concern over points of 'content'.

Such nuances of order, sound (especially in poetry), vocabulary, and so on, don't just *colour* the 'content' of a passage. They *constitute* its content. The passage may be badly written, but of interest as a description of an interesting event — traffic accident, a battle or a riot. But this event is not its 'literary content'. It's only the *subject*. Another passage may describe an apparently boring event, but bring to it a wealth of ideas and insights. And in this case we may speak of the author's 'style' as enlivening a banal 'content'. But this wealth of ideas and insights isn't 'mere' style — it is 'content'. And, here, to ask whether style or content is more important is like asking whether water is more important than H_2O. The words are different, the things's the same, which phrase one uses depends on one's context and emphasis. It is not the importance of their subjects, but the richness of their 'content-style' which distinguishes good artists from mediocre ones.

Another quite common and useful sense of the word 'style' is to refer to the whole mass of details which go into a film, but which happen to be confusing and difficult to describe in words. Thus a *specific* reaction

—horror, joy, etc.—tends to be called 'content' because it is easy to define, it offers a nice, solid idea to lean on. On the other hand, an actor's postures, gestures, smiles, the quality of his glance, the tension of his facial muscles, the director's spatial relationships, the tones of grey caught by the cameraman, all these may be very eloquent and forceful in communicating experience (and so are 'content'). But because it is difficult to analyse or explain their exact meaning in words they tend to be referred to, vaguely, as 'style'. But here again 'content' and 'style' are indissoluble. In fact, here, the 'content'—horror, joy—is a spectator's deduction from what the screen actually contains. This is why spectators

The Passion of Joan of Arc (1923) ". . . here again, 'content' and 'style' are indissoluble." The physical and spatial relationships are an essential part of the meaning of the scene. (Still courtesy of The Museum of Modern Art/Film Stills Archive.)

so often disagree on what a film's content is. The screen contains the style, but not the *content,* which is the spectator's deduction, and not contained on the *screen* at all!

If we speak of an artist's 'style' as being as individual as his face or his finger-prints, it is because he tends to bring similar insights and details to every subject which he treats. Dreyer's style is the visual expression of certain attitudes, interests and feelings which arise in him whether his subject is *La Passion de Jeanne d'Arc, Vampyr* (1932) or the naughty carry-ons of *The Parson's Widow* (1921). In this sense, 'content-style' is the quintessence of an artist—although often his choice of subject also is determined by his personality. Thus personal 'style' is a matter, not of mere visual mannerisms, but of plot, characterization, and so on. For example, King Vidor's heroines are tomboys expertly wielding shotguns in *Duel in the Sun* (1946), *Beyond the Forest* (1949) and *Ruby Gentry* (1952), and there are reminiscent traits of forceful independence in the heroines of *The Big Parade* (1925), *The Fountainhead* (1947), *Man Without a Star* (1955) and *Solomon and Sheba* (1959). His heroines' *style* is an important part of King Vidor's vision of the world. (Always when we speak of an artist's 'personal style' we might as well speak of his 'recurrent content'.)

In a sense, the total content of a film is made up of a vast array of details. But the meaning of each detail is heavily influenced by the context. For example, Karel Reisz writes '. . . the discreet distance which Ophuls' camera keeps from his players reflects a lack of identification', and Andrew Sarris '. . . Buñuel's . . . camera has always viewed his characters from a middle distance, too close for cosmic groupings and too far away for self-identification. Normally, this would make his films cold and his point of view detached. . . .'

These are fair enough as critical approximations, but it would certainly be wrong to conclude that identification is weak without a high proportion of close-ups. Silent films used far fewer close-ups than films of the 40's, and cinemascope Westerns use fewer again, but this has little effect on identification, compared with the main determinant, which is the spectator's affinities of emotion, experience and moral sympathy with the screen characters (their 'resonance' with him). Further, artists who don't know where the spectators' sympathies lie, how to make them chop and change from one character to another, how to create the anxious tensions and suspense of 'split sympathy', won't stay out of the bankruptcy court very long.

Where a film has a very popular star, the spectators so keep their eyes glued on him that even when he's in long-shot *physically,* he's in close-up *psychologically.* This is not to say that camera distance has no importance; only that it is only one of many elements of style-and-content working simultaneously. I'd suggest that the only partial identification made by most spectators when seeing a Buñuel film for the first time is mainly due to the fact that his characters are very complex individuals, and presented with a certain mystery. Seeing *El* (1953) for the first time, my principal emotion was one of fascination, of passionate curiosity; but at a second viewing, when the film's main pattern had been understood, a much stronger identification with the characters was possible. . . .

One or two further examples may make our point clearer. When the camera tracks forward swiftly (as in, say, a musical number) the spectator often feels a mild exhilaration, as if he in his seat were gliding effortlessly through the action. There is a general sense of well-being, of dynamic excitement. But in Truffaut's *Jules et Jim* (1961) the helicopter skims swiftly over a hilly landscape—and a hill rearing up before us suddenly reveals a sheer drop on the other side. Here any 'exhilaration' is modified by the turbulence of the landscape, and killed by the 'sudden drop'. In the same way, the film is about the turbulence and unsteadiness of human relationships. . . . In the same film, there is a sense of chaos, of confusion, when, seen from the helicopter, the train carrying one of the *ménage-à-trois* steams out of the country station. The last scenes of Joshua Logan's *Picnic* (1954) have a similar theme—a train seen from a helicopter, carrying William Holden away from Kim Novak. But the whole tone is different. Not only is the landscape different (level), but the dramatic context is different—this time the lovers are determined not to be separated for long. There is no sense of chaos—our helicopter shot is, so to speak, a 'fate's eye view', a map revealing that their paths will cross. It is the exact opposite of the 'similar' effect in *Jules et Jim*.

Within the general framework of a two-shot many different 'spatial relationships' are possible. In *The Magnificent Ambersons* (1942) Welles expertly puts his characters in tough, angular, separated compositions, creating an effect of loneliness-by-antagonistic-wills. In Renoir's *La Règle du Jeu* (1939), more fluent and informal arrangements leave plenty of space for the characters to move around, to change their minds, to remain individuals while being members of free and easy groupings.

Suppose a film ends with the camera tracking back from the lovers embracing alone on the beach. This may mean 'how tiny and unprotected they are' or 'how frail and futile their love' or 'the whole wide world is theirs' or 'this is the moment of destiny' (for plan views can suggest a 'God's-eye-view') or 'Good-bye, good-bye', depending on which emotions are floating about in the spectator's mind as a result of the rest of the film. Hence style is essentially a matter of intuition. There is no possibility whatsoever of an 'objective', 'scientific' analysis of film style — or of 'film' content. It is worse than useless to attempt to watch a film with one's intellect alone, trying to explain its effect in terms of one or two points of style. Few films yield any worthwhile meaning unless watched with a genuine interest in the range of feelings and meanings it suggests. To any work of art one must bring one's own experience if one is to take from it its experience. Indeed, professional film makers have a point when they accuse film 'highbrows' of an almost fetishistic attention to whichever aspect of style happens to be in intellectual fashion. In the 20's it was *Caligari* décor, from *Potemkin* (1925) on it was montage and it was dubious whether cinema art could survive the hideous barbarism of the spoken word, in the 40's it was camera angles and location photography, and today it's camera movements.

The reputation (rather than direct influence) of *Cahiers du Cinema* and of its late doyen, André Bazin, has recently been goading British critics to a new interest in style and theory. Yet a certain 'fetishism' often cramps Bazin's intelligence. For example, writing about William Wyler's *The Little Foxes* (1941) and *The Best Years of Our Lives* (1947) Bazin calls their deep focus more 'democratic' than shallow-focus because it enables the director to have more important characters on the screen simultaneously, thus permitting the spectator to choose whichever character he will look at and identify with. Yet in these films Wyler had effectively determined which characters the spectators would be interested in, by the moral and emotional traits with which he endowed them, and which he balances one against the other with just as much care and control as do such shallow-focus films as *Johnny Guitar* or *This Island Earth*. Within the limits of their tendencies to moral schematism, tendencies from which Wyler is not exempt, American directors can calculate audience sympathies to the nth decimal place, with a finesse which, given the cultural diversity of their audience, is a far from inconsiderable 'classicism'. The spectator is no freer, no more 'democratic', in Wyler's film than in the others.

Conversely, Welles uses deep focus in his *Citizen Kane* to present an extremely 'egocentric' universe, Kane's. There's no reason why Leni Reifenstahl, Hitler's cinéaste-laureate, shouldn't have used the 'hierarchical' possibilities implicit in deep focus to Fascist effect (the Leader in big close-up with 'the people' reduced to little faces peering hopefully up from far away, and so on. In practice of course the points made by the visuals would counterpoint rather than repeat those made by narrative or dialogue or audience assumption — e.g. one would enhance the Fuhrer's real grandeur by showing him far away and small).

Often the best way for a director to sensitively nuance every aspect of his medium is to forget about 'style' altogether and immerse his conscious mind in his feelings and ideas; just as the thoughtful spectator will often arrive at the most sensitive understanding of a film by giving the artists the benefit of any reasonable doubt, and, within the spirit of the word 'reasonable', assuming that every aspect of the film is the way it is as the result, not of mere 'mechanics', but of an intuitive intention'. . . .

'Style' — or rather, *nuance* — is conventionally associated with the creation of a personal, a subjective, a 'non-objective' world — a world that is *this* artist's (or *this* character's, or both). And in the next chapter we shall try and consider, in view of this, the cinema's reputation as a particularly 'realistic', 'objective' medium.

8

Anthony Schillaci

FILM AS ENVIRONMENT

Father Schillaci has had extensive practical experience in teaching film using
study groups, film festivals, institutes,
and weekend workshops. He wrote *Movies and Morals* (Fides Publishers, Inc.,
1968) and has another book on film
scheduled for publication. In this article
from the *Saturday Review*, (December 28,
1968) he examines the attitudes of young
people toward contemporary motion
pictures.

The better we understand how young people view film, the more we
have to revise our notion of what film is. Seen through young eyes, film
is destroying conventions almost as quickly as they can be formulated.
Whether the favored director is "young" like Richard Lester, Roman
Polanski, and Arthur Penn, or "old" like Kubrick, Fellini, and Buñuel,
he must be a practicing cinematic anarchist to catch the eye of the young.
If we're looking for the young audience between sixteen and twenty-
four, which accounts for 48 per cent of the box office today, we will
find they're on a trip, whether in a Yellow Submarine or on a Space
Odyssey. A brief prayer muttered for Rosemary's Baby and they're
careening down a dirt road with Bonnie and Clyde, the exhaust spitting
banjo sounds, or sitting next to The Graduate as he races across the
Bay Bridge after his love. The company they keep is fast; Belle de Jour,

Petulia, and Joanna are not exactly a sedentary crowd. Hyped up on large doses of *Rowan and Martin's Laugh-In,* and *Mission: Impossible,* they are ready for anything that an evolving film idiom can throw on the screen. And what moves them must have the pace, novelty, style, and spontaneity of a television commercial.

All of this sounds as if the script is by McLuhan. Nevertheless, it is borne out by the experience of teaching contemporary film to university juniors and seniors, staging film festivals for late teens and early adults, and talking to literally hundreds of people about movies. The phenomenon may be interesting, and even verifiable, but what makes it important is its significance for the future of film art. The young have discovered that film is an environment which you put on, demanding a different kind of structure, a different mode of attention than any other art. Their hunger is for mind-expanding experience and simultaneity, and their art is film.

Occasionally a young director gives us a glimpse of the new world of film as environmental art. The optical exercise known as *Flicker* came on like a karate chop to the eyes at Lincoln Center's Film Seminar three years ago. One half-hour of white light flashing at varied frequency, accompanied by a deafening sound track designed to infuriate, describes the screen, but not what happened to the audience. As strangers turned to ask if it was a put-on, if they had forgotten to put film in the projector, they noticed that the flickering light fragmented their motions, stylizing them like the actions of a silent movie. In minutes, the entire audience was on its feet, acting out spontaneous pantomines for one another, no one looking at the flashing screen. The happening precipitated by *Flicker* could be called the film of the future, but it was actually an anti-environment that gives us an insight into the past. By abstracting totally from content, the director demonstrated that the film is in the audience which acts out personal and public dramas as the screen turns it on. The delight of this experience opened up the notion of film as an environmental art.

Critics have noted the trend which leaves story line and character development strewn along the highways of film history like the corpses in Godard's *Weekend.* The same critics have not, in general, recognized that the growing option for nonlinear, unstructured experiences that leave out sequence, motivation, and "argument" is a vote for film as environment. Young people turn to film for a time-space environment in which beautiful things happen to them. The screen has, in a sense, less and less to do with what explodes in the audience. This new scene could mean either that film is plunging toward irrelevant stimulation, or that there is a new and unprecedented level of participation and involvement in young audiences. I prefer to think the latter is the case. Young people want to talk about Ben's hang-up, why Rosemary stayed with the baby, or what it feels like to be in the electronic hands of a computer like Hal. They do not forget the film the minute they walk out of the theater.

The attention given the new style of film goes beyond stimulation to real involvement. A generation with eyes fixed on the rearview mirror tended to give film the same attention required for reading—that is, turning off all the senses except the eyes. Film became almost as private as reading, and little reaction to the total audience was experienced. As the Hollywood dream factory cranked out self-contained worlds of fantasy, audiences entered them with confidence that nothing even vaguely related to real life would trouble their reveries. As long as one came and left in the middle of the film, it was relatively non-involving as environment. When television brought the image into the living room, people gave it "movie attention," hushing everyone who entered the sacred presence of the tube as they would a film patron who talked during a movie. One was not allowed to speak, even during commercials. It took post-literate man to teach us how to use television as environment, as a moving image on the wall to which one may give total or peripheral attention as he wishes. The child who had TV as a baby-sitter does not turn off all his senses, but walks about the room carrying on a multiplicity of actions and relationships, his attention a special reward for the cleverness of the pitchman, or the skill of the artist. He is king, and not captive. . . .

The new multisensory involvement with film as total environment has been primary in destroying literary values in film. Their decline is not merely farewell to an understandable but unwelcome dependence; it means the emergence of a new identity for film. The diminished role of dialogue is a case in point. The difference between *Star Trek* and *Mission: Impossible* marks the trend toward self-explanatory images that need no dialogue. Take an audio tape of these two popular TV shows, as we did in a recent study, and it will reveal that while *Mission: Impossible* is completely unintelligible without images, *Star Trek* is simply an illustrated radio serial, complete on the level of sound. It has all the characteristics of radio's golden age: actions explained, immediate identification of character by voice alone, and even organ music to squeeze the proper emotion or end the episode. Like *Star Trek,* the old film was frequently a talking picture. . . . It was the films of Fellini and Bergman, with their subtitles, that convinced us there had been too many words. Approximately one-third of the dialogue is omitted in subtitled versions of these films, with no discernible damage—and some improvement—of the original.

More than dialogue, however, has been jettisoned. Other literary values, such as sequential narrative, dramatic choice, and plot are in a state of advanced atrophy, rapidly becoming vestigial organs on the body of film art as young people have their say. *Petulia* has no "story," unless one laboriously pieces together the interaction between the delightful arch-kook and the newly divorced surgeon, in which case it is nothing more than an encounter. The story line wouldn't make a ripple if it were not scrambled and fragmented into an experience that explodes from a free-floating present into both past and future simultaneously. *Petulia* is like some views of the universe which represent the ancient past of events whose light is just now reaching us simultaneously with the future of our galaxy, returning from the curve of outer space. Many films succeed by virtue of what they leave out. *2001: A Space Odyssey* is such a film, its muted understatement creating gaps in the action that invite our inquiry. Only a square viewer wants to know where the black monolith came from and where it is going. For most of the young viewers to whom I have spoken, it is just there. *Last Year at Marienbad* made the clock as limply shapeless as one of Salvador Dali's watches, while $8\frac{1}{2}$ came to life on the strength of free associations eagerly grasped by young audiences. The effect of such films is a series of open-ended impressions, freely evoked and enjoyed, strongly inviting inquiry and involvement. In short, film is freed to work as environment, something which does not simply contain, but shapes people, tilting the balance of their faculties, radically altering their perceptions, and ultimately their views of self and all reality. Perhaps one sense of the symptomatic word "grooving," which applies to both sight and sound environments, is that a new mode of attention—multisensory, total, and simultaneous—has arrived. When you "groove," you do not analyze, follow an argument, or separate sensations; rather, you are massaged into a feeling of heightened life and consciousness.

If young people look at film this way, it is in spite of the school, a fact which says once more with emphasis that education is taking place outside the classroom walls. The "discovery" that television commercials are the most exciting and creative part of today's programming is old news to the young. Commercials are a crash course in speed-viewing, their intensified sensations challenging the viewer to synthesize impressions at an ever increasing rate. The result is short films like one produced at UCLA, presenting 3,000 years of art in three minutes. *God is Dog Spelled Backwards* takes you from the cave paintings of Lascaux to the latest abstractions, with some images remaining on the screen a mere twenty-fourth of a second! The young experience the film, however, not as confusing, but as exuberantly and audaciously alive. They feel joy of recognition, exhilaration at the intense concentration necessary (one blink encompasses a century of art), and awe at the 180-second review of every aspect of the human condition. Intended as a put-on, the film becomes a three-minute commercial for man. This hunger for overload is fed by the television commercial, with its nervous jump cuts demolishing continuity, and its lazy dissolves blurring time-space boundaries. Whether the young are viewing film "through" television, or simply through their increased capacity for information and sensation (a skill which makes most schooling a bore), the result is the same — film becomes the primary environment in which the hunger to know through experience is satisfied.

Hidden within this unarticulated preference of the young is a quiet tribute to film as the art that humanizes change. In its beginnings, the cinema was celebrated as the art that mirrored reality in its functional dynamism. And although the early vision predictably gave way to misuse of the medium, today the significance of the filmic experience of change stubbornly emerges again. Instead of prematurely stabilizing change, film celebrates it. The cinema can inject life into historical events by the photo-scan, in which camera movement and editing liberate the vitality of images from the past. *City of Gold,* a short documentary by the National Film Board of Canada, takes us by zoom and cut into the very life of the Klondike gold rush, enabling us to savor the past as an experience.

Education increasingly means developing the ability to live humanly in the technological culture by changing with it. Film is forever spinning out intensifications of the environment which make it visible and livable. The ability to control motion through its coordinates of time and space makes film a creative agent in change. Not only does film reflect the time-space continuum of contemporary physics, but it can manipulate artistically those dimensions of motion which we find most problematic. The actuality of the medium, its here-and-now impact, reflects how completely the present tense has swallowed up both past and future. Freudian psychology dissolves history by making the past something we live; accelerated change warps the future by bringing it so close that we can't conceive it as "ahead" of us. An art which creates its own space, and can move time forward and back, can humanize change by conditioning us to live comfortably immersed in its fluctuations.

On the level of form, then, perhaps the young are tuned in to film for "telling it like it is" in a sense deeper than that of fidelity to the event. It is film's accurate reflection of a society and of human life totally in flux that makes it the liberating art of the time. We live our lives more like Guido in $8\frac{1}{2}$ — spinners of fantasies, victims of events, the products of mysterious associations — than we do like Maria in *The Sound of Music,* with a strange destiny guiding our every step. Instead of resisting change and bottling it, film intensifies the experience of change, humanizing it in the process. What makes the ending of *The Graduate* "true" to young people is not that Ben has rescued his girl from the Establishment, but that he did it without a complete plan for the future. The film may fail under analysis, but it is extraordinarily coherent as experience, as I learned in conversations about it with the young. The same accurate reflection of the day may be said of the deep space relativity of *2001,* the frantic pace of *Petulia,* or the melodramatic plotting of *Rosemary's Baby.* Whether this limitless capacity for change within the creative limits of art has sober implications for the future raises the next (and larger) question of what young people look for and get out of film.

When the question of film content is raised, the example of *Flicker* and other films cited may seem to indicate that young people favor as little substance as possible in their film experiences. A casual glance at popular drive-in fare would confirm this opinion quickly. Nevertheless, their attitude toward "what films are about" evidences a young, developing sensitivity to challenging comments on what it means to be human. The young are digging the strong humanism of the current film renaissance and allowing its currents to carry them to a level deeper than that reached by previous generations. One might almost say that young people are going to the film-maker's work for values that they have looked for in vain from the social, political, or religious establishments. This reaction, which has made film modern man's morality play, has not been carefully analyzed, but the present state of evidence invites our inquiry.

As far as the "point" of films is concerned, young people will resist a packaged view, but will welcome a problematic one. The cry, "Please, I'd rather do it myself!" should be taken to heart by the film-maker. It is better to use understatement in order to score a personal discovery by the viewer. Such a discovery of an idea is a major part of our delight in the experience of film art. A frequent answer to a recent survey question indicated that a young man takes his girl to the movies so that they will have something important to talk about. It is not a matter of pitting film discussion against "making out," but of recognizing that a rare and precious revelation of self to the other is often occasioned by a good film. The young feel this experience as growth, expanded vitality, more integral possession of one's self with the consequent freedom to go out to others more easily and more effectively.

Very little of the business of being human happens by instinct, and so we need every form of education that enlightens or accelerates that process. While young people do not go to films for an instant humanization course, a strong part of the pleasure they take in excellent films does just this. Whether through a connaturality of the medium described earlier, or because of a freer viewpoint, young audiences frequently get more out of films than their mentors. It is not so much a matter of seeing more films, but of seeing more in a film. The film-as-escape attitude belongs to an age when the young were not yet born; and the film-as-threat syndrome has little meaning for the sixteen to twenty-four group. . . . A typical irrelevance that causes youthful wonder is the elderly matron's complaint that *Bonnie and Clyde* would teach bad driving habits to the young.

The performance of youthful audiences in discussions of contemporary film indicates their freedom from the judgmental screen which blurs so many films for other generations. In speaking of *Bonnie and Clyde,* late high school kids and young adults do not dwell upon the career of crime or the irregularity of the sexual relationship, but upon other things. The development of their love fascinates young people, because Clyde shows he knows Bonnie better than she knows herself. Although he resists her aggressive sexual advances, he knows and appreciates her as a person. It is the sincerity of their growing love that overcomes his impotence, and the relationship between this achievement and their diminished interest in crime is not lost on the young audience. The reversal of the "sleep together now, get acquainted later" approach is significant here. These are only a few of the nuances that sensitive ears and eyes pick up beneath the gunfire and banjo-plucking. Similarly, out of the chaotic impressions of *Petulia,* patterns are perceived. Young people note the contrasts between Petulia's kooky, chaotic life, and the over-controlled precision of the surgeon's existence. The drama is that they both come away a little different for their encounter. Instead of a stale moral judgment on their actions, one finds open-ended receptivity to the personal development of the characters.

Youth in search of identity is often presented as a ridiculous spectacle, a generation of Kierkegaards plaintively asking each other: "Who am I?" Nevertheless, the quest is real and is couched in terms of a hunger for experience. SDS or LSD, McCarthy buttons or yippie fashions, it is all experimentation in identity, trying on experiences to see if they fit. The plea is to stop the world, not so that they can get off, but so they can get a handle on it. To grasp each experience, to suck it dry of substance, and to grow in that process is behind the desire to be "turned on." But of all the lurid and bizarre routes taken by young people, the one that draws least comment is that of the film experience. More people have had their minds expanded by films than by LSD. Just as all art nudges man into the sublime and vicarious experience of the whole range of the human condition, film does so with a uniquely characteristic totality and involvement.

Ben, *The Graduate,* is suffocating under his parents' aspirations, a form of drowning which every young person has felt in some way. But the film mirrors their alienation in filmic terms, by changes in focus, by the metaphors of conveyor belt sidewalk and swimming pool, better than any moralist could say it. The satirical portraits of the parents may be broad and unsubtle, but the predicament is real and compelling. This is why the young demand no assurances that Ben and the girl will live happily ever after; it is enough that he jarred himself loose from the sick apathy and languid sexual experimentation with Mrs. Robinson to go after one thing, one person that he wanted for himself, and not for

The Graduate (1967) ". . . those who are not busy judging the morality of the hotel scenes will note that sex doesn't communicate without love." (Still from the motion picture "The Graduate," copyright © 1967 by Avco Embassy Pictures Corp.)

others. Incidentally, those who are not busy judging the morality of the hotel scenes will note that sex doesn't communicate without love. Some may even note that Ben is using sex to strike at his parents — not a bad thing for the young (or their parents) to know.

Emotional maturity is never painless and seldom permanent, but it can become a bonus from viewing good films because it occurs there not as taught but experienced. Values communicated by film are interiorized and become a part of oneself, not simply an extension of the womb that parents and educators use to shield the young from the world. Colin Smith, in *The Loneliness of the Long Distance Runner*, IS youth, not because he did it to the Establishment, but because he is trying to be his own man and not sweat his guts out for another. The profound point of learning who you are in the experience of freedom, as Colin did in running, is not lost on the young who think about this film a little. Some speak of Col's tragedy as a failure to realize he could have won the race for himself, and not for the governor of the Borstal. Self-destruction through spite, the pitfalls of a self-justifying freedom, and the sterility of bland protest are real problems that emerge from the film. The values that appeal most are the invisible ones that move a person to act because "it's me" (part of one's identity), and not because of "them." Because they have become an object of discovery and not of imposition, such values tend to make morality indistinguishable from self-awareness.

It should be made clear, however, that it is not merely the content, but the mode of involvement in the film experience that makes its humanism effective. In terms of "message," much of contemporary film reflects the social and human concerns that Bob Dylan, the Beatles, Simon and Garfunkel, and Joan Baez communicate. But the words of their songs often conceal the radical nature of the music in which they appear. The direct emotional appeal of the sound of "Eleanor Rigby," "Give a Damn," "I Am a Rock," or "Mr. Businessman" communicates before we have the words deciphered. Films with honest human concern, similarly, change audiences as much by their style as their message. *Elvira Madigan's* overpowering portrait of a hopeless love, *A Thousand Clowns'* image of nonconformity, *Zorba's* vitality, and *Morgan's* tragedy are not so much the content of the images as the outcome of their cinematic logic. If these films change us, it is because we have done it to ourselves by opening ourselves to their experiences.

Expo 67 audiences were charmed by the Czech Kinoautomat in which their vote determined the course of comic events in a film. Once again, we find here not a peek into the future, but an insight into all film experience. In one way or another, we vote on each film's progress. The passive way is to patronize dishonest or cynical films, for our box-office ballot determines the selection of properties for years to come. We have been voting this way for superficial emotions, sterile plots, and happy endings for a generation. But we vote more actively and subtly by willing the very direction of a film through identification with the character, or absorption into the action. The viewer makes a private or social commitment in film experience. He invests a portion of himself in the action, and if he is changed, it is because he has activated his own dreams. What happens on the screen, as in the case of *Flicker*, is the catalyst for the value systems, emotional responses, and the indirect actions which are the byproducts of a good film. Film invites young people to be part of the action by making the relationships which take the work beyond a mere succession of images. The reason why young people grow through their art is that they supply the associations that merely begin on the screen but do not end there. When parents and educators become aware of this, their own efforts at fostering maturity may be less frantic, and more effective.

It is not only the films that please and delight which appeal to the young, but also those which trouble and accuse by bringing our fears into the open. The new audience for documentary films highlights a new way of looking at film as an escape *into* reality. From *The War Game* to *Warrendale*, from *The Titicut Follies'* to *Battle of Algiers*, young audiences are relishing the film's ability to document the present in terms of strong social relevance. *Portrait of Jason* is more than a voyeuristic peak into the psyche of a male whore; it is a metaphor for the black man's history in America, and this is what young people see in that film. Even the most strident dissenters will appreciate the ambiguities of *The Anderson Platoon*, which leaves us without anyone to hate, because it is not about Marines and Vietcong, but about men like ourselves. In these as in other films, the social content is intimately wed to the film experience, and together they form a new outlook. Ultimately, we may have to change our views on what film art is about.

The foregoing analysis of how young people look at film will appear to some to constitute a simplistic eulogy to youth. For this reason, we may temper our optimism by a hard look at real problems with this generation. There is a desperate need for education. Although they cannot all be structured, none of the better youthful attitudes or responses described came about by chance. Mere screening of films, for example, whether they be classics or trash, does little good. Colleges can become places where the young are taught hypocrisy, being told they "should" like Fellini, Bergman, Antonioni, or Godard. They can accept these filmmakers just as uncritically as their parents adulated movie stars. Unless there is encouragement to reflect on film experience, its impact can be minimal and fleeting. Most of the responses I have mentioned came from students who were well into the habit of discussing film. These discus-

sions are best when they flow from the natural desire we have to communicate our feelings about a film. Nonverbalization, the reluctance to
betray by treacherous abstractions the ineffable experience of the film,
arises at this point. Real as it is, there must be found some middle
ground between a suffocatingly detailed dissection of a film, and the
noncommunicative exclamation, "like WOW!" Reflecting on one's
experience is an integral part of making that experience part of one's
self. Furthermore, one can see an almost immediate carry-over to other
film experiences from each film discussed.

A problem more crucial than lack of reflection is the poverty of
critical perspective. The young can plunge into their personal version
of the *auteur* theory and make a fad or fetish out of certain films and
directors. Roman Polanski has made some bad films, that is, films which
do not reflect his own experience and feelings honestly as did *Knife in
the Water*. Fascinating as *Rosemary's Baby* is, it suffers from an uncertain
relationship of the director to his work. Some directors are adulated for
peripheral or irrelevant reasons. Joseph Losey is a good film-maker, not
because of a cynical preoccupation with evil, but because, like Hitchcock
and Pinter, he makes us less certain of our virtue. And Buñuel, far from
being a cheerful anarchist attacking church and society with abandon,
is a careful surgeon, excising with camera the growths of degenerate
myth on the cancerous culture.

In their own work, young people can celebrate bad film-making
as "honest" and voyeuristic films as "mature." Criticism of poor films is
not "putting down" the director for doing his own thing, especially if his
thing is trite, dishonest, or so personal that it has no meaning accessible
to others. Criticism means taking a stand on the basis of who you are.
The current preference of spoof over satire is not just another instance
of cool over hot, but is symptomatic of a noncritical stance. *Dr. Strange-
love* makes comic absurdity out of the cold war from a certain conviction
about what mature political action should be. The *Laugh-In* has no con-
victions but a lot of opinions. If it is accused of favoring an idea or cause,
it will refute the charge by ridiculing what it holds. The cynical, sophisticated noninvolvement of the "won't vote" movement in the recent
election has its counterpart in film viewing.

A question that should perhaps have been asked earlier is: Why
should we be concerned with asking how young people look at film?
Tired reasons, citing *Time's* Man of the Year, the under-twenty-five
generation, or the youth-quake menace of *Wild in the Streets* (they'll be
taking over!) are not appropriate here. Anyone who is interested in the
direction taken by cinema, and its continued vitality in the current
renaissance of the art, will have to take the young into account as the
major shaping force on the medium. If the age group from sixteen to

twenty-four accounts for 48 per cent of the box office, it means that this
eight-year period determines the success or failure of most films. Fortunately, there has not yet appeared a formula for capturing this audience.
Variety described the youth market as a booby trap for the industry,
citing the surprise success of sleepers such as *Bonnie and Clyde* and *The
Graduate*, as well as the supposed youth-appeal failures *(Half a Sixpence,
Poor Cow, Here We Go Round the Mulberry Bush)*. The list may suggest a
higher level of young taste than producers are willing to admit. In any
case, if the young have influenced the medium this far, we cannot ignore
the fact. It is for this reason that we are encouraged to speculate on the
future in the form of two developments revolutionizing the young approach to film: student film-making and multi-media experiences.

More and more, the answer to how young people look at film is
"through the lens of a camera." In coming years, it will be youth as film-
maker, and not simply as audience, that will spur the evolution of the
cinema. Students want a piece of the action, whether in running a university, the country, or the world; in terms of our question, this means
making films. There is a strong resonance between film-making and the
increasingly sophisticated film experience. Young people delighted by
a television commercial are tempted to say: "I could do that!" Considering the cost and artistry of some commercials, this is a pretty naïve
statement, but it doesn't stop the young from taking out their father's
Super-8 or buying an old Bolex to tell their story on film. Today, anyone can make a film. Although Robert Flaherty's longed-for parousia,
when film is as cheap as paper, has not yet arrived, the art has come into
the reach of almost everyone. The Young Film-Makers Conference held
by Fordham University last February drew 1,200 people, 740 of them
student film-makers below college age. On a few weeks' notice, some 120
films were submitted for screening. Kids flew in from Richmond, California, and bussed in from Louisville, Kentucky, with twenty-seven
states and Canada represented. Numbers, however, do not tell the story.
One of the notable directors and actors present sized up the scene by
saying: "My God, I'm standing here in the middle of a revolution!" It
was the quality of the films that caused Eli Wallach to remark, only half
in jest, that some day he'd be working for one of these film-makers. The
young look at film as potential or actual film-makers, and this fact raises
participation to an unprecedented critical level. The phenomenon also
removes the last residue of passive audience participation from the
Golden Forties box-office bonanza.

Foolhardy though it may be, one can predict that the new interest
in film will take the direction of multi-media experimentation. Expo 67,
it seems, is *now*. Our new and growing capacity to absorb images and
synthesize sounds demands a simultaneity that cannot be met by tradi-

tional forms of film-making. The response so far has been the half-hearted multiple screens of *The Thomas Crown Affair*, not part of the conception of the film, but inserted as fancy dressing. The object of multiple images is not so much to condense actions as to create an environment such as the Ontario pavilion film, *A Place to Stand*. My own students have begun to relegate location shots such as street scenes or mood sequences to peripheral attention on side screens and walls, while the action takes place on the main screen. . . .

The young look at film is a revolutionary one, motivated more by love of the medium than hatred of the Establishment. In a sense, the new taste is liberating film for a free exploration of its potential, especially in the area of humanizing change. The hunger for a relativity of time and space will extend to morality, producing films that explore problems rather than package solutions. Nevertheless, the very intensity of young involvement gives promise of profound changes in the youth audience as people themselves to the reality of the medium. Whether as young film-maker or multi-media entrepreneur, the young will have their say. If we take the time to cultivate their perspective, we may learn an interesting view of the future of media, and a fascinating way to stay alive.

9

Stanley Kauffmann

THE FILM GENERATION: CELEBRATION AND CONCERN

Stanley Kauffmann, one of the major film critics writing today, reviews movies for *The New Republic*. This article, from his book *A World on Film*, examines the "new American film," a term used for filmmakers like Kenneth Anger and Stan Brakhage and other avant-gardist and underground filmmakers. He combines muted hope with uncertain optimism in a most perceptive way.

Some of the following remarks were included, in differing forms, in talks delivered recently at several universities, colleges, and seminars. In one of the audiences were a distinguished poet and a critic of the graphic arts. Afterward, the critic came up to me and said, "You destroyed us. You wiped out our professions. You rendered my friend and me obsolete." I said that I neither believed nor intended that. Then he said wryly, stroking his chin, "On the other hand, if I were twenty years younger, I know I'd go into films."

His dismal reaction had been prompted by my assertion that film is the art for which there is the greatest spontaneous appetite in America at present, and by my reasons for thinking so. I must be clear that this is not to say that it is the art practiced at the highest level in this country; the film public depends more on imports today than does any other art public. But observation and experience, and the experience of others, make me believe that this uniquely responsive audience exists.

Or, in another phrase, there exists a Film Generation: the first generation that has matured in a culture in which the film has been of accepted serious relevance, however that seriousness is defined. Before 1935 films were proportionately more popular than they are now, but for the huge majority of film-goers they represented a regular weekly or semiweekly bath of escapism. Such an escapist audience still exists in large number, but another audience, most of them born since 1935, exists along with it. This group, this Film Generation, is certainly not exclusively grim, but it is essentially serious. Even its appreciations of sheer entertainment films reflect an over-all serious view.

There are a number of reasons, old and new, intrinsic and extrinsic, why this generation has come into being. Here are some of the older, intrinsic reasons.

1. In an age imbued with technological interest, the film art flowers out of technology. Excepting architecture, film is the one art that can capitalize directly and extensively on this century's luxuriance in applied science. Graphic artists have used mechanical and electronic elements, poets and painters have used computers, composers use electronic tapes. These are matters of choice. The film-maker has no choice: he must use complicated electronic and mechanical equipment. This fact helps to create a strong sense of junction with his society, of membership in the present. American artists have often been ashamed of—sometimes have dreaded—a feeling of difference from the busy "real" American world around them. For the film-maker the very instruments of his art provide communion with the spirit of his age. I think that the audience shares his feeling of union, sometimes consciously (especially when stereophonic sound, special optical effects, or color processes are used). The scientific skills employed are thus in themselves a link between the artist and the audience, and are a further link between them all and the unseen, unheard but apprehended society bustling outside the film theater.

There is a pleasant paradoxical corollary. In an era that is much concerned with the survival of the human being as such, in an increasingly mechanized age, here a complicated technology is used to celebrate the human being.

2. The world of surfaces and physical details has again become material for art. Just as the naturalistic novel seems to be sputtering to

a halt, overdescribed down to the last vest button, the film gives some of its virtues new artistic life. A novelist who employs the slow steam-roller apparatus of intense naturalism these days is asking for an extra vote of confidence from the reader, because the method and effects are so familiar that the reader can anticipate by pages. Even when there is the interest of an unusual setting, the reader is conscious that different nouns have been slipped into a worn pattern. The "new" French novel of Robbe-Grillet, Duras, Sarraute attempts to counteract this condition by intensifying it, using surfaces as the last realities, the only dependable objective correlatives. Sometimes, for some readers, this works. But both the old and the latter-day naturalisms must strain in order to connect. Rolf Hochhuth, the author of *The Deputy*, has said:

> When I recently saw Ingmar Bergman's *The Silence*, I left that Hamburg movie house with the question, "What is there left for the novelist today?" Think of what Bergman can do with a single shot of his camera, up a street, down a corridor, into a woman's armpit. Of all he can say with this without saying a word.

Despite Hochhuth's understandable thrill-despair, there is plenty left for the novelist to say, even of armpits, but the essence of his re-mark rightly strips from fiction the primary function of creating material reality. The film has not only taken over this function but exalted it: it manages to make poetry out of doorknobs, breakfasts, furniture. Trivial details, of which everyone's universe is made, can once again be trans-muted into metaphor, contributing to imaginative act.

A complementary, powerful fact is that this principle operates whether the film-maker is concerned with it or not. In any film except those with fantastic settings, whether the director's aim is naturalistic or romantic or symbolic or anything else, the streets and stairways and cigarette lighters are present, the girl's room is at least as real as the girl—often it bolsters her defective reality. Emphasized or not, invited or not, the physical world through the intensifications of photography never stops insisting on its presence and relevance.

This new life of surfaces gives a discrete verity to many mediocre films and gives great vitality to a film by a good artist. Consciously or not, this vitality reassures the audience, tangentially certifying and com-menting on its habitat. Indeed, out of this phenomenon, it can be argued that the film discovered pop art years ago, digested this minor achieve-ment, then continued on its way.

3. The film form seems particularly apt for the treatment of many of the pressing questions of our time: inner states of tension or of doubt or apathy—even (as we shall see) doubts about art itself. The film can

externalize some psychical matters that, for example, the theater cannot easily deal with; and it can relate them to physical environment in a manner that the theater cannot contain nor the novel quite duplicate. The film can dramatize post-Freudian man, and his habitat—and the relation between the two. One does not need to believe in the death of the theater or the novel—as I do not—in order to see these special graces in the film.

4. Film is the only art besides music that is available to the whole world at once, exactly as it was first made. With subtitles, it is the only art involving language that can be enjoyed in a language of which one is ignorant. (I except opera, where the language rarely needs to be understood precisely.)

The point is not the spreading of information or amity, as in USIA or UNESCO films, useful though they may be. The point is emotional relationship and debt. If one has been moved by, for instance, Japanese actors in Japanese settings, in actions of Japanese life that have resonated against one's own experience, there is a connection with Japan that is deeper than the benefits of propaganda or travelogue. No one who has been moved by *Ikiru* can think of Japan and the Japanese exactly as he thought before.

Obviously similar experience—emotional and spiritual—is available through other arts, but rarely with the imperial ease of the film. As against foreign literature, foreign films have an advantage besides accessibility in the original language. The Japanese novelist invites us to re-create the scene in imagination. The Japanese film-maker provides the scene for us, with a vividness that our minds cannot equal in a foreign setting. Thus our responses can begin at a more advanced point and can more easily (although not more strongly) be stimulated and heightened.

This universality and this relative simultaneity of artistic experience have made us all members of a much larger empathetic community than has been immediately possible before in history.

5. Film has one great benefit by accident: its youth, which means not only vigor but the reach of possibility. The novel, still very much alive, is conscious of having to remain alive. One of its chief handicaps is its history; the novelist is burdened with the achievements of the past. This is also true of poetry. It flourishes certainly; as with fiction, the state of poetry is far better than is often assumed. But poetry, too, is conscious of a struggle for pertinent survival. In painting and sculpture, the desperation is readily apparent; the new fashion in each new season makes it clear. But the film is an infant, only begun. It has already accomplished miracles. Consider that it was only fifty years from Edison's camera to *Citizen Kane*, which is rather as if Stravinsky had written *Petrouchka* fifty years after Guido d'Arezzo developed musical notation. Nevertheless

the film continent has only just been discovered, the boundaries are not remotely in sight. It is this freshness that gives the young generation — what I have called the Film Generation — not only the excitement of its potential but a strong proprietary feeling. The film belongs to them.

These, I think, are some of the reasons for the growth of that new film audience. But they raise a question. As noted, these reasons have been valid to some degree for a long time, yet it is only in about the last twenty years that the Film Generation has emerged. Why didn't this happen sooner? Why have these reasons begun to be strongly operative only since the Second World War?

In that period other elements have risen to galvanize them. Some of these later elements come from outside the film world: the spurt in college education; political and social abrasions and changes; moral, ethical, religious dissolutions and resolutions. All these have made this generation more impatient and more hungry. But, since the Second War, there have also been some important developments within the film world itself.* These developments have been in content, not in form. Three elements are especially evident: increased sexuality, an increase in national flavor, and an increased stress on the individual. The latter two are linked.

As for the first, sex has been important currency in the theater since *The Agamemnon*, and with the first films came the first film idols. In fact there are scenes in many silent films that would have censor trouble today. But apart from sexual display or the sex appeal of any actor or actress, there is now — in many foreign films and some American ones — a sexual attitude that can be respected: an attitude closer to the realities of sexual life than the mythology that is preached by clergy of every faith, by mass media, by parents. This relative sexual freedom, long established in fiction and the theater, has been slower to arrive in films because of their wider availability to all ages and mentalities, and the consequent brooding of censors. Now, in a more liberal time, this freedom makes films even more pertinent to this generation. The mythology that still passes for sexual morality is prescriptive, these films are descriptive; but there is more to their merit than verisimilitude. Not by nudity nor bedroom calisthenics nor frank language but by fidelity to the

---

*These do not include linguistic developments. Nothing has changed the language of film as, for example, electronics has changed music or abstract expressionism has altered the vision of painting. There have been many technical film developments — wide screens, stereophonic sound, color refinements — but so far they have largely been peripheral to the art itself. They, and the improved hand-held camera and recorder, may affect the basic language of film in future; they have not yet markedly done so. This fact can be taken as an implied strength. Experiments in artistic technique are usually a sign that a boundary has been reached with old techniques. In film there is no hint of exhaustion in the techniques that were known to Griffith and Eisenstein forty years ago.

complexities of sexual behavior, these films provide more than recognition. By accepting and exploring complexities, they provide confidence in the fundamental beauty of those complexities, in the desirability of being human, even with all the trouble it involves.

The second element, national flavor, has been described by the English critic Penelope Houston in *The Contemporary Cinema* (1963):

> However partial or distorted an image one gets of a society through its cinema, it is still possible to discern the national face behind the screen. It is difficult to conceive of a neorealist idealism [in Italy] without the jubilant preface of the liberation of Rome; or to look at Britain's films of the past few years without reference to our redbrick radicalism; or to ignore the effect of the political climate on a French cinema which declares its awareness of strain in the very insistence with which it puts private before public life and creation for creation's sake before either.

It would be easy to add a similar sentence for almost every major film-producing country. Japanese films are concerned with contemporary unrest, directly and indirectly. Many of their costume pictures about samurai swordsmen are set in the 1860s when the feudal system was crumbling and immense social metamorphosis was taking place. The Soviet film has deepened in lethargy as revolutionary fervor wore off, as Stalinist despotism made it nervous, as some subsequent economic and scientific successes made it smug. It has become, with a few exceptions, either war glory or the ideologic equivalent of the petty bourgeois confection. As for America, the poor boy and rich girl story (or rich boy and poor girl) which was the staple of the popular film before the Second War has disappeared. Money as romance, the Gatsby dream, has receded, not because everyone is now rich but because the middle-class image has replaced both the poor image and the rich image. What American would now relish the ancient compliment "poor but honest"? And what is the difference *in appearance* between the clerk's car and the boss's? The much-mooted ascendancy of the middle class has reached the point where it is strong enough to control cultural forms, to magnify its own image in art.

With this ascendancy we have seen the emergence of a new romantic hero, posed against this bourgeois background, since all such heroes must contrast with their societies. The new romantic is the liberated prole, with a motorcycle or a Texas Cadillac, seeking his life by assaulting convention and morality, rather than by striving for success in accepted modes, either with money or with women. This hero scoffs at ideals of excellence and aspiration at the same time that he wants to dominate.

There are signs that this hero may have run his course, but in the last twenty years or so he was pre-eminent.

A lesser companion of his still continues: the Frank Sinatra-Dean Martin figure, the smart, cool operator just inside the law, a philanderer righteously resentful of any claims on him by women. His casual *persona* derives in part from the night-club microphone, which was first a necessity, then became a prop, then a source of power and ease for those who had little power and could achieve nothing but ease. The invisible hand-held microphone accompanies the crooner-as-hero wherever he goes. His oblique, slithering solipsism seems likely to persist after the Brando figure, more directly descended from the proletarian rebel and Byronic individualist, has passed. Mere "coolness" persists; purposeful rebellion fades.

All the national colors described above apply both to popular and serious films. If we concentrate on serious film — film made primarily as personal expression, not as contractual job or money-spinner — then we often find, besides intensified national color, an intensified introspection. This is the third of our elements: a concern with the exploration of the individual as a universe. It is not a novelty in films. No more introspective films have ever been made than Wiene's *The Cabinet of Dr. Caligari* (1919) or Pabst's *Secrets of a Soul* (1926). But merely to mention such names as Bergman, Antonioni, Fellini, Ozu, Torre Nilsson, Olmi, Truffaut is to see that, for many outstanding directors, there has lately been more reliance on inner conflict than on classic confrontation of antagonists. These men and others, including some Americans, have been extending the film into the vast areas of innermost privacy, even of the unconscious, that have been the province of the novel and of metaphysical poetry. Saul Bellow has complained that the modern novelist doesn't tell us what a human being *is* today. Bellow is a notable exception to his own complaint; but whether we agree or not, we can see that many contemporary film-makers have tried to answer that question, with a more consistent application than ever before in the history of the art.

These two elements — national color and the exploration of the individual — are obviously inseparable. Society and the man affect each other, even if it is in the man's withdrawal. These elements are further linked in a curious contradictory motion against our time. In an age when internationalism is promulgated as a solution to political difficulties, national colors have become more evident in films. In an age when social philosophers have begun to question the durability of individualism — which is, after all, a fairly recent concept in history and almost exclusive to the West — the film is tending to cherish the individual. Does this indicate a time lag between the film and the advances of political and social philosophy? On the contrary, I believe it indicates a perverse penetration to truth. The truth of art sometimes runs counter to what seems politically and intellectually desirable; that is always a risk of art. I think the film is showing us that nationalism, in the purely cultural sense, is becoming more necessary to us as jet plane and Telstar threaten to make us one world. I think that just at the time when technological and power structures challenge individualism, our own minds and souls have become more interesting to us. Up to now, technology has outraced self-discovery. Only now—in this postreligious, self-dependent age—are we beginning to appreciate how rich and dangerous each one of us is.

These elements have led, directly and by implication, to the phenomenon we are examining; the historical moment for the rise of the Film Generation, a surge of somewhat nostalgic revolution; a reluctance to lose what seems to be disappearing, accompanied by an impulse to disaffection, an insistence on an amorphous cosmos. ("Stay loose." "Swing.") Doubtless that nostalgia is sentimental, an unwillingness to be banned from an Eden of individualism that in fact never existed. But much of the revolution is clearheaded; not so much an attempt to halt change as to influence it; a natural and valuable impulse to scratch on the chromium fronts of the advancing tanks of factory-society "Kilroy was here."

The divided attitude toward social change leads to another, crucial polarity. This generation has an ambivalent view of cultural tradition. On the one hand there is a great desire for such tradition, admitted or not. Everyone wants to know that he came from somewhere; it's less lonely. But this desire is often accompanied by a mirror attitude that looks on the past as failure and betrayal. It is of course a familiar indictment, the young accusing the old of having made a mess, but now the accusation is more stringent and more general because of the acceleration of change and the diminutions of choice.

This ambivalence toward tradition—this polarity that both wants and rejects it—has created a hunger for art as assurance of origins together with a preference for art forms that are relatively free of the past. Outstanding among these is film. Even though it has been on hand for sixty-five years or so, the film seems much more of the present and future than other forms. It has its roots—of content and method—in older arts: drama, literature, dance, painting; yet it is very much less entailed by the past than these arts. It satisfies this generation's ambivalent need in tradition.

So far, this inquiry has been almost all celebration; now a concern must be raised. So far, we have discussed certain phenomena as cultural dynamics and social facts: now a word must be said in value judgment of the revolutionary standards involved. Not all the films that the Film

Generation venerates seem worth its energy and devotion. It is not my purpose to lay down an artistic credo: I could always think of too many exceptions. Taste is a matter of instances, not precepts. One forms an idea of another's taste — or of one's own — from the perspective of many instances of judgment and preference, and even then, general deductions must be drawn delicately. But, drawing them as delicately as I am able, I am left with a concern to posit against the foregoing celebration.

There are enthusiasms of this Film Generation that I do not share, there are many enthusiasms of mine that they seem not to share. For the most part this is nobody's fault and probably nobody's virtue. But there is one enthusiasm in particular that has taken many members of this generation — not all, but a large proportion — that seems potentially deleterious and therefore to need discussion.

On college campuses around the country, in some film societies and small theaters (there are at least three in New York at this writing), much is being made of certain experimental films. The passion for experiment, as such, is eternal and necessary, but out of disgust with much commercial and fake-serious fare, there is a strong tendency to value experiment for its own sake, to regard it as a value instead of a means to value. And since, at this period in social and political affairs, a passion for these films has been taken to have other significances as well, the phenomenon is especially important.

The films to which I refer are often called underground films. In America a large proportion of them come from a group centered in New York but not confined there, variously called New American Films or the Film-maker's Cooperative. It is an association of dedicated film-makers and dedicated apostles. (The apostles carry the word widely. Two minutes after I met Federico Fellini in Rome, he asked me whether I had seen Jack Smith's *Flaming Creatures*.) The group also has a circle of apostolic critics.

Predictably, this group considers itself the element of poetry in an otherwise prosaic film situation in this country and the world. Also predictably, its works are difficult to describe because it is not a school like neorealism or surrealism. It includes these and many more styles. It welcomes anyone who uses film as a form of personal expression. The most lucid general statement about this group that I know was written by Ken Kelman (*The Nation*, May 11, 1964). He divides their works into three main categories. First, "outright social criticism and protest" (Dan Drasin's *Sunday*, Stan Vanderbeek's *Skullduggery*). Second, "films which suggest, mainly through anarchic fantasy, the possibilities of the human spirit in its socially uncorrupted state" (Jack Smith's *Flaming Creatures* and *Normal Love*). The third group "creates, out of a need to fill our rationalistic void, those actual inner worlds which fall within the realm of myth" (Kenneth Anger's *Scorpio Rising*, Stan Brakhage's *Anticipation of the Night* and *Window Water Baby Moving*).

Kelman's article, like others on the subject, is a ringing statement written with inner consistency and a fire that outstrips mere sincerity. The difficulty is that, when one sees these films (I have seen all those cited and numerous others), one finds small consonance between the descriptions and the works. Not to belabor individual films, one can say that most of them represent the attitudes and intents that Kelman describes but that their acceptance as accomplishment reflects a deliberate disconnection from cultural and social history. For me, most of the "new" techniques are dated, most of the social criticism is facile or vacuous, the mythic content undernourishing, the general quality of inspiration tenuous, strained, trite. Much of the work seems made for a young audience that insists on having its *own* films, at any critical or cultural price.

One of the grave liabilities in the situation is that writing like Kelman's and the attitudes it promotes tend to encourage the symbiotic state that exists today in the graphic arts. There is not much direct relation between film and audience, nothing so simple as the audience coming to the theater and being affected, or not, by what it sees. The audience exists jointly with these films in a highly verbalized critical environment; its preformed attitudes are eager dramatizations of credos and exegeses. Much of modern painting—op, pop, collage, latter-day abstraction—seems to have its life almost as much in what is written about it as on canvas. Indeed many of the paintings seem to have been made to evoke aesthetic disquisition, to exist verbally and in viewers' attitudes. The underground film has entered this territory—of art as "position"—a position sustained as much by the polemic-conscious audience as by the material on the screen. It has long been an indictment of Broadway and Hollywood hits that the audience is preconditioned, whipped into line by newspaper raves. Here is very much the same situation at a higher intellectual altitude.

Another grave liability is the pressure brought to bear by the underground movement for disconnection from cultural history. Generally, as has been noted, the Film Generation has at least an ambivalent attitude toward tradition: this underground movement pushes—by implication and otherwise—for complete rejection of the standards that have been continuingly evolved through some centuries of Western art. They are not to be evolved further, they are to be discarded. It is easy to chuckle patronizingly at this belief as one more instance of the perennial artistic rebellion of the young, but current social upheavals give it a momentum that takes it out of the sphere of mere youthful high spirits—or low spirits. And the morning or the year or the decade after the excitements of rebellion have passed, it may be discovered that a valuable continuum in culture has been seriously injured—to the detriment of the very aims for which the action was taken.

I do not argue against change, including radical change. I do argue against nihilism as a necessary first step for progress. Besides, this film nihilism contains a bitter contradiction. It is often a manifestation in art of discontents elsewhere, of anger at older generations' betrayal of certain ideals. But the best art of the past—in all fields—is expression of those ideals, often despite society's apathy toward them. In discarding that inheritance of art, the rebels discard much of the best work that the human race has done for the very ideals that galvanize this new rebellion.

There is a parallel between this devotion to the underground film in many of the Film Generation and an element in the "new left," the new political radicalism. Some of radical youth are engaged in genuinely creative action: antimilitarism, antidiscrimination, support of various economic programs. But many of them equate radicalism with personal gesture and style—revolt consummated by bizarre hair and dress, unconventional sexual behavior, flirtations with drugs. One who is aware of the valid basis for disaffection can still regret the introversions and futilities of these gestures. Likewise, one hopeful for the invigoration of the American film can doubt the pertinence of comparable gestures in this field: the exaltation of meaninglessness in film as a statement of meaninglessness in the world: the praise of juvenile irreverence—perennial in art—as a new formulation of myth; the approval of a social criticism that is devoid of intellectual foundation and political belief.

I dwell on the partiality to these experimental films not to counterbalance the happy fact of the Film Generation's existence but precisely because of its existence. Art has never been well created for long independently of an audience; in fact, history shows that audience response feeds great eras of art (painting in Renaissance Italy, the drama in Elizabethan England and neoclassic France, the sudden, ravenous worldwide appetite for silent-film comedy).

Speaking in the large, I believe that the Film Generation has the power to evoke the films that it wants, even though that generation is a minority and despite the harsh conditions of production and exhibition around the world. *All* films will not alter, nor should they, but if the dynamics of cultural history still obtains, an insistent group of art takers can—sooner or later, one way or another—have an effect on art makers. The effect is circular. The audience obviously cannot do it alone; there have to be talented artists. But talent is a relative constant in the human race; it is sparked by response and, even at its best, can be dampened by neglect. (Think of Herman Melville's twenty years in the Customs House.)

Thus, by a logical progression, we can see that the Film Generation has extraordinary powers. If it is true (as I have claimed) that film is the most pertinent art at present; if it is true that the young generation is closer to the film than to other arts; if it is also true that audience appetite can evoke art; then, it follows that the Film Generation has the opportunity to help bring forth the best and most relevant art of our age. And it is the possible impediment to this opportunity that makes a devotion to culturally baseless, essentially sterile films seem wasteful.

I am aware that the above puts an almost ludicrously large burden on this Film Generation. In effect, it is almost to ask them to solve the problems of cultural transition, to define what culture will become. The problem is not to be solved in any one locus, even when the locus — film and its audience — has come into being quite naturally. It is never to be solved; it is only to be confronted continually, particularly in an age that is *not* an age, that is a rapid series of continually shifting points. But the size of the conclusion does not diminish the opportunity.

There is not much question among the thoughtful that we live in a time of the most profound cultural change, when the very purposes of art, as well as its content, are being transformed. The New American Cinema is one manifestation of that upheaval. In my view, most of its films that I have seen are of minuscule importance, but the implication in most of them is important: the implication that what's past is quite dead. The art of the future may be divorced from present concepts of humanism; it may find its pertinences in modes that, to most eyes, now look cold or abstract or even antihuman. But they will have been made by men who would not be what they are, whatever that may be, without the precedents of culture; and if that new art, whatever it may be, is to be held to its highest standards, the best of the past needs to be brought forward with us. The real *use* of our inheritance in the contemporary situation would throw a good deal of illumination on much of the new that is now adulated. The Kelmans tell us that an Antonioni is only seemingly free, that he is trapped by attempting to renovate the past. But, to take Antonioni as an example, it is precisely the effort to alter in an altered cosmos without returning Western culture to Year One that may keep a cultural future possible; may sustain us as we travel from a terrain that once was fruitful to one that has not yet been sighted. We don't want to starve en route.

As an important part of this process — this rescue operation, if you like — the Film Generation can demand a new film from the serious filmmaker that is more than a gesture of denial. Such a generation, joined with the past and therefore truly equipped to outgrow it, may eventually get in its films what the Kelmans have prematurely claimed: a new social cohesion, a new fertile and reassuring mythos. If these come, they will manifest their presence, not so much by the blown prose of rhapsodists as by an irony: middle-of-the-road art will imitate the new film. That film will certainly not be ignored, as the majority now ignore underground efforts. When the imitation begins, then authentically progressive artists and audiences will know that they have thus far succeeded, and will know it is again time to move forward.

So the Film Generation, flaws and all, represents both a circumstance and an opportunity. On the whole it is, I believe, the most cheering circumstance in contemporary American art. That generation can be a vital force, or it can twiddle its strength and chances away in irrelevant artistic nihilism, in engorged social petulance. One does not ask them to "save" film forever. In the long run, the history of the film will be the same as that of all arts: a few peaks, some plateaus, many chasms; but the present chance—a rare one—could save much time in the development of this young medium. The foreseeable future is all that, reasonably, we can have hopes or anxieties about in art. The Film Generation can help to make the foreseeable future of film interesting and important. Let us see.

Pygmalion (1938) Liza sells her flowers in Covent Garden in what George Bernard Shaw called one of "the new scenes that the screen makes possible" and which he wrote expressly for the film version of his play. (Courtesy of National Film Archives.)

Henry V (1944) The French horsemen encounter the English archers at Agincourt. The screen can provide spectacle impossible on the stage and enhance it with the effective contrast of the close shot. (Stills courtesy of the Rank Organisation, Ltd. Copyright © 1945 by United Artists Corporation.)

FROM WORDS TO
VISUAL IMAGES

10
**Robert
Richardson**

VERBAL AND VISUAL LANGUAGES

Professor Richardson, Chairman of the English Department at the University of Denver, expands the usual definition of literature to include filmscripts and screenplays. He contrasts modern poetry and contemporary cinema. With copious examples, he indicates that movies have a significant influence on modern writers. His book, *Literature and Film*, from which this selection is taken, is particularly stimulating.

Film, as we are considering it, is a narrative medium and, like literature, is an art based on language. One is accustomed to hearing the word language used rather freely for arts such as painting and architecture, meaning vaguely that the art so described communicates something in some way. But the elements of film narrative, as they have existed since the mid-twenties, form not a figurative but an actual language. Language consists of vocabulary, grammar, and syntax. Vocabulary consists of words, which represent things or abstractions, while grammar and syntax are the means by which the words are arranged. The vocabulary of film is the simple photographed image; the grammar and syntax of film are the editing, cutting, or montage processes by which the shots are arranged.

Single shots have meaning much as single words do, but a series of carefully arranged shots conveys meaning much as a composed phrase does. Shots of a house burning, a woman weeping, a plane flying close overhead have each a simple content, but if arranged in the order airplane/house/ woman the three together make a statement. Film has an immense, a virtually unlimited vocabulary; its problem has been to evolve a film grammar as subtle as that possessed by even the simplest verbal language. Hence a fade-out followed by a fade-in was early conventionalized to mean "time passes," while a dissolve meant "meanwhile in another place." Irising in and close-ups were originally used as italics or underlining. The silent film, as Balázs observed, has no past tense and no future tense, for pictures alone can express only the present. Flashbacks thus became the standard way to express time past, while future time could be conveyed by misty or slow motion, or "dream" editing. But one of the great benefits of the sound movie was that to the large and expressive vocabulary of the film were added the grammatical and syntactical resources of verbal language. The drawback, unfortunately, was that the film ceased to work to provide its own visual grammar, relying instead on its enormous and subtle vocabulary. What can be achieved by paying close attention to the pictorial composition of each shot with only rather simple editing can be seen in Carol Reed's *Odd Man Out*, John Ford's late and visually idyllic westerns, or Charles Laughton's version of Agee's *The Night of the Hunter*. On the other hand, a film such as *Last Year at Marienbad* could be said to use a limited vocabulary, and an abstract one at that, but a complex grammar of editing techniques so subtle as to evade comprehension more or less successfully.

At any rate, since the introduction of sound, the nature of film language has become more complex. Before sound, as the steady development of film from 1910 to 1925 showed, the visual shot was the basic unit. The single shot was analogous to the word, as Pudovkin saw, while the process of editing supplied the film's grammar. When sound was added to the films, however, the vocabulary of the film was in effect doubled, since it came to consist of both individual sights and individual sounds. As sound enlarged and changed film's basic vocabulary, so it enlarged and gave more variety to film's grammar.

This can be seen most vividly in the matter of verbs. One of the distinguishing marks of effective prose is a high percentage of verbs. Amateur writers, thinking to gain richness and amplitude, fill their prose with adjectives, but prose which lacks strong and frequent verbs lacks energy and movement and is hard to read. One of the reasons why the prose of Samuel Johnson is as effective as it is, despite the heavily Latinate language, is that Johnson uses more verbs than most writers. Now the film had, from the start, a built-in way to obtain the force and the movement which, in prose, comes from verbs. This was the simple fact that one could take pictures of things that were moving. When one photographed a man reaching for a gun on the wall, lifting it down, tucking it under his arm, opening the breach, inserting a shell, and swinging around to face the door, one had an image which requires six verbs to describe in words. Secondly, the camera itself could move, even if the subject stood still. In moving the camera three hundred and sixty degrees around an empty room, one adds the verbal force of turning, seeing, and following to a scene which in reality would be utterly motionless. Thirdly, when the peculiar power of editing had been discovered, film makers found that they had another verbal force at hand. One could join a series of static shots together in such a way as to produce a powerful tension, a sense of latent energy, an expectation of motion that would be hard to describe in prose (though perfectly possible) since one would need language that was at once static but compressed like a spring. Hitchcock is one master of this sort of editing, but it is a common quality in the film. The scenes in *High Noon* in which we are waiting for the train to arrive are a good example of this sort of editing of static material to produce an essentially verbal force. We see the railroad tracks shimmering in the heat, the waiting men, the town clock, the empty streets, the marshal's face. Nothing actually moves, but the editing unobtrusively drives the town toward violence. The fourth sort of verbal force available to the film is, of course, the actual verb on the sound track, where all the dramatic resources of the spoken word are just as available to the film as they have always been to the drama.

Verbs are only one part of speech, to be sure, but they are crucial and one of the reasons why nearly everyone will concede the potential, if not the actual, power of the film may be its rich and varied range of ways to express action as verbs express it in writing.

In addition to the parallels between language and film in matters of vocabulary and simple grammar, but closely connected with that subject, is the use of imagery. It can be argued that all words, even the most abstract, began as images. Emerson points out that "supercilious," cool and abstract as the word is now, means literally "raised eyebrow," and was once a vivid picture of an attitude. So, too, what I have been calling the vocabulary of film is, in ways that are largely obvious (because the film unlike most languages is still young), essentially a repertoire of images. Because language is by nature an image or symbol making process, literature has always been able to make effective, conscious use of it, and there exist, of course, numerous books on the subject. Film too, insofar as it thinks of its material as representations or images of reality and not as slices of life or actual reality, has an equally wide range of possibilities for conscious use of imagery. Film imagery has been, on the whole, rather simple compared with literary imagery, but there are signs that this is changing. It is hard, for example, to think of any film image with the force of, say, Marlowe's description of Helen—"Was this the face that launch'd a thousand ships,/And burnt the topless towers of Ilium?"[1] But the bolder editing that distinguishes the films of the last ten years is gradually increasing the film's command of imagery. One thinks of the profuse imagery of Fellini's recent films or of the subtle and powerful images of desolation which Antonioni drew out of the rocky island in *L'Avventura,* or the wit with which Truffaut made a stale oath come to comic life in a scene in *Shoot the Piano Player:* the hoodlum bragging about his possessions to the unimpressed youngster finally insists, "May my mother drop dead if I don't," whereupon is flashed on the screen an oval shot, framed in lace, of a little old lady keeling over.

Between the film's use of imagery and its literary uses there are both significant similarities and differences. Imagery is used both for vividness and for significance; and one might say that literature often has the problem of making the significant somehow visible, while film often finds itself trying to make the visible significant. Hence the differing emphases within what may be essentially the same technique.

In *Mother,* Pudovkin used film imagery to deepen the effect of a young man's release from prison:

> The son sits in prison. Suddenly, passed in to him surreptitiously, he receives a note that next day he is to be set free. The problem was the expression, filmically, of his joy. The photographing of a face lighting up with joy would have been flat and void of effect. I show, therefore, the nervous play of his hands and a big close-up of the lower half of his face, the corners of a smile. These shots I cut in with other and varied material—shots of a brook, swollen with the rapid flow of spring, of the play of sunlight broken on the water, birds splashing in the village pond, and finally a laughing child.[2]

As we see the scene then, the prisoner looks forward not just to release, but to a world of spring, sun, and water in which one has the freedom of a bird, and the innocence of a child. Or in another way, this could be described as a negative image of prison, the memory of which is to be cleansed by sun and water. A scene that is parallel in some ways

[1] Christopher Marlowe, *Doctor Faustus,* ed. J. D. Jump, Cambridge, Mass., Harvard University Press, 1962, p. 92.
[2] V. I. Pudovkin, *Film Technique and Film Acting,* trans. Ivor Montagu, London, Vision: Mayflower, 1958, p. 27.

to Pudovkin's occurs in the third act of Shakespeare's *Measure for Measure*. Claudio is in prison; his sister has just come to tell him that the price of his release is to be her chastity, and to ask him to die rather than see her dishonored. Shakespeare has Claudio reply:

> Ay, but to die, and go we know not where,
> To lie in cold obstruction and to rot,
> This sensible warm motion to become
> A kneaded clod; and the delighted spirit
> To bathe in fiery floods, or to reside
> In thrilling region of thick-ribbèd ice,
> To be imprisoned in the viewless winds
> And blown with restless violence round about
> The pendent world; or to be worse than worst
> Of those that lawless and incertain thought
> Imagine howling, 'tis too horrible.
> The weariest and most loathèd worldly life
> That age, ache, penury, and imprisonment
> Can lay on nature is a paradise
> To what we fear of death.[3]

These two passages are similar in that each records a prisoner's reaction to the announcement of his fate; each uses the fact and feeling of prison as a basis or a starting point; and each constructs the response as an imaginative flight, a sequence of images. The most interesting difference, though, is that Pudovkin's imagery is, in words, excessively sentimental; only by using pictures can Pudovkin avoid mawkishness. On the other hand, Shakespeare's description has extraordinary force just as it is, in language, while any attempt to redo the scene in pictures would give a surreal effect. Actual filmed images of "thrilling regions of thick-ribbèd ice" would probably only suggest that Claudio is somehow mad. Each scene works in its own medium; neither would work in the other medium; yet the technique is virtually the same in both.

There has been a great deal of discussion about the relative virtues of black and white versus color photography, and it seems generally agreed that widespread adoption of color film for most subjects tends to weaken rather than strengthen the film, since color tends to emphasize the naturalistic, the "real" quality of the image, while black and white makes a subtle but steady insistence that we are watching not reality, but an image of reality. When the color is controlled and made an important aspect of the film experience (*The Red Balloon, Orange and Blue*,

[3] William Shakespeare, *Measure for Measure*, Baltimore, Penguin Books, 1956, p. 72.

An American in Paris, The Red Desert), then, of course, no one would object. But generally speaking, black and white has produced a surprisingly effective style for the film. Among the reasons for this are those cited by Rudolf Arnheim:

> The reduction of all colors to black and white, which does not leave even their brightness values untouched (the reds, for instance, may come too dark or too light depending on the emulsion), very considerably modifies the picture of the actual world. Yet everyone who goes to see a film accepts the screen world as being true to nature. This is due to the phenomenon of "partial illusion." The spectator experiences no shock at finding a world in which the sky is the same color as a human face; he accepts shades of gray as the red, white and blue of the flag; black lips as red; white hair as blonde. The leaves on a tree are as dark as a woman's mouth. In other words, not only has a multicolored world been transmuted into a black-and-white world, but in the process all color values have changed their relations to one another: similarities present themselves which do not exist in the natural world; things have the same color which in reality stand either in no direct color connection at all with each other or in quite a different one.[4]

The fact that we do accept the peculiar, unreal world of black and white is very nearly analogous to the phenomenon which makes a reader accept the world, however strange, of a storyteller, a phenomenon Coleridge called the "willing suspension of disbelief." Further, the black and white world of film is simply a convention, albeit an effective one, in much the same way that verbal language is itself a widely accepted convention. We accept the word for apple as an actual apple much as we accept white hair for blonde in a film. To use E. H. Gombrich's terminology, each is an acceptable substitute for reality.[5]

To turn from the effect of the convention to artistic problems of controlling a convention, the peculiar and unreal relationships that exist in the black and white film world are much like those in language, but they must be recognized before they can be used. In reality, the leaves on a tree bear no relation to a woman's mouth, in film they can be made to bear such a relation. So in language, to use a crude example, objects do not rhyme with one another, but in language they can be

[4] Rudolf Arnheim, *Film As Art*, Berkeley and Los Angeles, University of California Press, 1957, p. 15.
[5] See the title essay in E. H. Gombrich's *Meditations on a Hobby Horse*, London, Phaidon, 1963.

made to. Ogden Nash's observation that ants are famous for being active, which is not surprising since no one with formic acid inside would be apt to be calm, is dull enough until the verbal world takes over.

> The ant has made himself illustrious
> Through constant industry industrious.
> So what?
> Would you be calm and placid
> If you were full of formic acid?[6]

So a routine novel called *The Night of the Hunter* became a powerful work when the world of the evil preacher was presented in a film style that used an almost savage alternation between brilliant whites and deep blacks. It has become common to refer the effectiveness of black and white to its relation to Western morality, but as the above may indicate, it may be more useful to consider it as a convention on the analogy of the convention of language.

Another aspect of film that has been virtually neglected and that may be related to analogous literary problems is the film's essential, but almost invisible, regularity. Film rests, we are told, on an illusion. There is no movement on the screen. The projection process is a matter of projecting a still picture on the screen, then blacking out the screen for a brief time while the machine removes the first still and positions the next. The black mask is then removed and we see the next still. The replacement process occurs twenty-four times a second, but we never "see" the blacked-out screen because of the phenomenon of "persistence of vision"; that is, the image remains on the retina of the eye for a fraction of a second longer than it is there on the screen, just long enough to allow the projector to black out the screen, get another picture in position and let the light through again. The entire process is supposed to be imperceptible; the perfect and subconscious illusion of motion is, for the film maker, an article of faith. But one wonders if the spectator is really totally unaware or unresponsive to what is actually going on before his eyes. Lawrence Durrell, in *Justine,* makes an interesting comment on this: "Are people continuously themselves or simply over and over again so fast that they give the illusion of continuous features — the temporal flicker of the old silent film?"[7]

At any rate, the projection process is completely rigid, utterly regular; nor is this the only rigid aspect of the film. One hears a good deal about the immense mobility and freedom of the film, all of which seems true enough. But one experiences a film under fixed and rigid

---

[6] Ogden Nash, *Verses from 1929 On.* Boston and Toronto, Little, Brown, 1959, p. 239.
[7] Lawrence Durrell, *Justine,* New York, Pocket Books, p. 199.

conditions. One cannot, as with a novel, slow down, speed up, or lay it aside; nor can one, as with a poem, consider it, turn it this way and that, or reread it several times running. Given the immense and often mechanical industry that literary criticism has become, it may be argued that the difficulty one has in actually studying film is to be applauded rather than lamented, but it remains true that the freedom of film form applies more to the film maker than to the viewer. Still, from one point of view, the fixed and immutable form of any given film, as it appears to the viewer, reminds one of some of the stricter literary forms. The sonnet, for example, has a fixed number of syllables, lines, and rhymes; in the hands of Milton or Wordsworth it is carefully enjambed, so that the technically rigid form seems to create or allow a single flowing statement, and a full appreciation of the poem depends upon the reader's being aware of the strict form within which the freely moving poem has been created. One wonders, then, if some aspect of film enjoyment does not arise from similar conditions, from our being vaguely aware of the completely mechanical form within which so much freedom can be somehow apprehended.

Another fixed quality the film has, which will come in for increasing attention as time passes, is its total visibility, a result of the film's inability to reject or ignore surfaces. This aspect of film raises the general problem of the function of detail. The completed work of literature is also fixed — this is not true of oral literature of course — no word can be changed, and from this viewpoint any work of art is complete and unalterable for as long as it lasts. Yet the work of literature can leave certain details to the imagination despite the unchangeable verbal content. A few lines from one of Shakespeare's sonnets will illustrate this:

> Alas, 'tis true I have gone here and there
> And made myself a motley to the view,
> Gored mine own thoughts, sold cheap what is most dear,
> Made old offenses of affections new.
> Most true it is that I have looked on truth
> Askance and strangely; . . .[8]

These lines are vivid and fresh; the images are as alive as the subject, yet there is no distracting detail and nothing to make the poem date. For one thing, the poem does not depend on topical material. The dress, manners, habits, the fashions and fads of the day are simply not used in this sort of writing. The reader, unhampered by detail, can concentrate on the human emotions and the thought involved, and the poem

[8]*Shakespeare's Sonnets*, ed. II. E. Rollins, New York, Appleton-Century-Crofts, p. 55.

will seem as applicable today as it was three hundred and fifty years ago. Apparently then, it is not true to think that great art requires a completely detailed setting, yet this is what any film is virtually forced to have.

If narrative film relies on a basic film language just as a novel or poem relies on a language, comparison between the two usually works to the film's disadvantage, since film language is not yet as supple, as varied, or as precise as written language. But such comparisons as are possible suggest that the film still has an open line for development in this direction. Film has barely reached the point of having, for example, a conditional tense, a way of showing "what if." In *La Guerre est Finie*, Resnais presents Diego's apprehensive speculations about the future in a series of shots of the same action, but with first one person, then another, first one place and then another. What we see are visual scraps of Diego's musings. Claude Lelouch in his color extravaganza, *A Man and a Woman*, has Anouk Aimée, the heroine, ask Jean-Louis Trintignant what he does. He races cars, but he won't tell her; he will only say that his work is "unusual." At once is cut in a black and white sequence, her amused and deliberately silly speculation, of him as a big city slicker collecting money from a string of B-girls like someone out of Damon Runyon. Resnais seems more concerned than any current film maker with deliberately extending the film's grammar and syntax, yet there remain areas, such as that of generalization, that are still extraordinarily difficult. How, for example, would one get a film equivalent of the famous opening sentence of *Anna Karenina*, "All happy families resemble one another, but each unhappy family is unhappy in its own way." The opening of Jane Austen's *Pride and Prejudice* would present the same problem; "It is a truth universally acknowledged, that a single man in possession of a good fortune must be in want of a wife." Film simply lacks the resources to make such brief generalized speculations. Yet it is perfectly capable of the sort of thing one finds in highly detailed prose. Salinger's description of Seymour's wife as "a girl who for a ringing phone dropped exactly nothing," because it is a description of a particular sight and a particular sound, is a kind of language the film can easily match.[9]

Despite occasional flurries of enthusiasm for what is called abstract film, film in general is not very well suited to abstractions. Samuel Johnson's "Nothing can please many and please long but just representations of general nature" cannot be "said" in film. But if film language has little in common with Johnson's prose, it has somewhat more in common with that of Edward Gibbon; "A candid but rational inquiry into the progress and establishment of Christianity," Gibbon wrote at the start

⁹ J. D. Salinger, "A Perfect Day for Bananafish," in *Nine Stories*, New York, New American Library, 1954, p. 7.

of the fifteenth chapter of *The Decline and Fall of the Roman Empire*, "may be considered as a very essential part of the history of the Roman empire. While that great body was invaded by open violence, or undermined by slow decay, a pure and humble religion gently insinuated itself into the minds of men, grew up in silence and obscurity, derived new vigour from opposition, and finally erected the triumphant banner of the Cross on the ruins of the Capitol." Gibbon's generalization takes a more or less concrete form, the argument proceeds by contrasted images, the elaborate prose is, in fact, a montage composed of several lines of images. This way of writing allows Gibbon to say two things simultaneously. The actual or literal meaning of the above is that while Rome grew weaker, Christianity grew stronger; but the sense that Gibbon's linguistic montage, his ironic juxtaposition of images, gives the sentence is that Christianity attacked and conquered Rome by stealth. A recent CBS documentary called *The Great Love Affair* showed a thorough mastery of this sort of ironic prose montage. Ostensibly about the Americans and their cars, the film was historical and factual. But the montage, the timing, the juxtaposition led one constantly to the film maker's other theme, the auto as the great mechanical curse of modern life. One cannot say then that film is to be compared only with simple prose. It seems more accurate to say that film as yet shows no talent for generalization or abstraction, whereas it is very close to the subtle, controlled, and concrete prose of an ironist such as Gibbon.

Film language seems also to have a hard time with complicated logic; the following bit from Thomas Aquinas is, I would guess, not translatable into film. "To say that a thing is understood more by one [person] than by another may be taken in two senses. First, so that the word *more* be taken as determining the act of understanding as regards the thing understood; and thus, one cannot understand the same thing more than another, because to understand it otherwise than as it is, either better or worse, would be to be deceived rather than to understand, as Augustine argues."[10] Yet this is not to say that the film is incapable of logic. Film logic tends, though, to be either the sort that works by analogy or the sort that draws a conclusion from a mass of evidence. Film has, for example, no trouble with the sort of logic that distinguishes John Donne's famous statement about involvement; "No man is an Iland, intire of it selfe; every man is a peece of the Continent, a part of the maine; if a Clod bee washed away by the Sea, Europe is the lesse, as well as if a Promontorie were, as well as if a Mannor of thy friends or of thine owne were; Any mans death diminishes me, because I am involved

---

[10]Thomas Aquinas, from the *Summa Theologica*, Q. 85, Art 7, in *Introduction to St. Thomas Aquinas*, New York, Random House, 1948, p. 419.

in Mankinde; And therefore never send to know for whom the bell
tolls; It tolls for thee."[11] This kind of logic of analogy has been used
innumerable times in film. A well-known example is the final sequence
of *Strike*, which goes, in part:

1. The head of a bull jerks out of the shot, beyond the upper frame-
   line, avoiding the aimed butcher's knife.
2. The hand holding the knife strikes sharply — beyond the lower
   frame-line.
3. 1,000 persons roll down a slope — in profile.
4. 50 persons raise themselves from the ground, arms outstretched.
5. Face of a soldier taking aim.
6. A volley of gun-fire.
7. The shuddering body of the bull (head outside the frame) rolls
   over.[12]

Eisenstein's logic here, like Donne's, is to insist on the truth or
applicability of his analogy, the "pacification" of the workers is an act of
simple butchery, and the underlying point, much like that of Donne, is
that this is wrong because it denies the idea of the human community.

A Japanese film called *The Island* makes a point the reverse of
Donne's by the technique of accumulated detail. After an hour and a half
of the painful particulars of life on a waterless island, the film's logic, that
men are indeed islands, seems inescapable. The logic here is like that of
Cassius in *Julius Caesar*, who after a long catalogue of Caesar's physical
ailments and shortcomings, has himself and us convinced that he, Cassius,
is the better man. As the film has difficulty with abstraction and generalization, so it is weak on abstract or abstruse reasoning, but highly capable
of even the subtlest reaches of argument by analogy or illustration.

Since Whitman and the rise of free verse, it has been difficult to
draw a clear line between prose and poetry. Indeed, there seems to be
no necessary distinction between free verse and prose except that with
the former, lines don't always go all the way to the right hand margin.
But between classical or regular verse and prose there is a clear distinction which has a bearing on film. Classical or regular poetry, meaning
here any kind of verse written in regular, repeated, and predictable
patterns of foot, line, and stanza, can have, and, with most good poets,
does have two rhythms: the steady metronomic beat of the pattern
rhythm, and the spoken, voiced rhythm. Thus the line from Milton's

[11] John Donne, *Devotions Upon Emergent Occasions*, Cambridge, Cambridge University
Press, 1923, p. 98.
[12] Sergei Eisenstein, *The Film Sense*, Cleveland and New York, World (Meridian),
1957, p. 234.

Samson Agonistes "Oh dark, dark, dark, amid the blaze of noon," has both a tick-tock iambic pattern and a great sweeping spoken rhythm. The effect, which has been called "the constant evasion and recognition of meter," is really an effect of counterpoint. As in music, one pattern is played against and with another. Thus a double rhythm is possible because of the fixed pattern which a poet adopts to underlie his work. In prose, which has no fixed line length and no necessarily repeated rhythms, this double rhythm cannot be managed, and in this connection film is usually more like prose or free verse than classical poetry. As the sentence is the unit in prose, and the line in free verse, so the shot is the unit in film. And in the absence of a fixed sentence pattern, a fixed line length, or a set shot pattern, all these forms can only achieve a single rhythm. This is not to say, of course, that the single rhythm cannot be superb — one thinks of Donne's sermons, or Whitman's verse, or the well controlled rhythm of Clouzot's *The Wages of Fear*.

Still the film need not be bound to a single rhythm. It would be interesting to see what could be done with a film which decided ahead of time to make all the shots the same length, or which decided to try visual rhyme, that is, making every tenth shot either the same as or very nearly the same as every fifth shot and so on. The effect would probably be very formal, but it would give the film an increased capacity for rhythm; indeed, it would give the film the double rhythm of classical poetry.

In this respect and in innumerable others, only a few of which are touched on above, the film language, which is the basis of film as a narrative art, seems still to be evolving, and it would be premature and rash to suggest that it will not eventually develop a language with the force, clarity, grace, and subtlety of written language. But film language may not evolve so far, or even in this direction; as Resnais has remarked, "the cinema is far from having found its true syntax," and the future of film as language is correspondingly uncertain.[13]

---

[13]Roy Armes, *French Cinema Since 1946*, Vol. 2, London, Zwemmer, 1966, p. 18.

11

Fred H. Marcus
and Paul Zall

CATCH-22: IS FILM FIDELITY AN ASSET?

This contrast in media article was written specifically for this book. Professor Zall, who specializes in nineteenth-century British literature, has taught seminars on satire, including Heller's Catch-22. Professor Marcus, the compiler of this anthology, has taught film courses, written articles on film, and co-authored The Motion Picture and the Teaching of English. Both are members of the English Department of California State College, Los Angeles.

The 1970 opening of Mike Nichols' film, Catch-22, adapted from the highly successful novel by Joseph Heller, opened gates to a flood of critical assessment. Film reviewers revealed themselves as latent literary critics, eager to evaluate the novel in addition to drawing inferences and making observations about the changes from book to movie.

A Vincent Canby review in The New York Times (June 25, 1970) concluded an opening laudatory paragraph with an encompassing summation, ". . . oh, to hell with it! — it's the best American film I've seen this year." Six paragraphs later, Canby voiced a demurrer, ". . . I'm not sure that anyone who has not read the novel will make complete sense out of the movie's narrative line . . ." In *New York* (June 29, 1970), Judith Crist mixed a moderate amount of praise for the film with some astute negative criticism, particularly since she valued the novel highly and found the movie lacking in "cohesion, style, and essential mood." She added, perceptively and properly, that ". . . devotees of the book will find themselves short-changed, but of course nothing less than a 12-hour film could capture the variety that Heller offered. . . ." In *The New Republic* (July 4, 1970), Stanley Kauffmann began his review with high praise for the initial promise in the opening scenes but quarreled with most of the film treatment thereafter. In the next to last paragraph of a fairly extended review, he wrote, "He (Nichols) seems to have realized too late the enormous difficulties of filming this book, of conveying its cosmos within a reasonable length, of making *visible* its understated lunacies. . . ."

Contrasts in media often begin with a truism. Novels are verbal; films are primarily visual. Heller's novel is more than conventionally verbal. The rich comic humor of *Catch-22* runs an astonishing gamut from hilarious one-liners to complex linguistic paradoxes. Verbal word play and wit spice the novel. The logic of *Alice in Wonderland* blends with the savage satire and venom of Jonathan Swift. Heller's novel begins with entertaining absurdities but closes with unbearable absurdities. As Crist notes in her review, man's inhumanity and capacity for self-destruction leaves an involved human being "only the alternatives of shrieking with horror or writhing with laughter." While Yossarian provides the reader with initial wild laughter, the insanities mount from aberration to explosive venality to physical and moral destructiveness. The structure of Heller's novel may begin with madcap humor but the corrosive denial of human dignity displaces humor on center stage by the novel's end. Heller's verbal fireworks permeates the book; because language use and abuse fill the novel, Shakespeare's statement in *Hamlet* is relevant in *Catch-22*: "There's nothing either good or bad but thinking (substitute *saying*) makes it so." Out of Heller's verbal flood tide, *language structures reality.*

The plot of the novel is deceptively simple, filled with description and narration of missions, hospital episodes, headquarters red tape and power struggles, wartime black market exploitation, and Roman orgies. It seems as if we were watching a consciousness that has been watching too many war movies. The form of the novel reinforces this impression. We note a random sequence of recollections caught in the act of being recollected. The plot lacks the conventional logical coherence of sequential narrative or the emotional coherence in stream of consciousness novels where the metaphorical stream implies a smooth continuity deriving from the association of ideas. Instead, *Catch-22* offers a bubbling up of random memories that assume coherence through repetitive patterns of events, images, and words.

The plot follows imaginative time rather than clock or calendar time. We see events only as and when they occur or happen to Yossarian. This differs from standard story-telling, which deals with past events and can thus sort them out, rearrange, and organize them. It also departs from narrative that requires the narrator to report only what he has witnessed physically, for here we are dealing with imaginative reconstruction rather than the reordering of personal experience.

It is fitting that the book opens and closes with Yossarian and the Chaplain. "It was love at first sight," the story begins, and the affection of Yossarion for Tappman provides a sane base beneath the absurd, often horrible cacophony of his relations with others and his view of himself — now a pop hero (Tarzan, Mandrake, Flash Gordon), now a classical hero (Ulysses, Deirdre of the Sorrows, Sweeney in the nightingales among trees), later an anti-hero as he rails against God ("Someday I'm going to make Him pay"), and eventually as Christlike ("the night was filled with horrors, and he thought he knew how Christ must have felt as he walked through the world"). The Armenian name Yossarian translates as "son of Joseph," thus opening the way to religious allegory. But Heller's first name is also Joseph, and it seems plausible to perceive Yossarian as a representative of twentieth-century consciousness faced with a significant moral decision. As the novel closes and Yossarian takes off, he leaves behind Chaplain Tappman, now prepared to persevere as a more effective disciple.

In Heller's novel, Yossarian's initial goal is survival in a world filled with people wanting to kill him. His primary concern is to save himself, first by playing the game — flying the specified number of missions. As the number rises beyond rational reach, he feigns physical and mental illness to save his skin. Eventually, he asserts his intellectual integrity by refusing to fly again. This threatens the entire system. Lt. Colonel Korn explains: "The men were perfectly content to fly as many missions as we asked as long as they thought they had no alternative. Now you've given them hope." Faced by the threat of Yossarian, the establishment offers him the attractive bribe of prosperous freedom and a hero's homecoming, if only he will say nice things about the Korns, Cathcarts, Dreedles, Peckems, et al. If he refuses this extravagantly attractive cop-out, he risks a rigged court martial. He elects the self-serving offer, but only temporarily, for he has come to see that his struggle is more than merely personal. "People kept popping up at him out of the darkness to ask him how he was doing, appealing to him for confidential information with weary, troubled faces on the basis of some morbid and clandestine kinship he had not guessed existed." In sane desperation, Yossarian elects a third course, refusing to sell out or cop-out. Like Orr before him, like Hemingway's hero, his farewell to arms stems from a personal separate peace, and he makes the break for freedom. Ironically, the alternatives posed by Heller in 1961 are equally relevant today in the context of an Asian war.

Catch-22 has brilliant visual episodes, but they play a secondary role to the verbal cornucopia Heller presents. On the second page of the novel, Yossarian is assigned the role of censoring letters, and he invents word games. One day, he deletes all modifiers; the next day he makes war on articles. When he blacks out everything but *a, an,* and *the,* the result is more "dynamic intralinear tensions."

Some pages later, Yossarian approves of Lt. Dunbar as ". . . a true prince. One of the finest least dedicated men in the whole world." Colonel Cargill is described as ". . . a self-made man who owed his lack of success to nobody." Cargill's speech to the men follows. He observes, "You're American officers. The officers of no other army in the world can make that statement. Think about it." The speech is ad- dressed to the enlisted men.

General Dreedle had demanded that both enlisted men and officers be required to shoot skeet at least eight hours a month because it was ". . . excellent training for them. It trained them to shoot skeet."

These lines all occur in the opening pages of the novel. By mid- novel lines of this sort have become less frequent. Instead, the episodic horrors and spasmodic insanities become more heavily concentrated in the latter half of the book. Heller's increasingly bitter satire accompanies the depressing flow of events. Even Snowden's death, a major episode in the novel, follows the same pattern. The statement that "Snowden had been killed over Avignon" (in chapter 4) is factual and brief. Yossarian seems almost untouched by it. Succeeding allusions become increasingly detailed. In mid-novel (chapter 22) the horror of the Snowden incident mounts and reaches a crescendo in Chapter 41, when Yossarian can no longer stave off the reality he has been repressing. The gory evisceration is experienced by Yossarian and reader simultaneously.

The novel's brilliant visual images, possibly even more striking because they are few relative to the emphasis on language, are structurally important. Heller uses a repetitive pattern. An example is the completely bandaged soldier in white. The first time Yossarian sees him, he jokes about him. The second time Yossarian's response is fretful. The third appearance finds Yossarian rejecting any implication that this is the same man. Other visual scenes reappear in the novel. Unlike the image of the soldier in white, which is detailed from its first appearance, the other images gain additional details each time they reappear. They surge onward despite Yossarian's efforts to suppress them. Visual episodes reveal Yossarian in ludicrous nakedness. He sits in the tree observing Snowden's funeral. He steps forward to receive his medal from General Dreedle. At the end of the book, he is a second Adam who has tasted from the tree of knowledge and sanity. He rejects an insane Eden.

Trying to make a movie from a long, language-saturated, structurally difficult novel with any degree of fidelity may seem an act of madness. Mike Nichols accomplishes the feat with reasonable success, marred by some flaws. The opening scene violates one of the cardinal clichés of contemporary film-making. Nichols fixes his camera, an utterly unmoving camera, on a black screen. Credits in white succeed each other; no sound intrudes. The sun, rising from below a mountain ridge etches a mountain silhouette in barely discernible light. A dog bays in the distance; the light inches up in intensity giving the mountains a halo-like effect. Suddenly, streaks of dawn shimmer on the water and race toward the island of Pianosa. The scene (one long fixed shot) closes with the roar of B-25s maneuvering for takeoff. The violation results in superb cinematic art. The sound of thundering engines links scene one to scene two. As the B-25s appear, Nichols uses surprising tracking shots. The planes extend beyond the outside frame of the screen and dominate the viewer's line of vision. Wheels roll by close to the camera and seem enormous. One bomber cannot be contained within the framing limits of the wide screen. The squadron can only be encompassed by the eye after they have taken off in tight formation. As Stanley Kauffmann observes in his review, a superb balance has been achieved: "Dawn blasphemed by the bombers." This second scene and its sequence of shots parallels the third scene. The camera focuses on the battered control tower; we see Yossarian to the right (foreground), Col. Cathcart, and Lt. Col. Korn. Lips move but the continuing roar of engines drowns out the words. We watch Yossarian shake hands with Cathcart and Korn, and the camera now pans to follow him down the steps. While Yossarian is the focal point, the camera eye enlarges the field of vision enough to include a figure, back to the camera, apparently engaged in some minor repair detail. When Yossarian stops the fourth figure takes on a frightening dimension by drawing a knife, stepping over to him, and stabbing him. Yossarian's face, now closeup, reveals his horror and anguish. The scene ends with his falling forward. Abrupt cut!

For the film viewer who has read the novel, the third and fourth scenes come as a surprise since their early appearance departs from the novel where they take place in the concluding segment of the book. For the filmgoer who has not read the novel, the fall of Yossarian marks the beginning of a complex film structure, a structure not yet comprehended. The two-scene sequence, extended in length and shorn of quick cutting (another cliché ignored) recurs late in the film. At that point, real time recommences.

With Yossarian's fall, the film moves spasmodically into a series of random flashbacks. One flashback, joining Captain Yossarian to the death of Lt. Snowden, reappears several times and each recurrence adds details to the totality of that interior flashback. The sickening whiteness of the flashbacks lead to Yossarian and the viewer experiencing the final shock at the same moment.

Heller's Yossarian wants to be grounded; Nichols' Yossarian seeks precisely the same objective. He tries to persuade Doc Daneeka; ground me because I am crazy. Doc refuses and cites Catch-22. Sure, Yossarian is crazy. Sure, he should be grounded. But a man cannot be grounded unless he formally requests it. If, however, anyone requests grounding— to avoid being killed—that proves he is not crazy and therefore cannot be grounded.

Most of Yossarian's actions stem from his increasing desire to be adjudged insane. His desperation is linked to Snowden's death; this point becomes increasingly clear to the viewer until the final gory evisceration leaves no room for failure to understand completely. Yossarian's actions are hilariously comic; in retrospect, they are hideously sane. At Snowden's funeral, we see the naked Yossarian watching from a tree. In another sequence, when General Dreedle presents medals to the men for valor in action, we observe the file of officers from a camera behind and above them. General Dreedle and his entourage face the audience. The men, with a single glorious exception, are smartly scrubbed and uniformed. Yossarian wears nothing. When the general reaches him, the situation contains the combustibles of a Marx Brothers routine. Dreedle's questions about Yossarian's nakedness pass down the line of command to the ingenious sergeant who improvises brilliant responses, ironically containing some seeds of accuracy. Dreedle doesn't really give a damn; he does care about his Wac, a sultry, mouth-watering, unspeaking, scene-stealer whom he orders back to his car.

Yossarian's earlier encounter with Dreedle's Wac does not involve any literal nudity. But the pulchritude of her tightly uniformed bottom and her sexy pout of apparent disinterest kindle appreciative animal noises from Captain Yossarian. As Major Danby briefs the man, Yossarian's kindling produces flickers of flame in others. The wolfish moans, groans, whistles, and wheezes create a bedlam that General Dreedle himself must override. His silent Wac says nothing—eloquently.

One of the earliest visual clues to Yossarian's role in the film occurs as the men prepare to take off on their mission; they are encouraged by a familiar "thumbs-up" gesture from a high-ranking officer—who is base-bound. The men grin and respond. Yossarian's response is a "finger" response, but the finger is not his thumb. And the gesture is not up as in victory. Since the mission is to be over Italy, it is doubly appropriate that his response be an ancient, familiar, Italian gesture which has long since earned international recognition.

Non-Yossarian scenes of visual potency and acidulous humor pepper the film. The completely bandaged soldier, arms and legs fastened to weights that maintain his grotesque position, has two jars attached to him. Fluid from one flows into him; fluid for the other flows out of him. When the upper jar is empty, and the lower one full, two nurses appear. Quickly and dexterously, without a hesitant break in their animated conversations, they tend the patient. The position of the two jars is reversed.

Another non-Yossarian-dominated scene underscores the "language structures reality" thesis. Doc Daneeka, fearful about flying, has found a way to keep his flight pay without leaving the ground. He has Captain McWatt list him as a passenger. In a scene that jars credibility, McWatt skims over the swimming dock. Possibly he miscalculates but he literally cuts the figure on the dock in two while buzzing the area. The scene seems unreal, in both novel and film, but the follow-up sequence is horrifyingly possible. People on the shore are aghast. They watch McWatt's plane in the sky. Someone realizes that he is heading for a mountain. Yossarian, sensing what's to come, screams at the pilot futilely. He, and others, join in shouting for him to return. Someone observes that Doc Daneeka is with him because *the flight slip says so.* Despite Doc's literal presence, the cries continue calling for McWatt to jump, calling for Doc to jump. Daneeka, standing on the sand, fails to convince them he is there. The flight slip says he's up there with McWatt. Just before the plane crashes into the mountain, Daneeka himself is caught up and yelling for himself to bail out. When the sequence ends, Doc's friends fail to "see" him; they walk past, through, around. Reality is in the mind of the beholder and language reality has greater validity than physical reality. Stanley Kauffmann's political analogy is frightening. He says, ". . . in the year when our president says he widened a war in order to hasten peace, the logic of this novel [film] is hardly unrecognizable."

Another example from the film merits attention. Yossarian finds fraternity man Aarfy in Rome. Good old Aarfy has just committed rape and murder. Yossarian sees the MP's coming; he's shocked by Aarfy's casual behavior. The two MP's blast into the room — and take Yossarian into custody. He's AWOL. Once again, insanity prevails. The hierarchy of sensible values is reversed.

The closing sequence of the movie parallels the end of the novel. In Heller's book, Yossarian "took off." The phrase is both ambiguous and abstract. Visualizing the concept, Nichols *shows* us Yossarian taking off. Following the lead of Orr, he races across the beach into the sea, inflates his life raft, and paddles away. He has left behind the Cathcarts and Korns, the Dreedles and Minderbinders, and the mind-forged manacles that dominate his society.

In adapting Heller's book, Nichols employs several crucial changes in accordance with the differences between the two media. Compressing a long novel demands cutting. The major deletions were events related to Peckem, Scheisskopf, ex-PFC Wintergreen, and the multiple repetitions that characterized the structure of the novel. While most of the film dialogue appeared in the novel, much of the language play and verbal pyrotechnics in the novel never reached the screen. The novel's plethora of medical officers, doctors, and undiluted satire aimed at the medical profession have all been compressed into Doc Daneeka, and the indictments reduced in the process. The novel's verbal Raskolnikov scene becomes a filmic scene in which Yossarian's compassion is assaulted by specific visual example of man's inhumanity to man and beast. However hard he tries, Yossarian cannot escape from the evidence that surrounds him, tangible evidence of a world filled with creatures created by a contemporary Hieronymous Bosch. Involvement and idealism are not Yossarian's initial weapons; they are forced upon him. When the film nears its end, we return to the third and fourth scenes. We hear and understand the deal offered Yossarian; we hear the words and see the handshake of agreement. But after scene four, Yossarian has time to think while recuperating in the hospital. His self-centered concern changes; how can he live on Cathcart's and Korn's terms? Spurred by news of Orr's escape to Sweden, Yossarian rejects the duality of choices. He rejects self-gain; he repudiates moral self-destruction. In his tiny raft on a large sea, he will seek out such sanity as a Sweden may afford.

While only time will determine the final reputation of Mike Nichols' movie, *Catch-22*, it is fascinating to observe his film techniques, his degree of fidelity to Heller's novel, and the results of his directorial style. We have already noted the effectiveness of the two opening scenes; the first utilizes a fixed camera position that captures instant audience attention and sets the scene, while the second uses the full dimension of the wide screen and creates the wonderful illusion of reality that represents film-making at its best. The third scene, with the planes drowning out voices, reinforces reality. Both the third and fourth scenes break from many modern films with their emphasis on long tracking shots rather than dependence on quick cuts to establish tension. The limited use of rapid intercutting persists throughout the film and reflects a more classical style than we find in most contemporary movies. Tracking shots produce two effects. First, there is the authenticity of real time and the concomitant feeling of realism which is essential to the film medium. There is, ironically, a simultaneous disadvantage in long tracking shots when the filmmaker adapts his film from a lengthy novel. Tracking shots are time consuming and force greater compression making it necessary to delete sections of the novel the director might ordinarily want to include. This point applies particularly to *Catch-22* where Nichols has been faithful to the spirit of the novel but cannot capture the full verbal spirit, which would demand a greater number of repetitions. When Nichols does use the technique of repetition, as in the evolving Snowden episodes, the results are potent and the viewer becomes involved.

Judith Crist's review of *Catch-22* suggests that Buck Henry's script ". . . is bogged down by its over-conscious fidelity to the scope rather than spirit of Heller's work. . . ." It would be impossible to argue the general thesis that Nichols sought fidelity. The language of the film emerges directly from the novel. The best visual elements of the novel can be found in the film, and are often wonderfully funny. If Nichols tried to encompass the literal totality of the novel, he would have to fail; but he obviously knew that, hence the selective omissions, most of them very wisely chosen. If there is a major weakness in *Catch-22*, it stems not from failure of spirit, but from success in capturing the spirit of the novel. Heller's novel is satirical; its style depends on *verbal* emphases. It appeals primarily to the mind, not to the emotions. Like any satire, the novel runs the risk of entertaining audiences rather than stimulating them to action. Even the increasing horrors of the events described in the book are muted by the language play that tickles the intellect. In the film revision of *Catch-22*, the greatest appeal is to the comic richness of both incidents and language. However, movies as a medium demand visceral involvement and *Catch-22* — novel and film — appeals more to head than gut. Thus, a lovely irony emerges. While lack of fidelity is often deplored by some film critics and many book-oriented film goers, the greatest weakness of Nichols' *Catch-22* is its fidelity. Moreover, since the movie does not *involve* the viewer deeply, he becomes detached and aware of the vignettes as incidents held together by a plot line. He perceives the film techniques, excellent though they are, because the movie does not grip him; instead, his mind assesses the flow of images.

One difference between novel and film works in *Catch-22* to the disadvantage of the movie. Because of the compression required in the film, the vicious absurdities cannot be as widely spaced as they are in the novel. The comic relief in Heller's long book has less space in Nichols' film; there is less time for healing between serious human offenses. Thus, on the one hand, Nichols uses visual/verbal comic absurdities while simultaneously not using enough language play to ease the viewer's discomfort at *Catch-22*'s dehumanizing events. Heller's virtuoso use of language tends to mitigate the horrors, although less so as the novel progresses. In the film the ugly realities mount, unrelieved by humor. The film shifts from its early satirical style to melodramatic anti-war statements, offering little relief from the increasing tension.

One major scene change illustrates Nichols as moralist. Nately is talking to the 107-year-old Italian man. Nately can hardly comprehend the Italian's thesis about the survival of the weakest. In the film, the scene is philosophic, intellectual, and amusing in concept as well as amusing in its effect upon Nately. In the book, however, the old man combines his philosophic observations with lecherous enjoyment of the girls in the house. The Heller incident adds attractive spice and reality to the paradoxical philosophic values of the scene. Nichols deliberately deletes feminine distraction from the message.

In the opening paragraph of this essay, we noted the inevitable tendency of critics to compare novel and film. Many critics seemed to feel that a knowledge of the novel enhanced appreciation of the film. This is partly true since each line of film dialogue or incident calls up in the viewer similar repetitions from the novel and adds more chuckles to each bit of film humor. On the other hand, the non-reader watching the film may get more emotionally involved; there are fewer remembered distractions. Since a function of art is to extend human experience — and since Heller's novel produces primarily an intellectual response — the film goer who has not read the novel may come closer to the experiences provided by images flashing across the screen.

Catch-22, a 1970 movie, lends itself to a barrage of criticism from readers of the novel who want more, more, more; from film buffs who are shocked by Nichols' reversal of several standard techniques; from critics who see the film techniques too clearly, but do not understand the novel's fatal flaw; from film goers (non-readers) who have difficulty with the complex film structure. While each may deplore some aspect of the film (one is reminded of the six blind men of Indostan and their experiences with an elephant), some truths cannot be denied. Mike Nichols' *Catch-22* is intelligent, technically excellent, filled with memorable sequences, verbally articulate, faithful to a difficult novel, daring in conception, and reasonably successful in execution. Finally, it is philosophic, compassionate, and frequently on target. Vincent Canby's closing paragraph captures the film's essence. He rejects any "black comedy" label which he defines as ". . . comedy bought cheaply at the expense of certain human values, so that, for example, murder is funny and assassination is hilarious." Instead, Canby concludes, "*Catch-22* . . . is almost beside itself with panic because it grieves for the human condition." He is absolutely accurate.

12

George
Bluestone

THE GRAPES OF WRATH

In this chapter from *Novels Into Film*,
George Bluestone contrasts Steinbeck's
Pulitzer Prize novel, *The Grapes of Wrath*,
with John Ford's Academy Award winning
film. Professor Bluestone has written
extensively on film and directed three
pictures, including an adaptation of
Herman Melville's *Bartleby the Scrivener.*

In his compact little study of California writers, *The Boys in the Back Room*,
Edmund Wilson comments on the problems inherent in the close affiliation between Hollywood and commercial fiction:

> Since the people who control the movies will not go a step
> of the way to give the script writer a chance to do a serious script,
> the novelist seems, consciously or unconsciously, to be going part
> of the way to meet the producers. John Steinbeck, in *The Grapes
> of Wrath*, has certainly learned from the films — and not only from
> the documentary pictures of Pare Lorentz, but from the senti-
> mental symbolism of Hollywood. The result was that *The Grapes
> of Wrath* went on the screen as easily as if it had been written in
> the studios, and was probably the only serious story on record that
> seemed equally effective as a film and as a book.[1]

[1] Edmund Wilson, *The Boys in the Back Room* (San Francisco, 1941), p. 61.

137

Indeed, not only did Steinbeck learn from Pare Lorentz; he also received, through Lorentz, his first introduction to Nunnally Johnson, the screen writer who did the movie adaptation of his novel.[2] And Bennett Cerf, the publishing head of Random House, must have had none other than Steinbeck in mind when he wrote, "The thing an author wants most from his publisher these days is a letter of introduction to Darryl Zanuck."[3] For if Steinbeck was fortunate in having Pare Lorentz as a teacher and Nunnally Johnson as a screen writer, he was one of the few who earned the coveted letter to Darryl Zanuck, the producer of *The Grapes of Wrath*. Add Gregg Toland's photography, Alfred Newman's music, and John Ford's direction, and one sees that Steinbeck had an unusually talented crew, one which could be depended upon to respect the integrity of his best-selling book.

Lester Asheim, in his close charting of the correspondence between twenty-four novels and films, seems to corroborate Edmund Wilson's conclusion about the easy transference of Steinbeck's book to John Ford's film. According to Asheim's analysis, the major sequences in the novel bear more or less the same ratio to the whole as the corresponding sequences do in the film:

	per cent of whole	
sequence	*book*	*film*
Oklahoma episodes	20	28
Cross-country episodes	19	22
General commentary	17	—
Government camp episodes	15	18
Hooverville episodes	10	13
Strike-breaking episodes	9	16
Final episodes	10	3
	100	100

And when Asheim goes on to explain that, if one ignores the major deletions which occur in the transference and considers only those episodes in the novel which appear in the film, the percentage of both book and film devoted to these central events would be virtually identical, his observation seems, at first, to be providing indisputable proof for Wilson's claim.[4]

[2] In conversation with Mr. Johnson.
[3] In *Hollywood Reporter* (January 9, 1941), p. 3; quoted in Leo C. Rosten, *Hollywood: The Movie Colony, The Movie Makers* (New York, 1941), p. 366.
[4] Lester Asheim, "From Book to Film" (Ph.D. dissertation, University of Chicago, 1949), pp. 55–56.

Yet, to follow through Wilson's primary analysis of Steinbeck's work is to come at once on a contradiction which belies, first, his comment on the ineluctable fitness of the novel for Hollywood consumption and, second, his implication that Steinbeck, like the novelists whom Bennett Cerf has in mind, had written with one eye on the movie market. For it is central to Wilson's critical argument that the "substratum which remains constant" in Steinbeck's work "is his preoccupation with biology."[5] According to Wilson's view, "Mr. Steinbeck almost always in his fiction is dealing either with the lower animals or with human beings so rudimentary that they are almost on the animal level."[6] Tracing the thematic seams that run through Steinbeck's prose, Wilson notes the familiar interchapter on the turtle whose slow, tough progress survives the gratuitous cruelty of the truck driver who swerves to hit it. This anticipates the survival of the Joads, who, with the same dorsal hardness, will manage another journey along a road, emerging like the turtle from incredible hardships surrounded by symbols of fertility, much like the turtle's "wild oat head" which spawns three spearhead seeds in the dry ground. And Wilson notes, too, the way in which the forced pilgrimage of the Joads, adumbrated by the turtle's indestructibility, is "accompanied and parodied all the way by animals, insects and birds," as when the abandoned house where Tom finds Muley is invaded by bats, weasels, owls, mice, and pet cats gone wild.

This primary biological analysis seems to contradict Wilson's more casual statement on the film, since the screen version, as evolved by Nunnally Johnson and John Ford, contains little evidence of this sort of preoccupation. And when Asheim concludes, after a detailed comparison, that to one unfamiliar with the novel there are no loose ends or glaring contradictions to indicate that alterations have taken place,[7] we begin to uncover a series of disparities which, rather than demonstrating the ease of adaptation, suggests its peculiar difficulties. We are presented in the film with what Asheim calls "a new logic of events," a logic which deviates from the novel in several important respects. Tracing these mutations in some detail will illuminate the special characteristics of book and film alike. The question immediately arises, how could *The Grapes of Wrath* have gone on the screen so easily when the biological emphasis is nowhere present?

Undeniably, there is, in the novel, a concurrence of animal and human life similar to that which appears in the work of Walter Van Tilburg Clark, another western writer who transcends regional themes.

[5] Wilson, p. 42.
[6] *Ibid.*, pp. 42–43.
[7] Asheim, p. 161.

Even from the opening of the chapter which depicts the pedestrian endurance of the turtle, creature and human are linked.

> The concrete highway was edged with a mat of tangled, broken, dry grass, and the grass heads were heavy with oat beards to catch on a dog's coat, and foxtails to tangle in a horse's fetlocks, and clover burrs to fasten in a sheep's wool; sleeping life waiting to be spread and dispersed, every seed armed with an appliance of dispersal, twisting darts and parachutes for the wind, little spears and balls of tiny thorns, and all waiting for animals and for the wind, for a man's trouser cuff or the hem of a woman's skirt, all passive but armed appliances of activity, still, but each possessed of the anlage of movement.

Here, the central motifs of the narrative are carefully, but unobtrusively enunciated, a kind of generalized analogue to the coming tribulations of the Joads: a harsh, natural order which is distracting to men and dogs alike; a hostile, dry passivity which, like the dormant blastema, is at the same time laden with regenerative possibilities. From the opening passages ("Gophers and ant lions started small avalanches . . .") to the last scene in which an attempt is made to beatify Rose of Sharon's biological act, the narrative is richly interspersed with literal and figurative zoology. Tom and Casy witness the unsuccessful efforts of a cat to stop the turtle's slow progress. In the deserted house, Muley describes himself as having once been "mean like a wolf," whereas now he is "mean like a weasel." Ma Joad describes the law's pursuit of Pretty Boy Floyd in animal terms: "they run him like a coyote, an' him a-snappin' an' a-snarlin', mean as a lobo." Young Al boasts that his Hudson jalopy will "ride like a bull calf." In the interchapter describing the change, the growing wrath triggered by the wholesale evictions of the tenant farmers, the western states are "nervous as horses before a thunder storm."

Later, Ma Joad savagely protests the break-up of the family: "All we got is the family unbroke. Like a bunch of cows, when the lobos are ranging." Later still, Tom tells Casy that the day he got out of prison, he ran himself down a prostitute "like she was a rabbit." Even the endless caravans of jalopies are described in terms which echo the plodding endurance of the turtle. After a night in which "the owls coasted overhead, and the coyotes gabbled in the distance, and into the camp skunks walked, looking for bits of food . . ." the morning comes, revealing the cars of migrants along the highway crawling out "like bugs." After the relatively peaceful interlude of the Government Camp, Al comments on the practice of periodically burning out the Hoovervilles where the dispossessed farmers are forced to cluster: ". . . they jus' go hide down in the willows an' then they come out an' build 'em another weed shack. Jus' like gophers." And finally, toward the end, Ma expresses her longing to have a settled home for Ruth and Winfield, the youngest children, in order to keep them from becoming wild animals. For by this time, Ruth and Winnie do, indeed, emerge from their beds "like hermit crabs from shells."

The persistence of this imagery reveals at least part of its service. In the first place, even in our random selections, biology supports and comments upon sociology. Sexual activity, the primacy of the family clan, the threat and utility of industrial machinery, the alienation and hostility of the law, the growing anger at economic oppression, the arguments for human dignity, are all accompanied by, or expressed in terms of, zoological images. In the second place, the presence of literal and figurative animals is more frequent when the oppression of the Joads is most severe. The pattern of the novel, as we shall see, is similar to a parabola whose highest point is the sequence at the Government Camp. From Chapter XXII to the middle of Chapter XXVI, which covers this interlude, the animal imagery is almost totally absent. Densely compacted at the beginning, when Tom returns to find his home a shambles, it recurs in the closing sequences of the strike-breaking and the flood.

The point is that none of this appears in the film. Even the highly cinematic passage depicting the slaughtering of the pigs, in preparation for the journey, is nowhere evident in the final editing. If the film adaptation remains at all faithful to its original, it is not in retaining what Edmund Wilson calls the constant substratum in Steinbeck's work. It is true, one may argue, that biological functions survive in the Joads' elementary fight for life, in the animal preoccupation with finding food and shelter, in the scenes of death and procreation, but this is not what Edmund Wilson has in mind. In the film, these functions are interwoven so closely with a number of other themes that in no sense can the biological preoccupation be said to have a primary value. This type of deletion could not have been arbitrary, for, as Vachel Lindsay showed as early as 1915, animal imagery can be used quite effectively as cinema. Reviewing Griffith's *The Avenging Conscience*, Lindsay is describing the meditations of a boy who has just been forced to say goodbye to his beloved, supposedly forever. Watching a spider in his web devour a fly, the boy meditates on the cruelty of nature: "Then he sees the ants in turn destroy the spider. The pictures are shown on so large a scale that the spiderweb fills the end of the theater. Then the ant-tragedy does the same. They can be classed as particularly apt hieroglyphics. . . ."[8] More recently, the killing of the animals by the boy in *Les Jeux Interdits*

[8] Vachel Lindsay, *The Art of the Moving Picture* (New York, 1915), p. 124.

shows that biology can still effectively support cinematic themes. In the particular case of *The Grapes of Wrath*, however, the suggestions of the book were abandoned. If, then, we are to understand the mutation, to assess the film's special achievement, we must look elsewhere.

Immediately, a number of other motifs strongly assert themselves in Steinbeck s model: the juxtaposition of natural morality and religious hypocrisy; the love of the regenerative land; the primacy of the family; the dignity of human beings; the socio-political implications inherent in the conflict between individual work and industrial oppression. Consider Casy's impulsive rationalizations in the very early section of the book where he tries, like the Ancient Mariner, to convince his listener and himself at the same time, that his rejection of religious preaching in favor of a kind of naturalistic code of ethics is morally acceptable. Tortured by his sexual impulses as a preacher, Casy began to doubt and question the assumptions which he had been articulating from his rough, evangelical pulpit, began to observe the discrepancy between theoretical sin and factual behavior. He repeats his conclusions to Tom, "Maybe it ain't a sin. Maybe it's just the way folks is. Maybe we been whippin' hell out of ourselves for nothin'. . . . To hell with it! There ain't no sin and there ain't no virtue. There's just stuff people do. It's all part of the same thing. And some of the things folks do is nice, and some ain't nice, but that's as far as any man got a right to say."

Casy retains his love for people, but not through his ministry, and later this love will be transmuted into personal sacrifice and the solidarity of union organization. This suspicion of a theology not rooted in ordinary human needs continues to echo throughout the novel. When Casy refuses to pray for the dying Grampa, Granma reminds him, quite offhandedly, how Ruthie prayed when she was a little girl: "'Now I lay me down to sleep. I pray the Lord my soul to keep. An' when she got there the cupboard was bare, an' so the poor dog got none.'" The moral is clear: in the face of hunger, religious piety seems absurd. After Grampa's death, the inclusion of a line from Scripture in the note that will follow him to his grave is parodied in much the same way, but Casy's last words at the grave echo his earlier statement: "This here ol' man jus' lived a life an' jus' died out of it. I don't know whether he was good or bad, but that don't matter much. He was alive, an' that's what matters. An' now he's dead, an' that don't matter. . . . if I was to pray, it'd be for the folks that don' know which way to turn." Ma Joad expresses the same kind of mystical acceptance of the life cycle when she tries to tell Rose of Sharon about the hurt of childbearing:

> They's a time of change, an' when that comes, dyin' is piece
> of all dyin', and bearin' is a piece of all bearin', an bearin' an' dyin'

is two pieces of the same thing. An' then things ain't lonely any more. An' then a hurt don't hurt so bad, 'cause it ain't a lonely hurt no more, Rose-asharn. I wisht I could tell you so you'd know, but I can't.

Because Ma is so firm in her belief in the rightness of natural processes, she becomes furious at the religious hypocrites who plague the migrants. At the Hoovervilles and in the government station, the evangelists whom Ma characterizes as Holy Rollers and Jehovites are grimly present, like camp followers. Beginning with polite acceptance, Ma becomes infuriated when one of these zealots works on Rose of Sharon, scaring her half to death with visions of hellfire and burning. Ma represents the state of natural grace to which Casy aspires from the beginning.

Just as the novel reveals a preoccupation with biology, it is also obsessed with love of the earth. From the opening lines of the book, "To the red country and part of the gray country of Oklahoma, the last rains came gently, and they did not cut the scarred earth," to the last scene of desolation, the land imagery persists. The earth motif is woven into the texture complexly, but on the whole it serves two main functions: first, to signify love; and second, to signify endurance. Tom makes the sexual connection when, listening to Casy's compulsive story, he idly, but quite naturally, draws the torso of a woman in the dirt, "breasts, hips, pelvis." The attachment of the men for the land is often so intense that it borders on sexual love. Muley's refusal to leave, even after the caterpillar tractors have wiped him out, looks ahead to Grampa's similar recalcitrance. At first, Grampa is enthusiastic about the prospect of moving to a more fertile land, and he delivers himself of words verging on panegyric: "Jus' let me get out to California where I can pick me an orange when I want it. Or grapes. There's a thing I ain't ever had enough of. Gonna get me a whole big bunch a grapes off a bush, or whatever, an' I'm gonna squash 'em on my face, an' let 'em run offen my chin." But when the moment for departures arrives, Grampa refuses to go. His roots in the ground are too strong; he cannot bear to tear them up. Very soon after the family leaves its native soil, Grampa dies of a stroke. And when Casy says to Noah, "Grampa an' the old place, they was jus' the same thing," we feel that the observation has a precision which is supported by the texture of the entire novel. When the Joads get to California, they will, of course, find that the grapes which Grampa dreamed of are inaccessible, that the grapes of promise inevitably turn to grapes of wrath. The land, one interchapter tells, has been possessed by the men with a frantic hunger for land who came before the Joads. And the defeated promise is bitterly dramatized in the last scene, when a geranium, the last flower of earth to appear in the novel, becomes an issue dividing Ruthie and Winfield, and results in Ruthie's pressing one petal against Winfield's nose, cruelly. Love and endurance have been tried to their utmost. When the land goes, everything else goes, too; and the water is the emblem of its destruction.

Love of family parallels love of the earth. During the threatening instability of the cross-country journey, Ma Joad acts as the cohesive force which keeps her brood intact. Whenever one of the men threatens to leave, Ma protests, and sometimes savagely. When she takes over leadership of the family, by defying Pa Joad with a jack handle, it is over the question of whether or not Tom shall stay behind with the disabled car. Even after Connie, Rose of Sharon's husband, and Noah, one of the brothers, desert the family, the identity of the clan remains Ma Joad's primary fixation. After half a continent of hardship, Ma articulates her deepest feelings. She tells Tom, "They was a time when we was on the lan'. They was a boundary to us then. Ol' folks died off, an' little fellas came, an' we was always one thing—we was the fambly—kinda whole and clear. An' now we ain't clear no more." The deprivation of the native land, and the alienation of the new, become more than economic disasters; they threaten the only social organization upon which Ma Joad can depend. The fertility of the land and the integrity of the clan are no longer distinct entities; both are essential for survival.

Closely bound up with this theme of familial survival is the theme of human dignity. Clearly, the exigencies of eviction and migration force the problem of brute survival upon the Joads. But just as important is the correlative theme of human dignity. The first time the Joads are addressed as "Okies," by a loud-mouthed deputy who sports a Sam Browne belt and pistol holster, Ma is so shocked that she almost attacks him. Later, Uncle John is so chagrined by Casy's sacrificial act (deflecting from Tom the blame for hitting the deputy, and going to prison in his stead) that he feels positively sinful for not making an equal contribution. At the Government Camp, a woman complains about taking charity from the Salvation Army because "We was hungry—they made us crawl for our dinner. They took our dignity." But it is Tom who makes the most articulate defense of dignity against the legal harassment to which the Joads have been subjected: " . . . if it was the law they was workin' with, why, we could take it. But it *ain't* the law. They're a-workin' away at our spirits. . . . They're workin' on our decency." And the final image of Rose of Sharon offering her breast to the starving farmer is intended as an apotheosis of the scared girl, recently deprived of her child, into a kind of natural madonna.

In short, if the biological interest exists, it is so chastened through suffering that it achieves a dignity which is anything but animal, in

Edmund Wilson's sense of the word. The conflicts, values, and recognitions of the Joads cannot, therefore, be equated with the preoccupations of subhuman life. The biological life may be retained in the search for food and shelter, in the cycle of death and procreation, but always in terms which emphasize rather than obliterate the distinctions between humans and animals. When Steinbeck reminisces about his carefree bohemian days in Monterey, he is just as nostalgic about the freedom of assorted drifters, his "interesting and improbable" characters, as he is about Ed Ricketts' "commercial biological laboratory."[9] Steinbeck's novel may be read, then, as much as a flight from biological determinism as a representation of it. The story of the pilgrimage to the new Canaan which is California, the cycle of death and birth through which the Joads must suffer, becomes a moral, as well as a physical, trial by fire.

The socio-political implications of the Joad story, more familiar than these correlative themes, serve to counterpoint and define the anger and the suffering. Throughout the novel, the Joads are haunted by deputies in the service of landowners, bankers, and fruit growers; by the contradiction between endless acres in full harvest and streams of migratory workers in dire straits; by unscrupulous businessmen who take advantage of the desperate, westbound caravans; by strike-breakers, corrupt politicians, and thugs. At first, the Joads must draw from their meager savings to pay for gas and half-loaves of bread; but as they draw West they must even pay for water. In California, they cannot vote, are kept continually on the move, are bullied by the constabulary, and must even watch helplessly as one of the Hoovervilles is burned out. The only time they earn enough money to eat comes when they are hired as strike-breakers. Gradually, there is the dawning recognition that the only possible response to these impossible conditions is solidarity through union organization, precisely what the fruit growers and their agents dread most. In order to overcome the fruit growers' divisive tactics, Casy becomes an active union organizer and gets killed in the process by a bunch of marauding deputies. At the end, Tom, in his familiar farewell to Ma Joad, is trembling on the verge of Casy's solution. "That the end will be revolution," one reviewer writes, "is implicit from the title onwards."[10] Steinbeck ultimately withdraws from such a didactic conclusion, as we shall see in a moment, but that the didactic conclusion is implicit in the narrative can hardly be denied.

> . . . the companies, the banks worked at their own doom
> and they did not know it. The fields were fruitful, and starving

[9]John Steinbeck, "Dreams Piped from Cannery Row," *New York Times Theater Section* (Sunday, November 27, 1955), p. 1.

[10]Earle Birney, "The Grapes of Wrath," *Canadian Forum*, XIX (June, 1939), 95.

men moved on the roads. The granaries were full and the children
of the poor grew up rachitic, and the pustules of pellagra swelled
on their sides. The great companies did not know that the line
between hunger and anger is a thin line. And money that might
have gone to wages went for gas, for guns, for agents and spies, for
blacklists, for drilling. On the highways the people moved like ants
and searched for work, for food. And the anger began to ferment.

Hence the symbolism of the title. Clearly woven through the novel, and
therefore inseparable from Steinbeck's prose, we find these sharp
political overtones. Besides being a novel, writes one reviewer, *The
Grapes of Wrath* "is a monograph on rural sociology, a manual of practical wisdom in times of enormous stress, an assault on individualism, an
essay in behalf of a rather vague form of pantheism, and a bitter, ironical
attack on that emotional evangelistic religion which seems to thrive
in the more impoverished rural districts of this vast country. . . ."[11]

Along the highways, a new social order is improvised, a fluid but
permanent council in which the family is the basic unit, an order reaching
its almost utopian operation at the Government Camp. According to
this scheme, the governing laws remain constant, while the specific
counters are continually replaced, one family succeeding another, a sort
of permanent republic which can accommodate a populace in constant
motion:

> The families learned what rights must be observed — the right
> of privacy in the tent; the right to keep the past black hidden in
> the heart; the right to talk and to listen; the right to refuse help or
> to decline it; the right of son to court and daughter to be courted;
> the right of the hungry to be fed; the rights of the pregnant and the
> sick to transcend all other rights. . . .
> And with the laws, the punishments — and there were only
> two — a quick and murderous fight or ostracism; and ostracism was
> the worst.

Within such a scheme, Ma Joad's fierce maintenance of the family
becomes more clear. For without the integrity of the clan, survival is all
but impossible. The alternatives are death, which does, in fact, snip the
Joad family at both ends, claiming both the grandparents and Rose of
Sharon's baby, or, on the other hand, militant struggle through union
organization.

[11]James N. Vaughan, "The Grapes of Wrath," *Commonweal*, XXX (July 28, 1949),
341–342.

If the biological motifs do not appear in the film, these correlative themes are adopted with varying degrees of emphasis. The religious satire, with a single exception, is dropped entirely; the political radicalism is muted and generalized; but the insistence on family cohesion, on affinity for the land, on human dignity is carried over into the movie version.

In the film, the one remnant of tragi-comic religious satire occurs in Tom's first talk with Casy on the way to the Joad house. Casy's probing self-analysis is essentially the same as in the book, and its culmination,

The Grapes of Wrath (1940) "At first, the Joads must draw from their meager savings to pay for gas and half-loaves of bread; but as they draw west they must pay even for water." (Still courtesy Twentieth Century-Fox Film Corporation.)

"There ain't no sin an' there ain't no virtue. There's just what people do," is a precise copy from the novel. Once the theme is enunciated, however, it is underplayed, recurring almost imperceptibly in the burial scene. Ma's anger at the evangelical camp followers is dropped entirely.

The film-makers must have known that the film was political dynamite. After a difficult decision, Darryl Zanuck began what turned out to be, thematically speaking, one of the boldest films in the history of the movies. The secrecy which surrounded the studios during production has become legend. Even as the film was being shot, Zanuck reportedly received 15,000 letters, 99 per cent of which accused him of cowardice, saying he would never make the film because the industry was too closely associated with big business.[12] And yet, fearful that the Texas and Oklahoma Chambers of Commerce would object to the shooting, on their territory, of the *enfant terrible* of the publishing world, the studio announced that it was really filming another story innocuously entitled, *Highway 66*.[13] It was precisely this fear of criticism, of giving offense to vested interests that was responsible for muting the film's political implications. Lester Asheim has pointed out how the film scrupulously steers clear of the book's specific accusations. Many small episodes showing unfair business practices, for example, were cut from the film version.[14] While the reference to the handbills which flood Oklahoma, luring an excess labor force out West, is carried over into the film, most of the corresponding details are dropped. The complaint about the unfair practices of used-car salesmen; the argument with the camp owner about overcharging; the depiction of the company-store credit racket; the dishonest scales on the fruit ranch; and even the practice, on the part of an otherwise sympathetic luncheon proprietor, of taking the jackpots from his own slot machines—none of these was ever even proposed for the shooting-script. Similarly, all legal authority is carefully exempt from blame. In Tom's angry speech about the indignities foisted upon the family by the local constabulary, everything is retained except his bitter indictment of the deputies, and his line, ". . . they comes a time when the on'y way a fella can keep his decency is by takin' a sock at a cop."[15] In Casy's discourse on the progress of the fruit strike, the line, "An' all the cops in the worl' come down on us" is deleted. Casy's announcement that the cops have threatened to beat up recalcitrant strikers is retained, but the film adds, "Not them reg'lar deputies, but them tin badge fellas they call guards. . . ."

In spite of the revolutionary candor of the interchapters, whenever the film raises questions about whom to see or what to do for recourse or

[12] Frank Condon, "The Grapes of Raps," *Collier's* (January 27, 1940), p. 67.
[13] *Ibid.*, p. 64.
[14] Asheim, p. 277.
[15] *Ibid.*, p. 256.

complaint, the novel's evasive answers are used in reply. When Tom asks the proprietor of the Government Camp why there aren't more places like this, the proprietor answers, "You'll have to find that out for yourself." When Muley wants to find out from the City Man who's to blame for his eviction, so that he can take a shotgun to him, the City Man tells him that the Shawnee Land and Cattle Company is so amorphous that it cannot be properly located. The bank in Tulsa is responsible for telling the land company what to do, but the bank's manager is simply an employee trying to keep up with orders from the East. "Then who do we shoot?" Muley asks in exasperation. "Brother, I don't know . . ." the City Man answers helplessly. To add to the mystification, the film supplies a few clouds of its own. In the scene where Farmer Thomas warns Tom and the Wallaces about the impending raid on the Government Camp, the recurring question of "red" agitation comes up again. The "red menace" has become the *raison d'être* for attacks against the squatter camps. Tom, who has heard the argument before, bursts out, "What is these reds anyway?" Originally, according to the script, Wilkie Wallace was to have answered, cribbing his own line from the novel, that according to a fruit grower he knew once, a red is anyone who "wants thirty-cents an hour when I'm payin' twenty-five." In the final print, however, Farmer Thomas answers Tom's question simply but evasively, "I ain't talkin' about that one way'r another," and goes on to warn the men about the raid.

Even Tom's much-quoted farewell to Ma Joad, retained in the film, is pruned until little remains but its mystical affirmation. And the final words, backing away from Casy's conscious social commitment, are carried over intact.

Ma: "I don' un'erstan . . ."

Tom: "Me neither, Ma. . . . It's jus' stuff I been thinkin' about. . . ."

In the world of the Ford-Johnson film, the politico-economic tendency is merely an urge in search of a name it is never allowed to find. And yet because of the naked suffering, the brute struggle to survive, devoid of solutions in either church or revolution, John Gassner finds that more appropriate than the image of God "trampling out the vintage where the grapes of wrath are stored," from which the title is derived, are the lines, "And here in dust and dirt . . . the lilies of his love appear,"[16] which connote neither religion nor politics. According to Gassner, bedrock is reached in this film, "and it proves to be as hard as granite and as soft as down."

If the religious satire is absent and the politics muted, the love of land, family and human dignity are consistently translated into effective

---

[16]John Gassner, *Twenty Best Film Plays*, ed. John Gassner and Dudley Nichols (New York, 1943), p. xxvi.

cinematic images. Behind the director's controlling hand is the documentary eye of a Pare Lorentz or a Robert Flaherty, of the vision in those stills produced by the Resettlement Administration in its volume, *Land of the Free* (with commentary by Archibald MacLeish), or in Walker Evans' shots for *Let Us Now Praise Famous Men* (with commentary by James Agee), which, like Lorentz's work, was carried on under the auspices of the Farm Security Administration. Gregg Toland's photography is acutely conscious of the pictorial values of land and sky, finding equivalents for those haunting images of erosion which were popularized for the New Deal's reclamation program and reflected in Steinbeck's prose. The constant use of brooding, dark silhouettes against light, translucent skies, the shots of roads and farms, the fidelity to the speech, manners and dress of Oklahoma farmers — all contribute to the pictorial mood and tone. I am told that some of these exteriors were shot on indoor sound stages at the studios,[17] but even this has worked to the advantage of the film-makers. In the studio, Ford was able to control his composition by precise lighting, so that some of the visuals — Tom moving like an ant against a sky bright with luminous clouds, the caravans of jalopies, the slow rise of the dust storm — combine physical reality with careful composition to create striking pictorial effects. Finally, generous selections of dialogue, culled from the novel, echoing the theme of family affiliation with the land, appear in the final movie version. Grampa's last minute refusal to go, as he clutches at a handful of soil, necessitates Tom's plan to get him drunk and carry him aboard by force. And, as Muley, John Qualen's apostrophe to the land, after the tractor has ploughed into his shack, is one of the most poignant anywhere in films.

In the same fashion, the central episodes depicting Ma Joad's insistence on family cohesion, and Tom's insistence on dignity, are either presented directly or clearly suggested. Ma, to be sure, is made a little less fierce than she is in the novel. Tom still tells Casy the anecdote about Ma's taking after a tin peddler with an ax in one hand and a chicken in the other, but the scene in which she takes a jack handle after Pa, originally scheduled according to the script, is deleted. We never see Ma physically violent.

Tracing through these recurring themes, comparing and contrasting the emphasis given to each, gives us all the advantages of content analysis without explaining, finally, the central difference between Steinbeck's artistic vision and that of the film-makers. This difference does emerge, however, when we compare the two structures.

Some deletions, additions, and alterations, to be sure, reflect in a general way the ordinary process of mutation from a linguistic to a visual

[17] In an interview with Mr. Ford.

medium. On the other hand, the characteristic interchapters in the novel are dropped entirely, those interludes which adopt the author's point of view and which are at once more lyric and less realistic than the rest of the prose. The angry interludes, the explicit indictments, the authorial commentary do not appear, indeed would seem obtrusive, in the film. Translated into observed reality, however, and integrated into the picture within the frame, certain fragments find their proper filmic equivalents. For example, the interchapters are mined for significant dialogue, and, in fact, Muley's moving lines, "We were born on it, and we got killed on it, died on it. Even if it's no good, it's still ours. . . . " appear originally in one of these interludes. In the second place, the themes of one or two of these interchapters are translated into a few highly effective montages — the coming of the tractors, the caravans of jalopies, the highway signs along route 66. As Muley begins telling his story, over the candle in the dimly lit cabin, the film flashes back to the actual scene. A series of tractors looming up like mechanical creatures over the horizon, crossing and criss-crossing the furrowed land, cuts to the one tractor driven by the Davis boy, who has been assigned the task of clearing off Muley's farm. Later, as the Joads' jalopy begins its pilgrimage, we see a similar shot of scores and scores of other jalopies, superimposed one upon the other, making the same, slow, desperate cross-country trek. Finally, the central episodes of the trip are bridged by montages of road signs — "Checotah, Oklahoma City, Bethany," and so on to California. These devices have the effect of generalizing the conflicts of the Joads, of making them representative of typical problems in a much wider social context. In every reversal, in every act of oppression, we feel the pressure of thousands.

If the film carries these striking equivalents of Steinbeck's prose, it is partly due to the assistance which Steinbeck offers the film-maker, partly to the visual imagination of the film-maker himself. Except for the freewheeling omniscience of the interchapters, the novel's prose relies wholly on dialogue and physical action to reveal character. Because Steinbeck's style is not marked by meditation, it resembles, in this respect, the classic form of the scenario. Even at moments of highest tension, Steinbeck scrupulously avoids getting inside the minds of his people. Here is Ma right after Tom has left her, and probably forever:

> "Good-by" she said, and she walked quickly away. Her footsteps were loud and careless on the leaves as she went through the brush. And as she went, out of the dim sky the rain began to fall, big drops and few, splashing on the dry leaves heavily. Ma stopped and stood still in the dripping thicket. She turned about — took three steps back toward the mound of vines; and then she turned quickly and went back toward the boxcar camp.

Although this is Steinbeck's characteristic style, it can also serve as precise directions for the actor. There is nothing here which cannot be turned into images of physical reality. Critics who seem surprised at the ease with which Steinbeck's work moves from one medium to another may find their explanation here. Precisely this fidelity to physical detail was responsible, for example, for the success of *Of Mice and Men* first as a novel, then as a play, then as a film. And yet, in *The Grapes of Wrath,* the film-makers rethought the material for themselves, and frequently found more exact cinematic keys to the mood and color of particular scenes in the book. Often their additions are most effective in areas where the novel is powerless—in moments of silence. Casy jumping over a fence and tripping, after the boast about his former preaching prowess; Ma Joad burning her keepsakes (the little dog from the St. Louis Exposition, the old letters, the card from Pa); the earrings

The Grapes of Wrath (1940) The Joads reach the Promised Land—California.

which she saves, holding them to her ears in the cracked mirror, while the sound track carries the muted theme from "Red River Valley"; the handkerchiefs which Tom and Casy hold to their mouths in the gathering dust; Tom laboriously adding an "s" to "funerl" in the note which will accompany Grampa to his grave; the reflection of Al, Tom, and Pa in the jalopy's windshield at night as the family moves through the hot, eery desert—all these, while they have no precedent in the novel, make for extraordinarily effective cinema. The images are clean and precise, the filmic signature of a consistent collaboration between John Ford and his cameraman.

The deletions, on one level, are sacrifices to the exigencies of time and plot. The dialogue is severely pruned. Most of the anecdotes are dropped, along with the curse words. And the leisurely, discursive pace of the novel gives way to a tightly knit sequence of events. The episodes involving the traveling companionship of the Wilsons; the desertions of Noah and Connie; the repeated warnings about the dismal conditions in California from bitterly disappointed migrants who are traveling home the other way; and countless other small events do not appear in the film story, though a few of them, like Noah's desertion, appeared in the script and were even shot during production. But the moment we go from an enumeration of these deletions to the arrangement of sequences in the final work, we have come to our central structural problem.

As I indicated earlier, the structure of the book resembles a parabola in which the high point is the successful thwarting of the riot at the Government Camp. Beginning with Tom's desolate return to his abandoned home, the narrative proceeds through the journey from Oklahoma to California; the Hooverville episodes; the Government Camp episodes; the strike-breaking episodes at the Hooper Ranch; Tom's departure; the flooding of the cotton pickers' boxcar camp; the last scene in the abandoned farm. From the privation and dislocation of the earlier episodes, the Joads are continually plagued, threatened with dissolution, until, through the gradual knitting of strength and resistance, the family finds an identity which coincides with its experience at the Government Camp. Here they are startled by the sudden absence of everything from which they have been running—dirty living conditions, external compulsion, grubbing for survival, brutal policemen, unscrupulous merchants. They find, instead, a kind of miniature planned economy, efficiently run, boasting modern sanitation, self-government, co-operative living, and moderate prices. After their departure from the camp, the fortunes of the Joads progressively deteriorate, until that desolate ending which depicts Rose of Sharon's stillborn child floating downstream. The critical response to Steinbeck's shocking ending was almost universally negative. Clifton Fadiman called it the "tawdriest kind of fake symbolism."[18] Anthony West attributed it to the novel's "astonishingly awkward" form.[19] Louis Kronenberger found that the entire second half of the book "lacks form and intensity . . . ceases to grow, to maintain direction,"[20] but did not locate the reasons for his dissatisfaction. Malcolm Cowley, in spite of general enthusiasm, found the second half less impressive than the first because Steinbeck "wants to argue as if he weren't quite sure of himself." [21] Charles Angoff was one of a small minority who defended both the ending and the "robust looseness" of the novel as squarely in the narrative tradition of Melville, Cervantes and Thomas Hardy.[22]

Contrast these objections with the general approval of the film's structure. Thomas Burton becomes adulatory over Ford's "incessant physical intimacy and fluency."[23] Otis Ferguson speaks in superlatives: "this is a best that has no very near comparison to date. . . . It all moves with the simplicity and perfection of a wheel across silk."[24] Why did the film-makers merit such a sharply contrasting critical reception? Simply because they corrected the objectionable structure of the novel. First, they deleted the final sequence; and second, they accomplished one of the most remarkable narrative switches in film history. Instead of ending with the strike-breaking episodes in which Tom is clubbed, Casy killed, and the strikers routed, the film ends with the Government Camp interlude. This reversal, effected with almost surgical simplicity, accomplishes, in its metamorphic power, an entirely new structure which has far-reaching consequences. Combined with the deletion of the last dismal episode, and the pruning, alterations, and selections we have already traced, the new order changes the parabolic structure to a straight line that continually ascends. Beginning with the desolate scene of the dust storm, the weather in the film improves steadily with the fortunes of the Joads, until, at the end, the jalopy leaves the Government Camp in sunlight and exuberant triumph. Even a sign, called for in the original script, which might have darkened the rosy optimism that surrounds the departing buggy, does not appear in the cut version. The sign was to

[18] Clifton Fadiman, "Highway 66 — A Tale of Five Cities," *New Yorker*, XV (April 15, 1939), 81.

[19] Anthony West, "The Grapes of Wrath," *New Statesman and Nation*, XVIII (September 16, 1939), 404–405.

[20] Louis Kronenberger, "Hungry Caravan: The Grapes of Wrath," *Nation*, CXLVIII (April 15, 1939), 441.

[21] Malcolm Cowley, "American Tragedy," *New Republic*, XCVIII (May 3, 1939), 382.

[22] Charles Angoff, "In the Great Tradition," *North American Review*, CCXLVII (Summer, 1939), 387

[23] Thomas Burton, "Wine from These Grapes," *Saturday Review of Literature*, XXI (February 10, 1940), 16.

[24] Otis Ferguson, "Show for the People," *New Republic*, CII (February 12, 1940), 212.

have read, "No Help Wanted." As in the novel, Tom's departure is
delayed until the end, but the new sequence of events endows his farewell speech with much more positive overtones. In place of the original
ending, we find a line that appears at the end of Chapter XX, exactly
two-thirds of the way through the book. It is Ma's strong assurance,
"We'll go on forever, Pa. We're the people." On a thematic level, as
Asheim points out, the affirmative ending implies that action is not
required since the victims of the situation will automatically emerge
triumphant. "Thus the book, which is an exhortation to action, becomes
a film which offers reassurance that no action is required to insure the
desired resolution of the issue."[25] But the film's conclusion has the advantage of seeming structurally more acceptable. Its "new logic" affords
a continuous movement which, like a projectile, carries everything before
it. The movie solution satisfies expectations which are there in the novel
to begin with and which the novel's ending does not satisfactorily fulfill.
Hence the critics' conflicting reaction to the two endings. Where the
book seems to stop and meander in California, the film displays a forward propulsion that carries well on beyond the Colorado River.

Is such an inversion justified? Nunnally Johnson reports that he
chose Ma's speech for his curtain line because he considered it the "real"
spirit of Steinbeck's book.[26] This might seem at first like brazen tampering. But Johnson further reports that from Steinbeck himself he
received *carte blanche* to make any alterations he wished. Steinbeck
defended his position on the grounds that a novelist's final statement
is in his book. Since the novelist can add nothing more, the film-maker
is obliged to remake the work in his own style. If Steinbeck's awareness of the adaptational process is not enough, we may also find internal
justification for the film-makers' brilliantly simple reversal. We have seen
how the production crew effected alterations which mute the villainy
of cops and tradesmen; underplay the religious satire; cloud over the
novel's political radicalism. But part of this withdrawal has precedent
in the novel itself. The city man's portrayal of the anonymity of the
banks; the proprietor's evasive answer to Tom in the Government Camp;
Ma and Tom's mystical faith—these are all Steinbeck's. So is the fact
that from the beginning Tom is on parole, which he technically breaks
by leaving the state. Already he is outside the domain of legal ordinance.
Tom is a fugitive who *has* to keep running. If the film's conclusion
withdraws from a leftist commitment, it is because the novel does also.
If the film vaporizes radical sociology, the novel withdraws from it, too,
with Rose of Sharon's final act. The familial optimism of the one and the
biological pessimism of the other are two sides of the same coin.

[25] Asheim, p. 157.
[26] In an interview with the author.

The structural achievement of the cinematic version may account, paradoxically, for the film's troubling reputation. On the one hand, acclamation, box-office success, critical enthusiasm; Jane Darwell winning an Academy Award for her portrayal of Ma Joad; the casting and acting of Henry Fonda, John Carradine, Charlie Grapewin, John Qualen, Frank Darien, Grant Mitchell, and the others, generally considered flawless; Nunnally Johnson sporting a gold plaque on the wall of his studio office in recognition of a fine screenplay; and one reporter poking fun at the grandiose premiere of the film at the Normandie Theater in New York, which was attended by glamorous stars adorned in jewels and furs, and, like a "Blue Book pilgrimage,"[27] by the representatives of the very banks and land companies that had tractored the Joads off their farms. Zanuck and his entourage must have known that the filmic portrait of Steinbeck's book was no serious threat.

On the other hand, the industry's discomfort. *The Grapes of Wrath* came as close as any film in Hollywood's prolific turnout to exposing the contradictions and inequities at the heart of American life. A new thing had been created and its implications were frightening. In spite of its facile conclusion, the film raises questions to which others, outside the fictive world, have had to supply answers. The film's unusual cinematographic accomplishments, its structural unity, its documentary realism, combine to fashion images, embodying those questions, which one may review with profit again and again. If the novel is remembered for its moral anger, the film is remembered for its beauty. And yet the industry has been a little embarrassed by its success. That success and that embarrassment may help explain why Nunnally Johnson has accomplished so little of lasting interest since his work on this film, and why he was last seen completing the scenario for Sloan Wilson's *The Man in the Gray Flannel Suit*, a book of a very different kind! It may explain why John Ford never lists *The Grapes* as one of his favorite films, and why Ford himself offers perhaps the best explanation for the film's unique personality. Tersely, but with just the slightest trace of whimsy and bravado, John Ford remarks, "I never read the book."[28]

---

[27] Michael Mok, "Slumming with Zanuck," *Nation*, CL (February 3, 1940), 127–28.
[28] In an interview with the author.

13
George W. Linden

THE STORIED WORLD

Reflections On the Screen, from which this excerpt has been taken, is a major contemporary work on film aesthetics. George W. Linden, like many excellent teachers, examines a failure in film adaptation to clarify differences between a novel and motion picture. His book contains brilliant generalizations about film as a medium and is filled with relevant examples.

The experience of the reader of the novel is analogous to the activity of the director of the film in the sense that the reader's contact with the world depicted in the novel is usually over an extended period of time. It takes longer to read a novel than to watch a film. No doubt this is one reason why the lazy say, "I won't read the book. I'll wait to see the film." Of course, being lazy, they overlook the fact that what they are seeing is not a novel on celluloid but a different object: a moving picture. It may be the novel in shadow but not in substance.

The experience of the reader is analogous to that of the director in another sense: it is intermittent. One usually reads a novel, then puts the book aside for the press of everyday life before once again resuming the illusory world. But the illusory world of experiencing the film is continuously present. One reason that it is possible for the reader to experience the novel intermittently is because the novel is a narrative. It is

157

something he must think together in imagination. The verbal symbols are constant and fairly simple to resume. The task of the director is much more difficult. He is working, not primarily with thoughts or with the verbal, but with the aural and visual; hence, he must be able to draw these disparate elements together on the basis of emotional rhythm. The necessity for emotional unity varies according to the type of film involved, of course. Hence, a documentary tends to be thought, while a fictional film is much more dependent upon feeling. In the novel, feeling is a precipitate of thought. In film, thought is a precipitate of feeling engendered by vision. In the novel, we see because we remember; in film, we remember because we see.

The experience of the reader of the novel is much more singular than that of the spectator of the film. The word "singular" is used here in various senses. The experience is singular in the sense that it is more rare and less frequent. At least in the modern world more people view films more often than read the novels on which those films are based, however loosely. The experience is also singular in the sense that one usually reads a novel alone. Rarely is novel reading a group experience; and, although in a very real sense each individual watching a film is in a theatre of his own, films are nevertheless a group experience. The reading of a novel is singular in the still further meaning that only one sense is usually involved: vision. One rarely reads a novel aloud; hence, the written symbols must carry the force to create the entire imaginary world. But it is precisely the counterpoint and fusion of sight and sound that are basic to the impact of film.

While the film and the novel are alike in that they are not primarily concerned with the imitation of an action, as is drama, but with the development of events, their approaches to the events differ due to their different demands and emphases. The novelist tends to reveal what people do through what they are; the director, to reveal what they are through what they do. What the novelist deploys, the director must display. It is exactly here that the film based on the novel usually fails. For a film to be an adequate rendition of a novel, it must not only present the actions and events of the novel but also capture the subjective tones and attitudes toward those events. This the novelist can do quite freely by using description and point of view. It is much more difficult for the director, since he must either discover or create visual equivalents for the narrator's evaluations. Let us examine two failures to find images of equal valency. One, *Hud*, was merely a limited failure, while the other, *Lord of the Flies*, was almost a total failure.

Hud is a good film, which has many brilliant moments in it. One must admire James Wong Howe's truly beautiful photography. He captures not only the clarity of the Western setting and its expansive

nature but also the emotional urgency and desperation of the destruction of the cattle due to foot-and-mouth disease. By shooting the burial
scene of the cattle from a low angle, he made the audience feel as though
it were being buried, and this greatly enhanced the desperation of the
situation presented. One also must admire the fine acting of Paul Newman and Brandon de Wilde and the beautiful strength and subtlety with
which Patricia Neal made an ordinary, middle-aged female into a woman.
Hers was probably one of the healthiest portrayals of the sexuality of
a real human being since Simone Signoret's performance in *Room at the
Top*. Alma (not Halmira) is forthrightly sexual, and she frankly wants
Hud; but she refuses to be subjected to physical or psychological rape.
She insists on being treated as what she is — a person and hence a center
of value. Martin Ritt should be praised not only for how he handled
these actors and the shooting but also for the way in which he utilized
the vast expanse of the wide screen to emphasize the open loneliness
of the West. But, being the director, he must also shoulder the blame.

Not only was he to blame for casting a man too old and weak,
Melvyn Douglas, for the part of the grandfather so that the main point
of the novel was lost, but he also violated the tone of the novel. The
theme of *Horseman, Pass By* is not really the growth of a young man,
Lonnie, to adulthood. After all, that is the subtheme of most novels,
and it was Hemingway's stock in trade. The theme is the dying of the
old ways and the conflict between the values of the past, as embodied
in the grandfather, and the new don't-give-a-damn self-aggrandizement
of the operator, the rich bum, Hud. Changing Halmira from Negro to
white makes Hud a bit less opportunistic and the film more commercial
but does not seriously damage the main theme. The weakness of the
grandfather does. The film thus becomes a story of two strong people,
Hud versus Alma, and of a boy's transition to disillusion, sex, and
adulthood. But the main failing was not being able to translate the basic
tone of the novel. The haunting and engaging quality of the book is
the lyrical love of the land and the tender regret at its despoiling. It
is a land that was won and held by hard men, but hard men of a new breed
are destroying its values and in the process are destroying themselves.
The meaning of the tone is this: Home is no longer a place. The home
place is deliberately negated, and everyone becomes a tumbleweed.
Hud Bannon, once he has destroyed, belongs no place and is going no
whither; he simply moves. In spite of the fine acting and the luminous
photography, the film lacked this sadness at the loss, not of innocence
and childhood ways, but of a real and tangible world of value, at the
destruction of place and the substitution of space.

As an attempt to translate the novel into film form, *Lord of the Flies*
was almost a total failure. Some critics praised it, of course; but even

assuming that they had good taste and understood film form (two vast assumptions), it is clear that they were praising their remembrances of an admired novel and not what they were actually seeing on the screen. It is highly doubtful that anyone who had not previously read the book could even have found the film intelligible. I attended the film with two educated and sensitive adults, neither of whom could figure out what the film was about or, most of the time, what was happening. Once I had briefly outlined the book for them, they were able to reconstruct some of the film and to view it as partially intelligible. But both agreed that the film was negligible, that is, a waste of time. Yet William Golding's novel is not only very popular, particularly with the young, but also well written and powerful. Why, then, was the motion picture such a disaster? The answer, I believe, is partly technical and partly methodological, but mostly the disaster resulted from a failure to translate ideas and descriptive events into appropriate visual analogues and to capture their human meaning.

Technically, the film was poor in quality. The editing was jumpy and erratic, and the camera work was murky and obscure. The visual quality of the film was thus inept enough to class it as amateur in the bad sense of the word "amateur." Had *Lord of the Flies* pretended to be an underground film, it would no doubt have won prizes for its incoherency. Certainly, it was superior to *The Do It Yourself Happening Kit, Prelude: Dog Star Man*, and other such "masterpieces" of episodic murk. But it was not designed nor was it intended to be an exercise in incoherent subjectivity. It was intended to be a feature film that expressed the novel. The examples of unclear camera work that concealed instead of revealing the thematic sense of the original are numerous. A few instances might suffice. There is a long build-up, in both the novel and in the film, of the importance of the monster. Golding's techniques are both narrative and dramatic; in the film, they are almost totally dramatic. But when the climactic scene comes in the film, the shots of the decayed parachutist are so unclear and so dim that the frantic reaction of the boys is not merely unjustified, it is unintelligible. One has to strain to look to see what is being shown. Golding's main point, irony, is totally lost. One may say the same thing for the chase of Ralph. Not only does the camera work detract from the event, but also the rhythm of the sequence does not build to the appropriate terror of the book. And the closing scene with the sailors loses the impact of the novel. The camera is in so tight that we fail to realize that the sailors are from a battleship — a man-of-war that is actually fighting in the adult world — and, again, the profound irony touched with hopelessness, which is a distinguishing quality of the novel, is lost. What has been lost is the *human meaning* of the events, the art of the novel.

The film itself is episodic. It lacks the internal unity and coherence of the novel. But internal unity is the prime condition of quality, whether in art, practical objects, or life. That which has internal unity is the least affected by external accident and idiosyncrasy. Lacking such qualitative coherence, the film was subject to manifold interpretations — many of which were not relevant to its theme — and to plain obscurity and puzzlement. It did not speak with one voice nor did it speak clearly. This disjointedness and the resultant working of the episodes to cross-purposes and irrelevancies were probably partly due to the lack of a script. I am told that the boys were merely given the book to read and then asked to improvise. Even accomplished actors have difficulty doing this. As Trevor Howard has remarked, the second *Mutiny on the Bounty* might not have been quite the disaster it was if the actors had known what they were doing and where they were going. As he said dryly, "It helps, at least, to have a script." When there is no script from the outset, the director and the actors have no narrative skeleton around which they may improvise. Without a skeleton, nothing holds; everything becomes an amorphous mess. Golding's novel is highly structured, and his techniques are masterfully utilized to enhance and to reveal the structural development of plot and theme. The lack of structure in the film, however, renders it so weak that no viable tension is developed between the foreground action of the plot and the thematic horizon. The two become confused, and the possibilities of contrast, complementation, reinforcement, cumulation, and revelation are lost.

The decision to use amateur actors and to shoot the film as a semi-documentary in the neo-realist tradition was a proper decision. The novel, after all, is almost a philosophical tract as well as a fictional narrative. Since the element of thought is so heavy and so meaningful in the novel, the methodological choice of documentary was correct. The documentary film does establish greater emotional distance and does move in a more intellectual context than does the straight dramatic or personal film, which has a unity of emotional quality as its core with concepts in the background. But the boys tried to act and not to react. These young actors were not handled as Vittorio De Sica could have handled them. The result is that the film is dead. The only scene that comes alive at all and has the ring of authenticity is the one in which Piggy is explaining the reason for town names. This boy is so remarkable that he becomes carried away by his own inspiration, and the camera captures that living time. The other scenes are flat, however. They are awkward, stiff, and stagy. There is nothing more awkward than the deliberately natural.

Most of these failures must be attributed to the director. A fine director does not need professional actors if he has control of his editing. Obviously, this presupposes that he has control of the shooting. If he can design visual analogues for the novel's descriptive events, he can, even with complete amateurs, turn out an impressive film. Robert Flaherty's work, with the exception of *Louisiana Story*, is a case in point. The director needs to be able to translate ideas into sights and sounds. He must be able to present us with what we would normally visualize or envision. It is precisely here that the film version of *Lord of the Flies* was such a dismal failure. We are not given visual equivalents of the narrative representations. Again, the failures are many. If I but mention the failure of a critical scene, however, that may suffice.

A crucial scene in the novel is Peter's mystic experience of the Lord. Peter is young and impressionable, but he is old enough to be torn by conflicting loyalties. The tension that builds in him reaches its climax in his mystic fascination with the decayed pig's head and the swarm of flies. This is a crucial scene in the novel, since without it one cannot understand Peter's character, his behavior and choices, or his death. The ironic choice of his name is enhanced by this scene, for his later death on the rocks is a bitter reversal of the Catholic claim. Golding's scene is powerful and profound. What do we see in the film? What we see is a young and very frail boy staring at a pig's head with flies buzzing around it. The camera draws in tight for extreme close-ups, but all we can get out of it is the image of a confused boy. There are many filmic ways this could have been handled, such as montage or flashback, but the scene is shot with straight realism. Such straight realism is the least appropriate tool for revealing the mystic depth of this scene. In some cases, such as this, it is necessary to be surreal in order to capture the human meaning of a reality. Remember, for a moment, the grisly scene of the mother carrying a slab of fetid meat in the dream episode of *Los Olvidados*. The master, Luis Buñuel, knows full well that in some cases the only way to capture the human depth meaning of reality is to enhance it with relevant fantasy.

From the viewpoint of the creator or the spectator, a film such as *Lord of the Flies* must be viewed as a disaster. Like the scientist, the aesthetician can learn as much from failures as he can from successes; usually, he can learn more. For reflection on different kinds of badnesses reveals the necessary conditions for art much more clearly than do the triumphs. One reason that the high points of an art are less revealing in this respect is simply because they *are* triumphs. Therefore, the hard work, the sweat, the brutal decisions, the agonizing technique, are usually hidden — the art of the artist is normally suppressed, and the values are centered, as is the spectator's attention, in the work. The fine work, consequently, often appears easy and artless. Certain inferior novelists, like inferior directors, constantly move themselves into the center of the picture and distract from their works. Such showboating detracts from the work at hand or at mind or at eye and ear. The artist who is sure of his voice lets his object speak.

What, then, can we conclude from reflecting upon the film *Lord of the Flies*? One thing we can conclude is that a director can change the plot of a novel, he can eliminate certain characters and scenes, and he can include scenes not included in the novel without violating it. But he cannot seriously violate the theme of the novel, and the one thing he must be able to translate into his new medium is its tone. If the tone of a work is lost, the work is lost; but the tone of the novel must be rendered in an aural/visual patterning instead of by the use of descriptive dialogue or other narrative device. The author's intellectual viewpoint must become the director's emotional standpoint. If this happens, the camera will capture the relevant visual analogues. If not, the meanings of the novel are lost. Of course, if the director succeeds in his effort, he will have produced not a copy of the novel, but a new object: an art film that aims at close targets in a different way.

Professor Battestin has come to many of the same conclusions we have by discussing a success, *Tom Jones*, instead of a failure, *Lord of the Flies*. He admits that the film does not have the moral earnestness of the novel nor does it express the belief in overriding Providence. Such a difference is inevitable, for John Osborne and Tony Richardson do not inhabit Henry Fielding's world. Nor do their audiences. We live in a time when such orderly beliefs as Fielding's seem naïve and irrelevant. We may be wrong, but this is our milieu. Hence, Osborne and Richardson cannot speak as Fielding spoke; and, if they did, they would not be understood. Nevertheless, as Battestin points out, the film is a successful rendition of the novel, and to say "that the film *Tom Jones* is a successful adaptation of the novel is not to equate the two works in purpose or effect." Each has its own purpose and its own effect, yet they are analogically identical.

As I have insisted, so has Battestin: analogy is the key.

14

Martin C.
Battestin

OSBORNE'S *TOM JONES:*
ADAPTING A CLASSIC

A professor of English at Rice University,
Battestin is a specialist on Henry Fielding,
the author of *Tom Jones.* In this article he
contrasts the eighteenth-century novel
with the 1963 film directed by Tony
Richardson from a screenplay by John
Osborne. In the article, Battestin reveals
his understanding of the differences between the two media.

The announcement in the late summer of 1962 that Britain's "Angry
Young Men" of the theater—John Osborne and Tony Richardson—were
making a movie of Henry Fielding's masterpiece occasioned among my
colleagues, the professional Augustans of the academy, a reaction closer
to shock than surprise. Neither was there much comfort in the knowledge that Albert Finney, fresh from his role in that equally angry film
Saturday Night and Sunday Morning, was to appear (think of it!) as
Fielding's open-hearted and bumptious hero. When one allowed oneself
to think of it at all, one had only uneasy expectations of the rowdy and
irreverent treatment Fielding's classic was in for. Instead, what one
saw on the screen was one of the most successful cinematic adaptations
of a novel ever made, and, what is more, one of the most imaginative of
comic films, a classic in its own right.

164

To understand the success of this film as an adaptation of the novel is, fundamentally at least, to notice the curious fact that some of the best writers of our own times have found congenial the literary modes and methods of the English Augustan Age — of which Fielding's comic epic of low life was the last major achievement. We are ourselves in a new age of satire, witnessing the dubious victories of what R. W. B. Lewis has called "the picaresque saint." Saul Bellow in *The Adventures of Augie March*, Jack Kerouac in *On the Road*, John Barth in *The Sot-Weed Factor* have exploited in various ways and for various effects the conventional form of the journey novel. George Garrett, whose recent book *Do, Lord, Remember Me* is a masterful comic celebration of the boundless possibilities of the human spirit for folly and degradation, and for love and glory, has traced the source of his inspiration to Chaucer and to Fielding. The spirit of Swift in *Gulliver's Travels* is not far from that of the "theater of the absurd," from Ionesco's rhinoceroses or Beckett's end-game — the symbolic fantasies of a fallen and dehumanized world. But the appeal of Fielding's comic vision for the contemporary writer has been nowhere better seen than in Kingsley Amis' healthy satire of the Establishment, *Lucky Jim*, and nowhere better expressed than by Bowen, the young writer of Amis' *I Like It Here*, who, standing before the white stone sarcophagus in which the author of *Tom Jones* rests near Lisbon, reflects on the significance of the master:

> Bowen thought about Fielding. Perhaps it was worth dying in your forties if two hundred years later you were the only non-contemporary novelist who could be read with unaffected and wholehearted interest, the only one who never had to be apologised for or excused on the grounds of changing taste. And how enviable to live in the world of his novels, where duty was plain, evil arose out of malevolence and a starving wayfarer could be invited indoors without hesitation and without fear. Did that make it a simplified world? Perhaps, but that hardly mattered beside the existence of a moral seriousness that could be made apparent without the aid of evangelical puffing and blowing.

There is, it would seem, a fundamental rapport between Bowen and his kind and the master novelist of an age which found satiric laughter the most congenial antidote to the perversion of order and the corruption of the Establishment, the most effective way of protesting the betrayal of humane ideals by the forces of venality and barbarism.

To say, however, that the film *Tom Jones* is a successful adaptation of the novel is not to equate the two works in purpose or effect. One of the most distinguished eighteenth-century scholars of our time — a man

of eminent wit and urbanity—told me that he walked out of the premiere
New York showing of the movie (October, 1963) dejected and irritated
at how widely Osborne and Richardson had missed the point of Fielding's
book. What my friend failed to find in the film was not Fielding's panoramic impression of English life two centuries ago, nor was it Fielding's
hearty, brawling comedy, which the film so admirably captures. What is
missing from the film is exactly that quality which Amis' hero singled
out as the distinctive characteristic of Fielding's fictional world—
namely, that "moral seriousness" which underlies all of Fielding's humor
and his satire and which makes of *Tom Jones* not merely a frivolous, if
delightful, romp through English society, but a complex symbolic expression of its author's Christian vision of life. Fielding's vision is comic
in an ultimate sense: it sees the human drama being enacted within a
cosmic system of order and of ascertainable moral values, a system in
which the great frame of the universe and of human society is presided
over by a just and benign Providence, which rewards the charitable and
the virtuous and punishes the selfish and the hypocritical. It is a vision
perhaps most succinctly summarized in these lines from the best philosophical poem of that age:

> All Nature is but Art, unknown to thee;
> All Chance, Direction, which thou canst not see;
> All Discord, Harmony, not understood;
> All partial Evil, universal Good. . . .

What occurs in the film—and, with the exception of Garrett's book,
in those other modern works we have mentioned—is close to the superficial impulse of Augustan satire, in which human folly or depravity is
the object either of olympian amusement or of savage indignation; but
what is lacking is the faith in an ultimate moral and providential design
which serves as a foil to vice and to social chaos. One cannot properly
understand Pope's *Dunciad* without knowing that it was written by the
author of the *Essay on Man*; one cannot understand *Gulliver's Travels*
without knowing that its author was Dean of St. Patrick's; one cannot
understand *Tom Jones* without being aware that its author was a staunch
defender of the established Church and government—and that he believed wholeheartedly in the responsibility of the individual both to
discipline his own passionate nature and to behave charitably toward
his fellow men. To the writers of our new age of satire, Osborne among
them, such faith in the order and coherency of things is naive; theirs
is not, as Bowen put it, "a simplified world." Thus, whereas Fielding's
novel is designed to fulfill his promise to recommend "the cause of
religion and virtue" by endeavoring "to laugh mankind out of their

favourite follies and vices," Osborne's film can make no more of this purpose than to prefer Tom's animal vitality and ingenuousness to the conniving of Blifil, or the pretentious metaphysics of Square, or the brutal pharisaism of Thwackum, or the jaded sexuality of Lady Bellaston. This moral opposition is, of course, very much a part of Fielding's own didactic intent, but in the novel a much larger and (to the dismay of self-complacent moderns let it be said) much less simplistic vision is operating. Ideally Fielding saw life, as he saw art, not merely as energy but as order: what he admired in men and in the natural world was a sort of benign exuberance rationally controlled and directed toward the achievement of a desirable end. The world of *Tom Jones* is dynamic, charged, as Coleridge remarked, with the energy of sunshine and laughter and love; and it is at the same time a celebration of that rational design which gives meaning to vitality, and which in fact alone makes it a source of joy and of wonder. *Tom Jones* is, on different levels, an assertion of the shaping powers of the Creator, of the artist (who, as Thackeray long ago observed, appears in this novel as a surrogate Providence), and of the moral man — the exemplar of what Fielding referred to in *Amelia* as "the Art of Life." Even the form of Fielding's novel embodies this meaning: the famous plot (Coleridge called it one of the three most perfect in all literature) in which every character and every event are organically interconnected and conspire to lead inexorably to the denouement; the much-discussed "hourglass structure" of the book, in which even the axioms of neo-classical aesthetics and architecture are scrupulously observed, producing a work balanced, symmetrical, proportionate, with the adventures at Upton standing as the keystone of the arch; the constant supervision of the narrative by the intrusive and omniscient author — such formal devices make the very fabric and texture of the novel a tacit assertion of the reality and value of design and order in the world.

The story itself is calculated to dramatize this lesson by depicting the near disastrous career of a young man possessed of every social and private virtue but one: Tom Jones is honest, brave, and generous, but he is imprudent. And prudence, as Allworthy explains, "is indeed the duty which we owe to ourselves"; it is the supreme rational virtue of both classical and Christian philosophy; it is the essence of wisdom, enabling the individual correctly to distinguish truth from appearances and to estimate the ultimate consequences of his actions. For want of this virtue Fielding's hero is cast out of "Paradise Hall," commits one good-natured indiscretion after another, and finds himself at last clapped into prison, rejected by Sophia and his foster father, and guilty (for all he knows) of incest and murder. In broad outline and in implication Jones's story is not unlike that of Spenser's Redcross Knight, who must also acquire prudence before he may be united with the fair Una—or, in Tom's case, with the "divine Sophia," whose name signifies that wisdom he has lacked. For Fielding a good heart and sexual prowess were much indeed, but they were not everything; for Osborne, apparently, they are all that really matters. In the film there is no sense of the hero's maturation, for there is never any question of his responsibility for what happens to him. In prison, having been informed that the woman he slept with at Upton was his own mother, Fielding's hero arrives at a crucial moment of self-recognition: "Sure . . . Fortune will never have done with me till she hath driven me to distraction. But why do I blame Fortune? I am myself the cause of all my misery. All the dreadful mischiefs which have befallen me are the consequences only of my own folly and vice." In the film, however, Jones is never informed of the supposed identity of Mrs. Waters, nor is he made to acknowledge his folly. His reunion with Sophie is not earned, nor, heralded by one of Finney's mischievous winks at the camera, does it have the joyous dignity and symbolic significance that Fielding invests it with. Osborne's happy ending is gratuitous, vintage Hollywood; Fielding's is—given the moral dimension which his comedy constantly implies—appropriate and necessary. Within the terms of his comic vision of an ordered and benign universe it is the only possible apocalypse. At the moment when Fielding's hero confesses his folly and learns the lesson of prudence, the prison doors miraculously open, his "crimes" are undone, his enemies exposed, his true identity discovered. His reconciliation with Allworthy and Sophia, the only father he has known and the only woman he has loved, follows inevitably.

My friend's feelings of dismay at the American première of the film were, one must grant, understandable. But if Osborne and Richardson missed a major intention behind Fielding's novel, they fully grasped and brilliantly re-created its essential spirit and manner. It is fruitless, of course, to require that the film reproduce the novel in its every scene and character. The problem of the adapter of fiction to the screen is more difficult by far than that of the translator of a novel or a play from one language to another. For one thing the rhetoric of the two art forms is fundamentally different: the arrangement of words in sequence is the business of the novelist, but the maker of a film deals in the arrangement of images. A second basic difference between the two forms is that of scope: Fielding may write on, as he does in *Tom Jones*, for a thousand pages or more, requiring the reader's attention for hours on end; Osborne and Richardson can expect us to lend them our eyes and ears for only a fraction of an evening, in this instance a little more than two hours. The two forms are similar, however, in that they may both be used for narrative purposes—for telling, or showing, a story—and they may adopt similar attitudes toward their subject and similar techniques of expression. They may be similar, but never identical. The "naturalism" of Zola in *Germinal*, let us say, is comparable to the stark realism of Rossellini's *Open City*; the symbolic fantasies of Kafka are comparable to the surrealism of Fellini's 8½: on the one hand, the manner of expression is close to the factual, expository method of the historian; on the other hand, it approaches the supralogical techniques of the poet.

Analogy is the key. To judge whether or not a film is a successful adaptation of a novel is to evaluate the skill of its makers in striking analogous attitudes and in finding analogous rhetorical techniques. From this point of view Osborne and Richardson produced in *Tom Jones* one of the most successful and imaginative adaptations in the brief history of film. This, as we have seen, is less true with regard to the authorial attitudes and ultimate thematic intentions of the two works. The real genius of the film as adaptation is in its brilliantly imaginative imitation of the *art* of the novel. Those "gimmicks" that so much surprised and delighted audiences may be seen as technical analogues of Fielding's own most distinctive devices.

Consider, for example, the opening sequence of the film. Before the title and credits we are presented with a rapid succession of scenes done in affected mimicry of the manner of the silent film, with subtitles supplying both commentary and dialogue (even Mrs. Wilkins' "aah!" as she sees Allworthy in his nightshirt), and with John Addison's spirited harpsichord setting the mood in the manner of the upright of the old "flicker" days. The device serves several practical purposes, of course: exposition which required the better part of two books in the novel is presented here swiftly and economically; a playful comic tone is at once established; and the reminiscence of the earliest era of the cinema also serves to remind us that Fielding's book appeared at a comparable moment in the history of that other peculiarly modern genre, the novel. Less obviously, in the use of out-dated acting styles, exaggerated reactions and posturing, and subtitles, Richardson and Osborne have translated into the medium of the cinema two aspects of Fielding's technique which contribute to the comic effect and distance. The overstated acting of the silent-film era is analogous to what may be called the "Hogarthian" manner (Fielding himself often made the comparison) of characterization in the novel. Even after spoken dialogue has been introduced (after the credits) and the need for pantomime is no longer present, Richardson continues to elicit heightened and hyperbolic performances from his actors—a style which, as in Hogarth and Fielding, serves not only to amuse, as caricature does, but also to reveal and accentuate the essential natures of the characters. As Fielding declared in *Joseph Andrews* (III, i), he described "not men, but manners; not an individual, but a species."

Richardson's actors rarely behave in the understated, naturalistic manner of the conventional film: smiles become leers, glances become ogles, gestures are heightened into stances, posturings. Similarly Fielding's characters, like Hogarth's, verge on caricature: they do not ask, as Moll Flanders or Clarissa Harlowe or Dorothea Brooke or Emma Bovary asks, to be accepted as real people, but rather as types and emblems of human nature; they have the reality of symbol rather than of fact.

Just as the miming of the actors during the opening sequence establishes the hyperbolic style of the performances throughout, so Osborne's initial use of subtitles prepares us for the spoken commentary of the narrator, whose voice is the first we hear in the film and who will accompany us throughout as an invisible guide and observer. Osborne's commentator is a clever adaptation of Fielding's celebrated omniscient narrator, whose presence is constantly felt in *Tom Jones*, describing the action, making apposite observations on the characters' motives and deeds, entertaining us with his wit and learning, controlling our attitudes and responses. It has been remarked that the most important "character" in Fielding's novel is the author-narrator himself, whose genial and judicious spirit pervades the entire work, presiding providentially over the world of the novel and reminding us at every point that the creation we behold is his own. He it is who, more than any character in the story itself—more than Tom, more even than Allworthy—provides the moral center of the book. Osborne's commentator functions correspondingly: when first we see Tom, now a full-grown young scamp prowling for nocturnal sport in the woods, the over-voice of the commentator informs us that Tom is "far happier in the woods than in the study," that he is "as bad a hero as may be," that he is very much a member of the generation of Adam. Like Fielding's, Osborne's narrator presents his fallible hero, but the tone of wry amusement and clear affection for the character controls our own attitude, establishes that tolerant morality which makes Tom's peccadilloes far less important than his honest, warm-hearted zest for life. Though Fielding's narrator has the advantage of being continually present, Osborne's commentator is heard often enough so that his own relationship with the audience is sustained, and with each intrusion his own "personality" becomes more sharply defined: in matters of morality he is tolerant of everything but hypocrisy and inhumanity; he knows his Bible and his Ovid; he can recite a verse or apply an adage; he has a becoming sense of decorum in turning the camera away from a bawdy tumble in the bushes. Though necessarily a faint echo, he is very much the counterpart of Fielding's authorial voice.

A further effect of the constant intrusion of the narrator in both the film and the novel is to insure that the audience remains aloof and detached from the drama. We are never allowed to forget that this is

not a slice of life, but only a tale told (or shown). The narrator is always
there between the audience and the images on the screen, preventing
the sort of empathic involvement which generally occurs in movies, or
in fiction. Such detachment is very much a part of Fielding's comic purpose: his fictional world never pretends to be an imitation of life in any
realistic sense, but is offered to us as a consciously contrived and symbolic representation of human nature and society. We are asked to be-

Tom Jones (1963) The off-screen voice
speaks, "As bad a hero as may be, with
many a weakness," but the tone is affectionate and understanding. (Still courtesy
Woodfall Films Ltd; © Copyright 1963
by United Artists Corporation.)

hold it from a distance, at arm's length, as it were, to enjoy it and to learn from it.

The use of type characters and a self-conscious narrator are, moreover, only two of the means by which Fielding achieves this comic distance. The style of *Tom Jones* is itself highly mannered, not unlike the artful compositions of Hogarth, and it is often deliberately "rhetorical," not unlike the poetic diction of Pope and Gay. To reproduce this feature of Fielding's book, Osborne and Richardson similarly flaunt every conceivable device in the rhetoric of their own medium. Just as Fielding indulges in amplifications, ironies, similes, mock-heroics, parodies, etc., so the film exploits for comic effect a circusful of wipes, freezes, flips, speed-ups, narrowed focuses—in short, the entire battery of camera tricks. The effect of this is again to call attention to the skill of the artist, to the intelligence manipulating the pen or the camera, as the case may be. Particularly remarkable in this respect is the most celebrated of Richardson's tricks—his deliberate violation of the convention that actors must never take notice of the camera, because to do so is to dispel the illusion of life on the screen, to call attention to the fact that what the audience is seeing is a play being acted before a camera. But Richardson's actors are constantly winking at us, appealing to us to settle their disputes, thrusting their hats before our eyes, etc. The effect, paradoxically, is not to involve us in their drama, but to remind us of the presence of the camera and, consequently, to prevent us, in our darkened seats, from achieving that customary magical identification with the vicarious world unfolding on the screen. In just this way Fielding's rhetorical somersaults keep us aware that his own fictional world, like the macrocosm itself, is being supervised and manipulated by a controlling and ultimately benign intelligence. This, though tacitly achieved, is the supreme statement of his comedy.

The brilliance of Osborne's adaptation may be seen not only in the general handling of character, narrator, and rhetoric, but in his treatment of particular scenes from the novel as well. Certainly one of the most delightful and significant of these is the sequence in which Tom, concerned that he has got Molly Seagrim with child, pays an unexpected visit to her in her garret bedroom, only to find that he has been sharing her favors with the philosopher Square. At the critical moment a curtain falls away and the august metaphysician—who has made a career of denouncing the body—stands revealed in his hiding place, clad only in a blush and Molly's nightcap. In both the novel and the film this scene is shaped as a sort of parabolic dramatization of Fielding's satiric theory and practice: satire, as he had pointed out in the preface to *Joseph Andrews*, deals with "the true Ridiculous," which was his term for affectation and pretense—for those whose deeds did not match their professions. As a graphic enactment of this comic theory — the hilarious revelation of the naked truth behind the drapery — the exposure of Square is the quintessential scene in all of Fielding's fiction.

But the most impressive single instance of Osborne's and Richardson's genius in translating Fielding's style, attitudes, and intentions into their own medium is the famous eating scene at Upton. It may surprise those whose memory of the novel is vague that virtually every gesture and every grimace in the film sequence — and, indeed, its basic metaphorical equation of lust and appetite — originated with Fielding. The passage in question is Book IX, Chapter V, entitled "An apology for all heroes who have good stomachs, with a description of a battle of the amorous kind." The chapter begins with the reluctant admission that even the most accomplished of heroes have more of the mortal than the divine about them: even Ulysses must eat. When Jones and Mrs. Waters sit down to satisfy their appetites — he by devouring three pounds of beef to break a fast of twenty-four hours, she by feasting her eyes on her companion's handsome face — Fielding proceeds to define love, according to the modern understanding of the word, as "that preference which we give to one kind of food rather than to another." Jones loved his steak and ale; Mrs. Waters loved Jones. During the course of the meal the temptress brings to bear on her companion "the whole artillery of love," with an efficacy increasing in direct proportion to Jones's progress in appeasing his hunger. Fielding, invoking the Graces, describes the lady's artful seduction of his hero in the amplified, hyperbolic terms of a mock-epic battle: "First, from two lovely blue eyes, whose bright orbs flashed lightning at their discharge, flew forth two pointed ogles; but happily for our hero, hit only a vast piece of beef which he was then conveying into his plate, and harmless spent their force. . . ." Mrs. Waters heaves an epic sigh, but this is lost in "the coarse bubbling of some bottled ale." The assault continues as, "having planted her right eye sidewise against Mr. Jones, she shot from its corner a most penetrating glance. . . ." Perceiving the effect of this ogle, the fair one coyly lowers her glance and then, having made her meaning clear even to the unassuming Jones, lifts her eyes again and discharges "a volley of small charms at once from her whole countenance" in an affectionate smile which our hero receives "full in his eyes." Jones, already staggering, succumbs when his delicious adversary unmasks "the royal battery, by carelessly letting her handkerchief drop from her neck. . . ." No one who has seen the film will need to be reminded how brilliantly Joyce Redman and Finney conveyed, in images only, the sense of Fielding's metaphor of lust and appetite and how well Miss Redman visually rendered the epic sighs and ogles and leers of Mrs. Waters. This scene is not only the funniest in the film; it is a triumph of the art of cinematic

translation. Both the form of the adaptation and the supremely comic
effect could have been achieved in this way in no other genre: they are,
in other words, the result of the collaborative exploitation (by writer,
director, photographer, actors, and editor) of peculiarly cinematographic
techniques—here, specifically, a series of close-ups arranged and controlled by expert cutting. An entirely verbal effect in the novel has been
rendered in the film entirely in terms of visual images.

Tom Jones (1963) Mrs. Waters brings to
bear on Tom "the whole artillery of love":
Fielding's verbal metaphor of lust, battle,
and appetite is rendered in visual images.
(Still courtesy Woodfall Films, Ltd.;
© Copyright 1963 by United Artists
Corporation.)

Consideration of the ways in which the film is a successful imitation of Fielding's novel can go no farther than this scene of amorous gastronomics at Upton. Let us turn, then, briefly, to an analysis of the film as a skillful work of art in its own right, for ultimately, of course, it is meant to be judged as such. Here perhaps it will be best to discuss those elements and techniques for which there is only the barest suggestion in the book. Most impressive of these is the use of visual contrasts in setting and situation for symbolic purposes. For instance, to establish at once the difference in nature between Jones and Blifil — the one free and wild and open-hearted, the other stiff and artful and cold — Osborne introduces each character in diametrically opposing situations. We first see Jones as he prowls in the wild woods at night, breaking the game laws and tumbling in the bushes with Molly: Tom is at home with the fox and the beaver; he returns the wink of an owl; and Molly, dark and dishevelled, flips a fern as she lures him to another kind of illicit sport. Blifil, on the other hand, is first seen in Allworthy's sun-drenched formal garden: he is dressed in formal frock coat and walks sedately, holding a book in his fastidious hands and obsequiously following those twin custodians of virtue and religion, the deist Square and Thwackum the divine. The contrast between Tom's two sweethearts, the profane and the sacred, is equally deliberate. After we have been shown another night scene of Tom and Molly among the bushes, the camera shifts abruptly to a bright, idyllic setting: we see Sophia's image reflected in a pond; swans swim gracefully about, and Sophie is as fair and white as they. When Tom appears, bringing her a caged song bird (nature not wild, but tame and lovely), the lovers run from opposite sides of the water to meet at the center of a bridge. Sophie has been presented as the very image of purity and light, the proper emblem of that chastity of spirit which (in Fielding's story at least) Tom must learn to seek and find. The film is visually organized according to a scheme of such contrasts — Allworthy's formal estate with Western's sprawling, boisterous barnyard; Molly's disordered bedroom with Sophie's chaste boudoir. Even such a fundamental element as the color itself is varied in this way to signal the shift from the naturalness and simplicity of the country to the affectation and luxury, and man-made squalor, of London: the scenes in the country are done predominantly in greens and browns, and in black, grey, and white; but London is revealed in a shock of violent colors. The entry of Tom and Partridge into town is meant to recall the stark and vicious scenes of Hogarth's "Rake's Progress" and "Gin Lane." And soon thereafter the screen is flushed with reds, purples, and oranges as Tom enters the gaudy masquerade at Vauxhall, where he will meet Lady Bellaston.

Such contrasts are based, of course, on similar oppositions, thematic

and structural, in the novel. For two of the film's most effective sequences, however, Osborne had scarcely any help from Fielding at all,
and yet both these scenes serve independently to convey attitudes and
themes consonant with Fielding's intentions and essential to the film Osborne is making. The first of these sequences is the stag hunt, for which
there was no basis in the novel, except for the fact that Fielding represents Squire Western as almost monomaniacal in his devotion to the
chase. In general effect the hunt serves a function similar to the shots of
Western's licentious table manners or of the gastronomic encounter
between Tom and Mrs. Waters: it serves, in other words, visually to
emphasize the brutal, predatory, appetitive quality of life in the provinces
two centuries ago. It is, as Osborne meant it to be, "no pretty Christmas
calendar affair." No one who has seen this chase will forget the furious
pace of it, the sadistic elation of the hunters—the lashing of horses, the
spurt of crimson as spur digs into flesh, the tumbling of mounts and
riders, the barnyard and the broken-necked goose trampled in the pursuit, the uncontrollable surge of the dogs as they tear the stag's throat
out, and Western's triumphant display of the bloody prey. This, surely,
is one of the most perfectly conceived and skillfully realized sequences
in the film.

    In sharp antithesis to the violence of this passage is the lyricism
of the montage sequence portraying the courtship and deepening love of
Tom and Sophie as Tom recovers from his broken arm on Western's
estate. Richardson has achieved here a sense of arcadia—an unfallen,
Edenic world of bright flowers and placid waters, of gaiety and innocence.
The growing intimacy and communion of the lovers is expressed in a
series of playful images in which their roles are interchanged or identified: first Sophie poles Tom around the lake while he lolls and smokes
a pipe, then their positions are reversed; Sophie appears on horseback
followed by Tom awkwardly straddling an ass, then vice versa, then they
both appear on the same horse; Sophie shaves Tom, and Tom later wades
into mud chest-deep to fetch her a blossom. They sing, skip, and lark
about together. When at length they do silently declare their love with
a deep exchange of glances and a kiss, the tone of the sequence is softly
modulated from the frivolous to the sincere. The entire passage is
altogether brilliant, done with exquisite sensitivity and a nice control.
Richardson has managed to communicate in a few frames skillfully juxtaposed the way it feels to fall in love. From this moment we can never
doubt the rightness and warmth of Tom and Sophie's affection—not
even when, afterwards, Tom will succumb to the temptations of Molly,
Mrs. Waters, and the demi-rep Lady Bellaston.

    It is pleasant to think of this film, a comic masterpiece of our new
Age of Satire, standing in the same relation to Fielding's classic as, say,

Pope's free imitations of Horace stand in relation to their original. In an impressive variety of ways, both technical and thematic, Osborne and Richardson's *Tom Jones* is a triumph in the creative adaptation of a novel to the very different medium of the cinema. Ultimately, of course, the film is not the novel, nor, doubtless, was it meant to be. It does capture an essential part of Fielding's spirit and intention in its depiction of the sweep and quality of eighteenth-century English life, in its celebration of vitality and an open heart, and in its ridicule of vanity and sham. But Osborne's vision is narrower than Fielding's: this is a function partly of the necessary limitations of scope in the film, partly of commercial pressures precluding "moral seriousness" in a work designed to entertain millions, and partly of the different *Weltanschauung* of the twentieth century. We are not left with a sense of Fielding's balanced and ordered universe, nor are we made aware of the lesson Fielding meant to impart in the progress of his lovable, but imperfect hero. And because the vision behind the film is different in kind, even those techniques of characterization, narration, and rhetoric which have been so effectively adapted from the novel do not serve, as they do in Fielding, as the perfect formal expression of theme. Despite these limitations and discrepancies, however, Osborne's *Tom Jones* is a splendid illustration of what can be done in the intelligent adaptation of fiction to the screen.

15

Eric R. Birdsall
and Fred H. Marcus

SCHLESINGER'S
MIDNIGHT COWBOY:
CREATING A CLASSIC

This article parallels the preceding one.
Here, a moderately effective novel has
been transformed into a superb film.
Birdsall is currently working on his doc-
torate at Johns Hopkins University. He
and Marcus wrote the article while Mr.
Birdsall was still an undergraduate English
major.

John Schlesinger's film *Midnight Cowboy* captured the 1969 Academy
Award for best motion picture of the year. In this instance, popular
acclaim and artistic achievement meshed appropriately. The award was
justified.

It seems unlikely that many of the film's viewers noted or cared
that *Midnight Cowboy* had been adapted from a novel. In 1965 James Leo
Herlihy's book attracted little critical or popular attention. Anyone
reading the novel and seeing the movie would recognize a family re-
semblance. But Schlesinger's transformation of novel to film underscores
a crucial point: the film medium differs radically from the literary
medium.

First published in this book.

Herlihy's novel tells the three-part story of Joe Buck, a sturdy and very naive Texan, who dreams of making his fortune serving as a stud to rich New York women. The opening section of the novel explores Joe's life prior to the moment he boards a Greyhound bus bound for New York. In part two, he arrives in the city, where he is victimized by several of its predatory denizens. The final section begins with Joe attending a Warholish party, where he encounters the first woman willing to pay for his services; the novel ends with another bus journey, this time culminating in Miami.

Through his use of compression, expansion, and imaginative visual invention, Schlesinger reshapes the novel. Using the language of film, he alters the structure of the book and creates a film of great beauty, insight, and emotional feeling. The movie concentrates on the last two sections of the novel. Only fifteen minutes of the 110-minute film have elapsed when Joe arrives in New York. Schlesinger reveals important background details in Joe's life by using relevant flashbacks from part one of Herlihy's novel. By cutting and compressing the first two-fifths of the novel, Schlesinger shifts the central focus of the story. The novel belongs to Joe, whose naive dreams are crushed by harsh reality. But the film is more tender—without sentimentality—and emphasizes the human relationship between Joe and Ratso; it focuses upon a fragile but growing friendship in a hostile environment.

In Herlihy's novel, Joe's radio plays a symbolic role. In much the same way that romantic novels supplied world views to the innocent Americans of Henry James, Joe's radio supplies his view of reality. When he arrives in New York, he promptly unpacks his radio, "hoping its sounds would give him the feeling of having truly arrived in this new place." The radio links Joe with the world; it filters and translates reality into something he can understand. In New York, the first thing he hears is a woman's cure for insomnia: to get up and stay awake. Joe reacts significantly: he "felt sorry for the lady but at the same time he was delighted by what he'd heard. For it seemed to bear out all those rumors about Eastern women." Joe hears and believes. He assumes that his radio reveals reality

Schlesinger recognizes the utility of the radio symbol; he also expands it and adds television touches (which Herlihy suggests but develops less fully). Joe's bus trip from Texas to New York shows Joe's dependence on his ever-present eight-transistor radio. This sequence of shots illustrates how a movie director can convert a concept into the visual, concrete language of film. Quick cuts depict the passage of time and individual shots characterize Joe Buck as well as his surroundings. The sequence begins with the bus in Texas. Joe and his radio. The countryside in bright daylight. Inside the bus with Joe, radio tuned to another station. Faces (close-ups) on the bus. Different countryside. A small town. A long shot of the bus moving down the highway at night. Morning in a new town. Different people. Another station on the radio glued to Joe's ear. Change in countryside. Joe walking through the bus, radio to his ear. More quick cuts — with the radio on the film's sound track punctuating the journey.

The film director supplements novelistic details with small, nicely ironic touches. It is the radio which announces the arrival of the bus in New York. In a second, more significant addition, Schlesinger foreshadows Joe's future relationship with the city. Arriving in his hotel room, resplendent in a cowboy shirt and movie cowboy boots, Joe turns on the television. It doesn't work. He thumps it with his hand; it still doesn't work. Finally, Joe realizes he will have to pay — it takes a quarter to operate the television set. Schlesinger visually says: nothing is free, not even "free" TV. Joe will pay, and pay again, for everything he gets in the city.

Schlesinger communicates his view of the city through a series of short visuals, invented entirely for the film. For example, Joe goes looking for his first "customer." In a series of quick cuts, we watch him following first one woman, then another. Cut to a jewelry store; close-up of a huge gem in the window of the store. Cut back to Joe, following another woman, looking delighted. A bank with the vault open; huge piles of cash seen through the window. Another woman. Quick cut to a long shot of a man passed out on the sidewalk (in front of Tiffany's!). Passers-by scarcely glance at him. Joe walks into view, one of many pedestrians. He alone stops, looks down. His face shows concern. Joe's stop contrasts with the rapid, unchanging pace of the city. He looks up at the people passing; he looks down again. Confusion replaces concern on his face. Hesitantly, he moves off, glancing back at the still figure. Joe has encountered his initial example of the inhumanity of the city; his reluctant retreat is his first defeat.

Joe Buck's optimistic and simplistic approach to his "career" begins with a calculated walk along Park Avenue. His ingenuous "line" about being new in the city and looking for the Statue of Liberty produces two responses. One, almost a motherly rebuke, declares he ought to be ashamed of himself. The second brings us closer to the ugly reality of the city. Joe's "rich New York lady" is walking her French poodle. Joe's Statue of Liberty gambit is almost beyond belief, but her harsh, "It's up in Central Park taking a leak" retort, taken from the novel, succeeds in establishing the vast gulf between Joe, the ingenuous would-be hustler, and this professional city-dweller. The second "rich lady" leads; Joe merely follows. The sexual sequence which follows underscores the pattern of exploitation; Joe is hustled, not hustler. Indeed, the lady's ardor evaporates rapidly into viciousness when Joe hints delicately that he receive his "stud fee." Violent reaction and phony weeping reduce Joe to an abject state. Ironically, his first hustling "success" costs him twenty dollars. His next experience, encountering Enrico (Ratso) Rizzo, continues the irony of the hustled hustler, but leads the film into a new and major dimension.

Schlesinger's characterization of Ratso demonstrates the ability of film to translate verbal symbols into concrete images which enable the viewer to "see, feelingly." The novel describes Ratso as a "skinny,

Midnight Cowboy (1969) The hustler hustled: Joe Buck's first "success" in the big city costs him twenty dollars. (© Copyright 1969 by United Artists Corporation; produced by Jerome Hellman; directed by John Schlesinger; screenplay by Waldo Salt.)

child-sized man of about twenty-one or twenty-two," with "big brown
eyes" and "big ears that [stick] straight out. . . ." He is a cripple, his
left leg "small and misshapen." As he walks, "his entire body [dips] to
the side so that his walk [has] a kind of rolling motion to it like the
progress of a lopsided wheel." Much of Herlihy's description is concrete,
but words are, inevitably, more abstract than film particulars. (What, for
example, does twenty-one or twenty-two really *show*?) In the film, Schlesinger's direction and Dustin Hoffman's superlative acting transform
Herlihy's words into a character so specific and immediate that the
viewer physically experiences his presence and character long after the
movie ends. He wears a slightly soiled white suit, a marvellously ironic

---

Midnight Cowboy (1969) Ratso is a creature of the city who knows its way and
is quick to exploit any available opportunity. (© Copyright 1969 by United
Artists Corporation; produced by Jerome
Hellman; directed by John Schlesinger;
screenplay by Waldo Salt.)

contrast to his venal character. Physically, Ratso has dirty, stringy hair, yellow-green slime on his teeth, and a three-day beard compounded equally of whiskers and city grime. When he walks, his crazy, rolling gait makes his whole body seem deformed. In Dustin Hoffman's portrayal, a reader/watcher perceives a twentieth-century Dickensian figure whose exterior reflects the interior man.

Since film must *show* character, Schlesinger visualizes Ratso in actions. Herlihy's novel tells us that Ratso is a creature of the city who knows its ways intimately, that he has a shrewd resourceful mind, and that he is quick to exploit any available opportunity. Schlesinger uses incidents to show us such characterization. Shortly after Joe and Ratso meet, they cross a busy street. A taxi bears down on them, braking just in time. Ratso knows his rights. He hammers on the hood of the taxi; he snarls at the driver, "I'm walkin' here. Ya hear dat? I'm walkin' here!" As he continues across the street, the driver mutters something. Ratso immediately executes a nice pirouette on his good leg, throws his arm in the air in a classic Italian gesture of contempt, and at the top of his lungs cries, "Up yours, ya son-of-a-bitch!" The incident takes place in the center of a busy street, in less time than it takes to describe. Ratso continues on as though nothing untoward had occurred; for him, it is commonplace action. This richly comic scene does not occur in the novel, but it is superb visual characterization.

An earlier scene also *pictures* Ratso's fine scheming mind. The plot details approximate Herlihy's narration. Ratso meets Joe in a bar (where Joe is recovering from the "lady with the French poodle" sequence). Ratso learns that Joe perceives himself as a hustler, a stud in the service of rich ladies. Schlesinger and Herlihy both utilize the irony of the hustler hustled. Ratso encourages Joe's fantasy; all Joe needs is proper "management," which, for a small fee, Ratso will provide. He tells Joe how he set up a similar fellow "just the other day," and adds that the other fellow really isn't much of a stud. Off they go to see Mr. O'Daniel, who will manage Joe. In a visual addition not in the Herlihy novel, Ratso waves toward a couple at a table, a man and a wealthy looking woman, and calls out, "Hiya Bernie, how ya doin', kid?" The implication is clear; Joe assumes that this is one of the men Ratso has set up in business. The audience can see, if Joe cannot, that "Bernie" is a complete stranger to Ratso.

In another scene created visually by the film director, Ratso and Joe walk past a telephone booth. Without interrupting his conversation, almost without missing a step, Ratso automatically slides into the booth and rattles the coin return, checking for forgotten dimes. Finding nothing, he swivels back out and continues along with Joe. The purely automatic action by Ratso is perfect cinematic characterization. Ratso is so well schooled in the minutiae of his daily grubbing that his routine scavenging is almost unconscious.

But Ratso is also complex. While both novel and film emphasize his ratlike ability to survive, both also recognize that the death of his father has left him desperately lonely. Nor is successful scavenging likely to ease his special need. In Herlihy's book, we learn about his father when Ratso speaks about him, a man who died as unimpressively as he lived, but who left at least one void. Schlesinger must modify the *telling*; the quicker pace of the film requires showing. So he invents a brilliant short sequence. The scene: a small cemetery in the city where Ratso takes Joe to visit the grave of his father. The sky is gray behind a small marble headstone. While Joe looks both uncomfortable and sympathetic, Ratso's words and appearance reveal him in a new light. In a close-up, the director demonstrates Ratso's strong and sincere emotion. But Schlesinger avoids a sentimentality that could destroy the film's credibility. In a master stroke, he has Ratso nab a floral offering from a nearby grave and place it on his father's. The gesture defines the character: emotional and exploitive. It also foreshadows the ironic film ending. Joe's loneliness has led him through suspicion of Ratso to concern, and finally, real affection. When Joe arrives at the readiness for a meaningful friendship, Ratso dies. When Ratso finds someone to give to and lean on, it is too late.

By expanding the role of Ratso and using quick intercut flashbacks to suggest much of Herlihy's first section on Joe's background, Schlesinger maintains the theme of loneliness—and even expands it—but changes the focus from Joe's story to an exploration of the relationships between Joe and Ratso and the city. The themes are universal; the plot and visual characterization are unique. A film must necessarily be concrete and individual. But extension of the unique to universality explains the richness of the film experience.

Technically, Schlesinger achieves his creation through several necessary transformations from the novel. In Herlihy's *Midnight Cowboy* Ratso first appears in chapter 6 of part two, almost midway through the novel. In the film, he appears in all but some twenty-five minutes of the 110-minute film. The director compresses and eliminates many of the particulars in part one, the section which explains *why* Joe is lonely and hungry for friendship. Yet Schlesinger retains essential clues. He shows, through quick flashbacks, Joe's fatherless boyhood and his sexual relationship with Annie, an illusion-ridden relationship that Herlihy describes didactically. Joe is illusion-prone and the novelist tells us so—literally. In one two-sentence paragraph, Herlihy completes a piece of narration with, "That was the way Joe imagined it. This is what actually took place."

Midnight Cowboy (1969) Ratso steals a floral offering to place on his father's grave. The gesture defines the character: emotional and exploitive. (© Copyright 1969 by United Artists Corporation; produced by Jerome Hellman; directed by John Schlesinger; screenplay by Waldo Salt.)

Schlesinger's compression gives the film a kind of tightly knit unity the book doesn't achieve. Necessary background is woven into the main stream of the plot through judicious juxtaposition. Herlihy's authorial intrusions, particularly on the subject of Joe's daydreaming and illusions, are replaced by sequences which create the fantasies visually.

Twice, in the short space of two pages, Herlihy suggests that the city is a force acting upon Joe and debilitating him, but he tends more often to use New York merely as the place in which his characters move. Using invented concrete examples, Schlesinger amplifies the concept

Midnight Cowboy (1969) Joe and Ratso are trapped by the city, which increasingly becomes a destructive, debilitating force. (© Copyright 1969 by United Artists Corporation; produced by Jerome Hellman; directed by John Schlesinger; sceenplay by Waldo Salt.)

of the city as an evil and destructive force. While Joe's innocence and naivete are apparent prior to his arrival in New York, the most destructive brutality and the most heinous experiences occur in the city itself. Indeed, it is the ever-colder city that has reduced Ratso to the dying parasitic exploiter we see and experience.

In the film, we twice see that Joe is capable of brutality. In each case, Schlesinger alters Herlihy's material. In the first instance, Joe allows a young homosexual to perform fellatio on him—for a price. The economic realities of the city already have begun to take their toll. When he finds that the young man has no money to pay him, Joe begins to rough him up. He quickly softens, though, recognizing that the boy is in terror, and allows him to leave. Through foreshadowing, Schlesinger demonstrates Joe's potential brutality. But in the novel, there is no violence; Joe never touches the boy. Herlihy makes a point ot it: "Joe looked at him hard, restraining an impulse to hit him across the face." Joe is angry, of course, and his impulse is to strike out, but he can still restrain himself.

In the second instance, Joe is consciously brutal, even sadistic, in his treatment of Towny. Joe allows Towny, a well-to-do homosexual, to lure him up to his hotel room. Joe's purpose — possibly a mitigating reason — is to get enough money to take the critically-ill Ratso to Florida. Towny resists giving him the money he needs, and Joe, desperate, decides to take it. He uses more force than necessary to take the money. At the end of the scene, Joe snatches the telephone from Towny and brutally jams the receiver into his mouth, hurting him badly, perhaps killing him.

In the novel, the scene plays differently. Joe (as in the film) is desperate for the money. But this time Towny encourages brutality; he is a masochist. The film hints at masochism only at the end of the sequence. In the novel, when Joe hits him, Towny is ecstatic: "I'm bleeding! Oh, thank God, I'm bleeding! I deserve to bleed!" When Joe realizes that Towny solicits and enjoys violence, it sickens him. Even the telephone is used differently; Herlihy explains that when Joe becomes brutal, it stems from fear and confusion. In the novel, as Joe begins to leave, Towny tries to use the telephone to call for help. Joe reacts by pulling the telephone out of the wall. In the meantime, Towny begins to run toward the door to call for help. Joe throws the receiver at him to stop him. Finally, when Joe stuffs the receiver into Towny's mouth, it is because:

> Joe still held in his mind the image of the man and the telephone, the telephone and the man, and in his confusion he still felt it necessary to subdue the two of them. He therefore pushed [Towny] to the floor, sat astride his chest, and shoved the telephone's receiver into the toothless mouth.

Schlesinger's portrait of Joe's capacity for brutality is not the only change he makes in Joe. He also supplies a significant addition which makes Joe seem more selfless than in the novel. After he successfully sells himself to Sylvia following the party, Sylvia calls a friend and recommends Joe to her. She agrees to sample his particular brand of service, and makes an appointment for later in the week. (Joe's "success" as a stud does *not* occur in the Herlihy novel.) Joe seems, finally, to be on his way to realizing his dream. He has been a success, and there is the promise, now, of a brighter future. Immediately after this scene, which Schlesinger added, Joe returns elated only to find Ratso ill, and decides to take him to Florida immediately. The function of this addition, then, is to underscore Joe's self-sacrifice, for, in a crucially ironic decision, he gives up precisely what he had sought in order to help a friend—his only friend.

Both Herlihy and Schlesinger envision individual humanity as a forceful agent for change. When Joe optimistically vows to earn enough money to take both Ratso and himself to Florida, Ratso's first response is one of incredulity. Does Joe really intend to take him along? Assured, he worries about Joe's actions. Not quite out of character, he warns Joe not to run foolish risks. Schlesinger enlarges upon Herlihy's brief indication in Ratso. His faltering invitation to Joe to share lodgings, his stealing a coat too large for himself, exposing his sentiment for his father: these all prepare the viewer for the change in Ratso.

If human caring for other human beings represents earthly salvation, Schlesinger presents the decadence of the city as antagonistic to such human trust and involvement. Schlesinger fills *Midnight Cowboy* with visions of decadence. In one scene, Ratso, cold and lonely, appears in front of a display window filled with elegant furs. Joe and Ratso share an unspeakable condemned tenement flat, without gas or electricity. Ratso's progressive illness accelerates with the oncoming of winter. Indeed, an icebox graces the apartment, not to keep food cold, but to keep the cockroaches out. To Schlesinger, the city is both degrading and vulgar. Before Joe loses his room and prized horsehide suitcase, the most dramatic image he sees from the window of his cheap hotel is a sign advertising Mutual of New York—M. O. N. Y.—which is how Joe thinks "money" is spelled. It is the city which strips Joe of his illusions, forcing him to sell himself to homosexuals, and to become increasingly brutal. The viewer experiences the degrading force of the city because the film's visual images are specific, powerful, and immediate.

The closing film sequences maintain Schlesinger's dark view of the city's corrupting power. On the bus to Florida, Joe discards his gaudy cowboy shirt symbolic of his earlier "stud" ambitions; he and Ratso wear new clothes bought by Joe. Ratso's shirt with palm trees symbolizes the final break from the bondage of New York. But Ratso dies on the bus—and the difference in emphasis between Schlesinger's film and Herlihy's novel becomes apparent. The closing lines of the book read:

> He [Joe] put his arm around him to hold him for a while, for these last few miles anyway. He knew this comforting wasn't doing Ratso any good. It was for himself. Because of course he was scared now, scared to death.

Herlihy has come full circle. The story is still Joe's and the didactic tendency of the novelist persists. But Schlesinger expands Herlihy's verbal suggestions to close his film with a series of superb visual shots: a close-up of Joe that takes the viewer into the guts of his feeling; other passengers gawking at the specter of death; an unconcerned woman powdering her nose (recalling the experience of the stricken man ignored by New York's hurrying throng). The final shot is from outside the bus, looking in at Joe and Ratso's body; the camera reveals Joe's pain. Reflected in the bus window we visualize the Miami (big city) skyline.

Are all dreams so ephemeral, so without hope of realization as Joe's? Schlesinger's final ambiguity—humanity coexistent with man's inhumanity—seems to tip in the direction of tentative hope for the human spirit. Joe Buck, despite the Miami skyline and his New York experiences, has come a long and human way since leaving Houston, Texas. In the film, his pain is not self-centered; love, not loneliness, symbolizes the human condition.

16

Allardyce Nicoll

FILM REALITY:
THE CINEMA
AND THE THEATRE

Professor Nicoll directed the Drama
Workshop at Yale and the Shakespeare
Institute at Stratford-on-Avon. He wrote
Film and Theatre in 1936, but as this
selection indicates, it reads like a contemporary classic. Extracts from his work
continue to appear in modern anthol-
ogies—and deservedly so.

. . . When we witness a film, do we anticipate something we should
not expect from a stage performance, and, if so, what effect has this upon
our appreciation of film acting? At first, we might be tempted to dismiss
such a query or to answer it easily and glibly. There is no essential
difference, we might say, save in so far as we expect greater variety and
movement on the screen than we do on the stage; and for acting, that,
we might reply, is obviously the same as stage acting although perhaps
more stabilised in type form. Do we not see Charles Laughton, Cedric
Hardwicke, Ernest Thesiger, Elizabeth Bergner now in the theatre,
now in the cinema? To consider further, we might say, were simply to
indulge in useless and uncalled for speculation.

190

Nevertheless, the question does demand just a trifle more of investigation. Some few years ago a British producing company made a film of Bernard Shaw's *Arms and the Man*. This film, after a few exciting shots depicting the dark streets of a Balkan town, the frenzied flight of the miserable fugitives and the clambering of Bluntschli onto Raina's window terrace, settled down to provide what was fundamentally a screen-picture of the written drama. The dialogue was shortened, no doubt, but the shots proceeded more or less along the dramatic lines established by Shaw and nothing was introduced which he had not originally conceived in preparing his material for the stage. The result was that no more dismal film has ever been shown to the public. On the stage *Arms and the Man* is witty, provocative, incisively stimulating; its characters have a breath of genuine theatrical life; it moves, it breathes, it has vital energy. In the screen version all that life has fled, and, strangest thing of all, those characters — Bluntschli, Raina, Sergius — who are so exciting on the boards, looked to the audience like a set of wooden dummies, hopelessly patterned. Performed by a third-rate amateur cast their life-blood does not so ebb from them, yet here, interpreted by a group of distinguished professionals, they wilted and died — died, too, in such forms that we could never have credited them with ever having had a spark of reality. Was there any basic reason for this failure?

THE CAMERA'S TRUTH

The basic reason seems to be simply this — that practically all effectively drawn stage characters are types and that in the cinema we demand individualisation, or else that we recognise stage figures as types and impute greater power of independent life to the figures we see on the screen. This judgment, running so absolutely counter to what would have been our first answer to the original question posited, may seem grossly distorted, but perhaps some further consideration will demonstrate its plausibility. When we go to the theatre, we expect theatre and nothing else. We know that the building we enter is a playhouse; that behind the lowered curtain actors are making ready, dressing themselves in strange garments and transforming their natural features; that the figures we later see on the boards are never living persons of king and bishop and clown, but merely men pretending for a brief space of time to be like these figures. Dramatic illusion is never (or so rarely as to be negligible) the illusion of reality: it is always imaginative illusion, the illusion of a period of make-believe. All the time we watch Hamlet's throes of agony we know that the character Hamlet is being impersonated by a man who presently will walk out of the stage-door in ordinary clothes and an autograph-signing smile on his face. True, volumes have been written on famous dramatic characters — Greek, Elizabethan English and modern Norwegian — and these volumes might well seem to give the lie to such assumptions. Have not Shakespeare's characters seemed so real to a few observers that we have on our shelves books specifically concerned with the girlhood of his heroines — a girlhood the dramas themselves denied us?

These studies, however, should not distract us from the essential truth that the greatest playwrights have always aimed at presenting human personality in bold theatric terms. Hamlet seizes on us, not because he is an individual, not because in him Shakespeare has delineated a particular prince of Denmark, but because in Hamlet there are bits of all men; he is a composite character whose lineaments are determined by dramatic necessity, and through that he lives. Fundamentally, the truly vital theatre deals in stock figures. Like a child's box of bricks, the stage's material is limited; it is the possibilities in arrangement that are well-nigh inexhaustible. Audiences thrill to see new situations born of fresh sociological conditions, but the figures set before them in significant plays are conventionally fixed and familiar. Of Romeos there are many, and of Othellos legion. Character on the stage is restricted and stereotyped and the persons who play upon the boards are governed, not by the strangely perplexing processes of life but by the established terms of stage practice. Bluntschli represents half a hundred similar rationalists; the idealism of thousands is incorporated in Sergius; and Raina is an eternal stage type of the perplexing feminine. The theatre is populated, not by real individuals whose boyhood or girlhood may legitimately be traced, but by heroes and villains sprung full-bodied from Jove's brain, by clowns and pantaloons whose youth is unknown and whose future matters not after the curtain's fall.

In the cinema we demand something different. Probably we carry into the picture-house prejudices deeply ingrained in our beings. The statement that "the camera cannot lie" has been disproved by millions of flattering portraits and by dozens of spiritualistic pictures which purport to depict fairies but which mostly turn out to be faintly disguised pictures of ballet-dancers or replicas of figures in advertisements of night-lights. Yet in our heart of hearts we credit the truth of that statement. A picture, a piece of sculpture, a stage-play — these we know were created by man; we have watched the scenery being carried in back stage and we know we shall see the actors, turned into themselves again, bowing at the conclusion of the performance. In every way the "falsity" of a theatrical production is borne in upon us, so that we are prepared to demand nothing save a theatrical truth. For the films, however, our orientation is vastly different. Several periodicals, it is true, have endeavored to let us into the secrets of the moving-picture industry and a few favored spectators have been permitted to make the rounds of the studios; but for ninety per cent of the audience the actual methods employed in the preparation of a film remain far off and dimly realised. "New York," we are told,

struts when it constructs a Rockefeller Center. A small town chirps when it finishes a block of fine cottages. The government gets into the newspapers for projects like Boulder Dam. It takes Hollywood approximately three days to build Rome and a morning to effect its fall, but there is very little hurrah about it. The details are guarded like Victorian virtue.

There is sound reticence on the part of a community that is usually articulate about its successes. Hollywood is in the business of building illusion, not sets. . . . The public likes to feel that the stork brought *The Birth of a Nation*. It likes to feel that a cameraman hung in the clouds — mid-Pacific — the day that Barrymore fought the whale.

That audience, accordingly, carries its prejudices with it intact. "The camera cannot lie" — and therefore, even when we are looking at Marlene Dietrich or Robert Montgomery, we unconsciously lose sight of fictional surroundings and interpret their impersonations as "real" things. Rudolph Valentino became a man who had had innumerable Sheikish adventures, and into each part she took the personality of Greta Garbo was incorporated. The most impossible actions may be shown us in a film, yet Laurel and Hardy are, at their best, seen as individuals experiencing many strange adventures, not as virtuoso comedians in a vaudeville act.

How true this is was demonstrated by a film, *Once in a Blue Moon*, which has been shown only in a few theatres. The general tone of *Once in a Blue Moon* was burlesque. In it was a "take-off" of certain Russian films, incidental jibes at a few popular American examples, and occasional skits directed at prominent players; Jimmy Savo took the rôle of Gabbo the Great while one of the actresses made up to look like Katherine Hepburn. The result was dismal. In Charlie Chaplin's free fantasy there is life and interest; throughout the course of *Once in a Blue Moon* vitality was entirely lacking. Nor was the reason far to seek. We cannot appreciate burlesque in the cinema because of the fact that in serious films actor and rôle are indistinguishable; on the stage we appreciate it since there, in serious plays, we can never escape from separating the fictional character and its creator. Stage burlesque is directed at an artistic method, generally the method employed by an individual player in the treatment of his parts. To caricature Irving was easy; hardly would a cinematic travesty of Arliss succeed. The presentation of this single film proved clearly the difference in approach on the part of cinema and theatre public respectively. These, so generally considered identical, are seen to be controlled by quite distinct psychological elements.

Charlie Chaplin's free fantasy has been referred to above. This, associated with, say, the methods of René Clair, might well serve to demonstrate the true resources of the film; comparison with the erring tendencies of *Once in a Blue Moon* brings out clearly the genuine frontiers of the cinematic sphere. In *The Ghost Goes West* there was much of satire, but this satire was directed at life and not at art and, moreover, was kept well within "realistic" terms. Everything introduced there was possible in the sense that, although we might rationally decide that these events could not actually have taken place, we recognized that, granted the conditions which might make them achievable, they would have assumed just such forms as were cast on the screen. The ghost was thus a "realistic" one, shown now in the guise of a figure solid and opaque and now in that of a transparent wraith, capable of defying the laws of physics. In a precisely similar way is the fantasy of the Chaplin film bound up with reality. We know that the things which Charlie does and the situations in which he appears are impossible but again, given the conditions which would make them possible, these are the shapes, we know, they would assume. Neither René Clair nor Charlie Chaplin steps into the field occupied by the artistic burlesque; neither are "theatrical." The former works in an independent world conceived out of the terms of the actual, and the latter, like George Arliss in a different sphere, stands forth as an individual experiencing a myriad of strange and fantastic adventures.

The individualising process in film appreciation manifestly demands that other standards than those of the stage be applied to the screen-play. In the theatre we are commonly presented with characters relatively simple in their psychological make-up. A sympathetically conceived hero or heroine is devoted in his or her love affairs to one object; at the most some Romeo will abandon a visionary Rosaline for a flesh-and-blood Juliet. For the cinema, on the other hand, greater complexity may be permitted without loss of sympathy. . . .

The strange paradox, then, results: — that, although the cinema introduces improbabilities and things beyond nature at which any theatrical director would blench and murmur soft nothings to the air, the filmic material is treated by the audience with far greater respect (in its relation to life) than the material of the stage. Our conceptions of life in Chicago gangsterdom and in distant China are all colored by films we have seen. What we have witnessed on the screen becomes the "real" for us. In moments of sanity, maybe, we confess that of course we do not believe this or that, but, under the spell again, we credit the truth of these pictures even as, for all our professed superiority, we credit the truth of newspaper paragraphs.

TYPE CASTING

This judgment gives argument for Pudovkin's views concerning the human material to be used in a film — but that argument essentially differs from the method of support which he utilised. His views may be briefly summarised thus: — types are more desirable in film work because of the comparative restrictions there upon make-up; the director alone knows the complete script and therefore there is little opportunity for an individual actor to build up a part intelligently and by slow gradations; an immediate, vital and powerful impression, too, is demanded on the actor's first entrance; since the essential basis of cinematic art is montage of individual shots and not the histrionic abilities of the players, logic demands the use of untrained human material, images of which are wrought into a harmony by the director.

Several of the apparent fallacies in Pudovkin's reasoning have been discussed above. There is, thus, no valid objection to the employment of trained and gifted actors, provided that these actors are not permitted to overrule other elements in the cinematic art and provided the director fully understands their essential position. That casting by type is desirable in the film seems, however, certain. Misled by theatrical ways, we may complain that George Arliss is the same in every screen-play he appears in; but that is exactly what the cinema demands. On the stage we rejoice, or should rejoice, in a performer's versatility; in the cinema unconsciously we want to feel that we are witnessing a true reproduction of real events, and consequently we are not so much interested in discerning a player's skill in diversity of character building. Arliss and Rothschild and Disraeli and Wellington are one. That the desire on the part of a producing company to make use of a particular "star" may easily lead to the deliberate manufacturing of a character to fit that star is true; but, after all, such a process is by no means unknown to the theatre, now or in the past. Shakespeare and Molière both wrote to suit their actors, and Sheridan gave short sentimental scenes to Charles and Maria in *The School for Scandal* because, according to his own statement, "Smith can't make love — and nobody would want to make love to Priscilla Hopkins."

To exemplify the truth of these observations no more is demanded than a comparison of the stage and screen versions of *The Petrified Forest*. As a theatrical production this play was effective, moving and essentially harmonised with the conventions applying to its method of expression; lifeless and uninteresting seemed the filming of fundamentally the same material. The reasons for this were many. First was the fact that the film attempted to defy the basic law which governs the two forms; the theatre rejoices in artistic limitation in space while the film demands movement and change in location. We admire Sherwood's skill in confining the whole of his action to the Black Mesa but we condemn the same confining process when we turn to see the same events enacted on the screen. Secondly, since a film can rarely bear to admit anything in the way of theatricality in its settings, those obviously painted sets of desert and mountain confused and detracted from our appreciation of the narrative. A third reason may be sought for in the dialogue given to the characters. This dialogue, following the lines provided for the stage play, showed itself as far too rich and cumbersome for cinematic purposes; not only was there too much of it, but that which sounded exactly right when delivered on the boards of the theatre (because essentially in tune with theatrical conventions) seemed ridiculous, false and absurd when associated with the screen pictures. Intimately bound up with this, there has to be taken into account both the nature and the number of the *dramatis personae*. Sherwood's stage characters were frankly drawn as types—an old pioneer, a killer, an unsuccessful littérateur, an ambitious girl, a veteran, a business-man, a businessman's wife—each one representative of a class or of an ideal. Not for a moment did we believe that these persons were real, living human beings; they were typical figures outlining forces in present-day society. This being so, we had no difficulty in keeping them all boldly in our minds even when the whole group of them filled the stage. When transferred to the screen, however, an immediate feeling of dissatisfaction assailed us; these persons who had possessed theatrical reality could have no reality in the film; their vitality was fled; they seemed false, absurd, untrue. Still further, their number became confusing. The group of representative types which dominated the stage proved merely a jumbled mass on the screen. . . . A Leslie Howard whose stage performance was right and just became an artificial figure when, before the camera, he had to deliver the same lines he had so effectively spoken on the stage. From the lack of individualisation in the characters resulted a feeling of confusion and falsity; because of the employment of conventions suited to one art and not to another vitality, strength and emotional power were lost.

PSYCHOLOGICAL PENETRATION

The full implications of such individualisation of film types must be appreciated, together with the distinct approach made by a cinema audience to the persons seen by them on the screen. Because of these things, allied to its possession of several technical devices, the cinema is given the opportunity of coming into closer accord with recent tendencies in other arts than the stage. Unquestionably, that which separates the literature of today from yesterday's literature is the former's power of penetrating, psychoanalytically, into human thought and feeling. The discovery of the sub-conscious has opened up an entirely fresh field of investigation into human behaviour, so that whereas a Walter Scott spread the action of a novel over many years and painted merely the outsides of his characters, their easily appreciated mental reactions and their most obvious passions, James Joyce has devoted an extraordinarily lengthy novel to twenty-four hours in the life of one individual. By this means the art of narrative fiction has been revolutionised and portraiture of individuals completely altered in its approach.

Already it has been shown that normally the film does not find restrictions in the scope of its material advantageous; so that the typical film approaches outwardly the extended breadth of a Scott novel. In dealing with that material, however, it is given the opportunity of delving more deeply into the human consciousness. By its subjective method it can display life from the point of view of its protagonists. Madness on the stage, in spite of Ophelia's pathetic efforts, has always appeared rather absurd, and Sheridan was perfectly within his rights when he caricatured the convention in his Tilburina and her address to all the finches of the grove. On the screen, however, madness may be made arresting, terrifying, awful. The mania of the lunatic in the German film, M, held the attention precisely because we were enabled to look within his distracted brain. . . .

Regarded in this way, the cinema, a form of expression born of our own age, is seen to bear a distinct relationship to recent developments within the sphere of general artistic endeavour. While making no profession to examine this subject, one of the most recent writers on *This Modern Poetry*, Babette Deutsch, has expressed, *obiter dicta*, judgments which illustrate clearly the arguments presented above. "The symbolists," she says, "had telescoped images to convey the rapid passage of sensations and emotions. The metaphysicals had played in a like fashion with ideas. Both delighted in paradox. The cinema, and ultimately the radio, made such telescopy congenial to the modern poet, as the grotesqueness of his environment made paradox inevitable for him.". . .

If the cinema has thus influenced the poets, we realise that inherently it becomes a form of art through which may be expressed many
of the most characteristic tendencies in present-day creative endeavour.
That most of the films so far produced have not made use of the peculiar
methods inherent in the cinematic approach need not blind us to the fact
that here is an instrument capable of expressing through combined visual
and vocal means something of that analytical searching of the spirit
which has formed the pursuit of modern poets and novelists. Not, of
course, that in this analytic and realistic method are to be enclosed the
entire boundaries of the cinema. The film has the power of giving an
impression of actuality and it can thrill us by its penetrating truth to
life: but it may, if we desire, call into existence the strangest of visionary
worlds and make these too seem real. The enchanted forest of *A Midsummer Night's Dream* will always on the stage prove a thing of lath and
canvas and paint; an enchanted forest in the film might truly seem
haunted by a thousand fears and supernatural imaginings. . . .

That the cinema has ample opportunities in this direction has been
proved by Max Reinhardt's *A Midsummer Night's Dream*, which, if un-
satisfactory as a whole and if in many scenes tentative in its approach,
demonstrated what may be done with imaginative forms on the screen.
Apart from the opportunity offered by Shakespeare's theme for the
presentation of the supernatural fairy world, two things were specially
to be noted in this film. The first was that certain passages which, spoken
in our vast modern theatres with their sharp separation of audience and
actors, become mere pieces of rhetoric devoid of true meaning and
significance were invested in the film with an intimacy and directness
they lacked on the stage. The power of the cinema to draw us near to an
action or to a speaker served here an important function, and we could
at will watch a group of players from afar or approach to overhear the
secrets of a soliloquy. The second feature of interest lay in the ease
with which the cinema can present visual symbols to accompany language. At first, we might be prepared to condemn the film on this ground,
declaring that the imaginative appeal of Shakespeare's language would
thereby be lost. Again, however, second thoughts convince us that much
is to be said in its defence; reference once more must be made to a subject already briefly discussed. Shakespeare's dialogue was written for
an audience, not only sympathetic to his particular way of thought and
feeling, but gifted with certain faculties which today we have lost.
Owing to the universal development of reading, certain faculties possessed by men of earlier ages have vanished from us. In the sixteenth
century, men's minds were more acutely perceptive of values in words
heard, partly because their language was a growing thing with constantly
occurring new forms and strange applications of familiar words, but

largely because they had to maintain a constant alertness to spoken speech. Newspapers did not exist then; all men's knowledge of the larger world beyond their immediate ken had to come from hearing words uttered by their companions. As a result, the significance of words was more keenly appreciated and certainly was more concrete than it is today. When Macbeth, in four lines, likened life to a brief candle, to a walking shadow and to a poor player, one may believe that the ordinary spectator in the Globe theatre saw in his mind's eye these three objects referred to. The candle, the shadow and the player became for him mental realities. . . .

The theatre, however, can only do so much. It may visually create the setting, but it cannot create the stimulus necessary for a keener appreciation of the imagic value of Shakespeare's lines. No method of stage representation could achieve that end. On the screen, on the other hand, something at least in this direction may be accomplished. In *A Midsummer Night's Dream* Oberon's appearance behind dark bespangled gauze, even although too much dwelt on and emphasised, gave force to lines commonly read or heard uncomprehendingly — "King of Shadows," he is called; but the phrase means little or nothing to us unless our minds are given such a stimulus as was here provided. Critics have complained that in the film nothing is left to the imagination, but we must remember that in the Shakespearean verse is a quality which, because of changed conditions, we may find difficulty in appreciating. Its strangeness to us demands that an attempt be made to render it more intelligible and directly appealing. Such an attempt, through the means of expression granted to the cinema, may merely be supplying something which will bring us nearer to the conditions of the original spectators for whom Shakespeare wrote.

Normally, however, verse forms will be alien to the film. Verse in itself presupposes a certain remoteness from the terms of ordinary life and the cinema, as we have seen, usually finds its most characteristic expression in the world that immediately surrounds us. The close connection, noted by Babette Deutsch, between cinematic expression and tendencies in present-day poetry will declare itself, not in a utilisation of rhythmic speech but in a psychological penetration rendered manifest through a realistic method.

THE WAY OF THE THEATRE

If these arguments have any validity, then clearly a determined revision is necessary of our attitude towards the stage of today. That the theatre ought not servilely to follow cinematic methods seems unnecessary of proof, even although we may admit that certain devices of the film may profitably be called into service by playwright and director. . . .

When the history of the stage since the beginning of the nineteenth century comes to be written with that impartiality which only the viewpoint of distant time can provide, it will most certainly be deemed that the characteristic development of these hundred odd years is the growth of realism and the attempted substitution of naturalistic illusion in place of a conventional and imaginative illusion. . . .

The film has such a hold over the world of reality, can achieve expression so vitally in terms of ordinary life, that the realistic play must surely come to seem trivial, false and inconsequential. The truth is, of course, that naturalism on the stage must always be limited and insincere. Thousands have gone to *The Children's Hour* and come away fondly believing that what they have seen is life; they have not realised that here too the familiar stock figures, the type characterisations, of the theatre have been presented before them in modified forms. From this the drama cannot escape; little possibility is there of its delving deeply into the recesses of the individual spirit. That is a realm reserved for cinematic exploitation, and, as the film more and more explores this territory, does it not seem probable that theatre audiences will become weary of watching shows which, although professing to be "lifelike," actually are inexorably bound by the restrictions of the stage? Pursuing this path, the theatre truly seems doomed to inevitable destruction. Whether in its attempt to reproduce reality and give the illusion of actual events or whether in its pretence towards depth and subtlety in character-drawing, the stage is aiming at things alien to its spirit, things which so much more easily may be accomplished in the film that their exploitation on the stage gives only an impression of vain effort.

Is, then, the theatre, as some have opined, truly dying? Must it succumb to the rivalry of the cinema? The answer to that question depends on what the theatre does within the next ten or twenty years. If it pursues naturalism further, unquestionably little hope will remain. . . . We admire the playhouses of Periclean Athens and Elizabethan England; in both a basis was found in frank acceptance of the stage spectacle as a thing of pretence, with no attempt made to reproduce the outer forms of everyday life. Conventionalism ruled in both, and consequently out of both could spring a vital expression, with manifestations capable of appealing not merely to the age in which they originated but to future generations also. Precisely because Aeschylus and Shakespeare did not try to copy life, because they presented their themes in highly conventional forms, their works have the quality of being independent of time and place. Their characters were more than photographic copies of known originals; their plots took no account of the terms of actuality; and their language soared on poetic wings. To this again must we come if our theatre is to be a vitally arresting force. So long as the stage is bound by the fetters of realism, so long as we judge theatrical characters by reference to individuals with whom we are acquainted, there is no possibility of preparing dialogue which shall rise above the terms of common existence.

From our playwrights, therefore, we must seek for a new foundation. . . . Boldly must they turn from efforts to delineate in subtle and intimate manner the psychological states of individual men and women, recognising that in the wider sphere the drama has its genuine home. The cheap and ugly simian chatter of familiar conversation must give way to the ringing tones of a poetic utterance, not removed far off from our comprehension, but bearing a manifest relationship to our current speech. To attract men's ears once more to imaginative speech we may take the method of T. S. Eliot, whose violent contrasts in *Murder in the Cathedral* are intended to awaken appreciation and interest, or else the method of Maxwell Anderson, whose *Winterset* aims at building a dramatic poetry out of common expression. . . . The poetic play may still lag behind the naturalistic or seemingly naturalistic drama in general esteem, but the attention paid in New York to Sean O'Casey's *Within the Gates* and Maxwell Anderson's *Winterset* augurs the beginning of a new appreciation, while in London T. S. Eliot's *Murder in the Cathedral* has awakened an interest of a similar kind. Nor should we forget plays not in verse but aiming at a kindred approach; Robert Sherwood's *The Petrified Forest* and S. N. Behrman's *Rain from Heaven*, familiar and apparently realistic in form, deliberately and frankly aim at doing something more than present figures of individuals; in them the universalising power of the theatre is being utilised no less than in other plays which, by the employment of verse dialogue, deliberately remove the action from the commonplaces of daily existence. . . .

THE WAY OF THE FILM

For the film are reserved things essentially distinct. Possibility of confusion between the two has entered in only because the playhouse has not been true to itself. To the cinema is given a sphere, where the subjective and objective approaches are combined, where individualisation takes the place of type characterisation, where reality may faithfully be imitated and where the utterly fantastic equally is granted a home, . . . where a visual imagery in moving forms may thrill and awaken an age whose ears, while still alert to listen to poetic speech based on or in tune with the common language of the day, have forgotten to be moved by the

tones of an earlier dramatic verse. Within this field lies the possibility
of an artistic expression equally powerful as that of the stage, though
essentially distinct from that. The distinction is determined by the
audience reactions to the one and to the other. In the theatre the spectators are confronted by characters which, if successfully delineated,
always possess a quality which renders them greater than separate
individuals . . . . All the well-known figures created in tragedy and
comedy since the days of Aristophanes and Aeschylus have presented in
this way the lineaments of universal humanity. If the theatre stands thus
for mankind, the cinema, because of the willingness on the part of spectators to accept as the image of truth the moving forms cast on the screen,

Hamlet (1948) ". . . reality may faithfully be imitated, and the utterly fantastic
equally granted a home." (Still by courtesy
of The Rank Organization, Ltd.)

stands for the individual. . . . The sense of reality lies as the foundation of the film, yet real time and real space are banished; the world we move in may be far removed from the world ordinarily about us; and symbols may find a place alongside common objects of little or no importance. If we apply the theory of "psychological distance" to the theatre and film we realise the force of each. For any kind of aesthetic appreciation this distance is always demanded; before we can hope to feel the artistic qualities of any form we must be able to set ourselves away from it, to experience the stimulus its contemplation creates and at the same time have no call to put the reactions to that stimulus into play. This distance obviously may be of varying degrees; sometimes it is reduced, sometimes it provides a vast gulf between the observer and the art object. Furthermore the variation may be of two kinds—variation between one art and another, and variation between forms within the sphere of a single art. Music is further removed from reality than sculpture, but in music there may be an approach towards commonly heard sounds and in sculpture abstract shapes may take the place of familiar forms realistically delineated. Determination of the proper and legitimate approach will come from a consideration of the sense of distance between the observer and the object; the masterpieces in any art will necessarily be based on an adaptation to the particular requirements of their own peculiar medium of expression.

Applying this principle to theatre and cinema, we will recognise that whereas there is a strong sense of reality in audience reactions to the film, yet always there is the fact that the pictures on the screen are two-dimensional images and hence removed a stage from actual contact with the spectators. What may happen if successful three dimensional projection is introduced we cannot tell; at present we are concerned with a flat screen picture. This gulf between the audience and the events presented to them will permit a much greater use of realism than the stage may legitimately employ. The presence of flesh-and-blood actors in the theatre means that it is comparatively easy to break the illusion proper to the theatre and in doing so to shatter the mood at which any performance ought to aim. This statement may appear to run counter to others made above, but there is no essential contradiction involved. The fact remains that, when living person is set before living person—actor before spectator—a certain deliberate conventionalising is demanded of the former if the aesthetic impression is not to be lost, whereas in the film, in which immediately a measure of distance is imposed between image and spectator, greater approaches to real forms may be permitted, even although these have to exist alongside impossibilities and fantastic symbols far removed from the world around us. This is the paradox of cinematic art.

Herein lies the true filmic realm and to these things the cinema, if it also is to be true to itself, must tend, just as towards the universalising and towards conventionalism must tend the theatre if it is to find a secure place among us. Fortunately the signs of the age are propitious; experiments in poetic drama and production of films utilising at least a few of the significant methods basically associated with cinematic art give us authority for believing that within the next decade each will discover firmer and surer foothold and therefore more arresting control over their material. Both stage and cinema have their particular and peculiar functions; their houses may stand side by side, not in rivalling enmity, but in that friendly rivalry which is one of the compelling forces in the wider realm of artistic achievement.

17

Albert R. Cirillo

THE ART
OF FRANCO ZEFFIRELLI
AND SHAKESPEARE'S
ROMEO AND JULIET

An English Renaissance scholar, Cirillo's article endorses Franco Zeffirelli's film adaptation of *Romeo and Juliet*. Writing in *TriQuarterly*, a Northwestern University journal, he refutes critics who objected to the many deletions. Cirillo understands the film medium and links the youth and ardor of Zeffirelli's tragic figures to the spirit of an early Shakespearean play.

We shall have done one braver thing than all the Worthies did when we can understand that a truly creative artist with imagination and insight can do more to make a classic live and breathe than we ever can with all of the scholarly and critical skills available to us. Once we have come to this understanding, unlike Donne's lover whom I have just irreverently paraphrased, perhaps we should not keep it hid. This ability to make a classic live is no more apparent than in Franco Zeffirelli's screen version of Shakespeare's *Romeo and Juliet*; and I hope that in the following pages my readers will remember that I *am* talking about a film, not a stage performance. Failure to distinguish the different demands of stage and film has frequently led to bad films being made of good plays, even of great stage performances (Olivier's recent *Othello* is a case in point). Just as often, failure on the critic's part to realize the different demands of the different mediums has led him to find a film wanting in those qualities which it really should not have if it is to be successful *as a film*. What might be a virtue in one medium is not necessarily a virtue in the other. In the theater where the audience is distant from the action on stage, where certain things simply cannot be staged because of the physical limitations of even the best equipped theater, we need dialogue and expository scenes to explain events and provide transitions. In a film, which can and should be more flexible, which can and does give us that sense of closeness and intimacy by which the expression on an actor's face as well as his gestures can be pregnant with significance, many of the words and scenes necessary on the stage are merely a detriment.

Even if we allow the mistaken theory that every one of his plays automatically provides a good script, transferring Shakespeare from stage to film does not always lead to success. It is to Franco Zeffirelli's credit (he has worked successfully for both stage and screen) that he has recognized and used the differences between stage and film to make his *Romeo and Juliet* one of the most unified films ever made. Although he and his script-writers have cut the play more than many would like, the cuts are essentially cinematic; they make the story move as a film. *Romeo and Juliet* is a play of Shakespeare's artistic youth, full of poetic excesses in imagery and language that he was later to outgrow and refine; cutting should not, therefore, be regarded as tampering with holy writ. Because it is a play about the joy and pain of youthful love it has become enormously popular, even overfamiliar; for it can still speak to us about the basic truths of experience, but not when, as so often happens in the theater, they are made incredibly distant and alien by the kind of stodgy treatment which makes the play an object of idolatry rather than an intimate and shared experience.

One has only to recall the version which Hollywood filmed during the '30s. Unless my memory of a recent revival fails me, the text was presented virtually uncut. Nearly every line was there, literally filmed, and reverently pronounced by mature actors. It was an extremely dull movie, a museum performance of what was obviously regarded as a museum piece in one of Hollywood's occasional, ceremonious bows to "culture," that remains memorable only for the Mercutio of John Barrymore, then in the twilight of his career. At least one of the major difficulties with this version was its too strict adherence to the text, which made its adaptation to film, in spite of an elaborate production, a superficial one at best. Hollywood wanted to prove to the professional Shakespeareans that it had the proper reverence towards that poet whom we have made a distant god. This kind of literalism Zeffirelli has thrown to the winds as unessential to his medium; he understands and makes part of his design precisely the kind of effect which can be achieved by a perfect synthesis of color and sound, of visual and aural techniques. In short, he understands the differences between a filmed play and a play adopted and adapted to a visual medium in such a way that visual as well as aural techniques become poetic, or, if you prefer, in such a way that poetic techniques are realized in visual and aural terms; the film is, in this respect, one of the perfect examples of the historic cultural phenomenon which Fr. Walter Ong and Marshall McLuhan have been analyzing at some length during the last decade: the transference of a verbal mode to a visually oriented culture. Zeffirelli shows that his apprenticeship to the great Luchino Visconti has not been in vain. From his master he has learned that suggestive blending of color, of groupings, and of pictorial composition, of gesture and movement, that every viewer of Visconti's stage and screen productions recognizes as contributory to the tone of a work.

Examples will illustrate what I mean about this use of visual communication particularly as it is related to cuts in the text as they contribute to the pacing of the film. In the play, Romeo's first appearance, announced by Benvolio shortly after the opening fray between the Capulets and the Montagues, leads into a long discussion of Romeo's obvious melancholy, the cause of which is, we learn only after some discussion, his infatuation with Rosaline. It takes a long expository dialogue filled with the kind of wit-writing typical of Shakespeare at this stage of his career to reveal this. Romeo is the romantic young lover, the expository scene suggests, in love with love. Indeed, the name of his infatuation, Rosaline, should immediately alert one to its potential symbolic character. By Shakespeare's time *Rosaline* had become almost a stock name for the object of a young male's affection; she is that which one loves. Yet, Zeffirelli eliminates all of this in the film; no mention is made of Rosaline until the later scene with Friar Laurence, after Romeo has decided to marry Juliet. The reason for this omission is simple, but subtly handled. On the stage where visual communication would be vitiated by the distance, both actual and psychological, between the audience and what is transpiring on the stage, we need to have these relationships articulated. In a film, they can be communicated with more immediacy without dialogue. What is important in the Rosaline business is simply that Romeo is ripe for love; he is a romantic young dreamer, an idealist ready for Cupid's arrow. In the space of a short but exquisitely beautiful scene, Zeffirelli communicates this visually.

As Romeo first enters the film, immediately after the opening battle, he is in the distance, coming up one of those quaint, narrow streets so common in the Italian hill towns. The camera pans in on him through a soft-focus lens; he is dressed in deep blue (Romeo wears blue or blue tones throughout the film; it is the color associated with him), and the scene is suffused with a bluish tint. Up the street he walks with a slight, youthful jaunt, oblivious of his surroundings, a rather silly, sickly-sweet, moonish smirk on his face as he smells a flower which he holds in his hand. All of this action is orchestrated in the sound track by a predominance of wind instruments playing, in hauntingly melancholic strains, a theme which will recur when he first sees Juliet at the Capulet ball. With this scene — which could be played convincingly only by a very young actor (a mature actor would look rather ridiculous trying to appear sheepish while smelling a flower) — we need no lengthy dialogue to tell us what is wrong with Romeo. We have *seen* his malady in his appearance, in his gestures, in his movement. He is quite clearly in a romantic dream-world. The soft-focus lens, the bluish hues, as well as the music, are used, not to make an already very young actor look younger, but to surround him with the soft, dreamy quality of his romantic illusions, to suggest, better and more effectively than any dialogue could, the emotional state of this *young* man. When, later in the same scene, he tosses his flower away angrily after seeing evidence of the battle he has missed (". . . what fray was here?/Yet tell me not, for I have heard it all./Here's much to do with hate . . ."), the simple gesture of tossing aside the flower tells us immediately that he wants nothing to do with a feud that represents values alien to him.

In the second half of the film (all that follows the wedding sequence) Zeffirelli cuts Juliet's famous "Gallop apace, you fiery-footed steeds" speech as well as her potion scene, that favorite of auditioning actresses. These scenes are, of course, highlights of any stage performances, moments for which we wait as an opera buff waits for a virtuoso aria. They can be very effective in the theater, but even a reasonably casual viewer may notice that in this half of the film Zeffirelli is increasing the pace of the action to suggest and heighten the sense of a swift movement towards the inevitable tragic climax of the crypt scene; all of the forces of circumstance are propelling the lovers towards that moment in the crypt when they will miss one another (and a possible happy ending) by a breath. Zeffirelli uses his medium to suggest this: he cuts rapidly from one scene to another. The potion scene (which, I understand, was actually filmed but cut from the final print), even if well done, would have dragged terribly here; it would have been an isolated moment rather than part of a unified design.

When Zeffirelli cuts Juliet's brief scene alone after she has dismissed the nurse, following the powerful confrontation with her father about her refusal to marry Paris, it is not only because the cut contributes to this "pacing," but because the scene is wholly unnecessary. In it Juliet tells us that she will no longer trust the nurse ("Thou and my bosom henceforth shall be twain"); but we do not need to be *told* this since we have seen disillusionment and maturity registered on Juliet's face, "heard" it in the music that italicizes those facial expressions to make this one of the most graphic scenes in the film. As the nurse answers Juliet's desperate request for advice and counsel with the suggestion that she should marry Paris and abandon Romeo to his exile, Juliet suddenly grows up before our eyes with the realization that her only companion among her elders is a hypocrite. The camera focuses on Juliet's youthful but serious face as it reacts to every line the nurse speaks; the eyebrows arch when the nurse calls Romeo a dishclout to Paris; the mouth sets firmly as the nurse tells Juliet that this match excels her first, blessing herself in what we have come to recognize as one of her habitual gestures even from her first scene. All of these details expose the nurse—with whom Juliet has been closer than with any adult—as a hypocrite, and we can chart this realization on Juliet's face, hear it in the tone with which she tells the nurse to "go in" as she forcefully shoves back the curtains of her bed, significantly, pulling away from the nurse's attempt to *touch* her sympathetically. This is to transfer to visual terms what needs to be verbalized on the usual stage.

When Romeo sees Juliet for the first time at the Capulet ball, we know he is originally looking for another girl who is no girl in particular; his face and manner tell us so. As the camera lingers on a very Italianate lady dancing gaily in the foreground he seems to have found her. Immediately, something happens. With the face of this nameless lady (obviously Rosaline) still in the foreground, a swirl of crimson velvet comes around a pillar behind her, and suddenly the face of Rosaline blends into, becomes, the face of Juliet—that incredibly beautiful face with its large, melting eyes, and olive-toned skin, which Zeffirelli seems to have cut out of a Botticelli. *The* moment has arrived. There have been no real transitions, either verbal or visual, because Zeffirelli can rely on an audience acclimatized to the cinema and its techniques where explicit transitions are not necessary. In visual terms, he has shown us the indefinable, general object of a young man's erotic awakenings yield to the particular object, a definite young lady who has already been identified for us a little earlier in the film. Juliet becomes the particular of which the nameless (in this film) Rosaline is the general, all without dialogue, in a series of frames so incredibly beautiful that the viewer wishes they would remain on the screen forever. Repeating—as Juliet whirls into view—the music which accompanied Romeo's first appearance, now orchestrated as a typical Renaissance dance, joins or relates the two scenes in a way similar to that in which a poet suggests the relation of one scene to another through the use of recurrent imagery.

The entire ballroom sequence is one of the masterpieces of the film. Here—as throughout the film—Zeffirelli and his cinematographer, Pasqualino De Santis, display that uncanny sense of color and pictorial quality that seems to give the film different textures to suit different scenes, from the grainy quality of the duel sequences which capture the bright yellow glare and dry dusty atmosphere of a hot Italian afternoon, to the smoky quality of the ball sequence here, with its shadows and lights suffused through a burnished gold patina splashed with crimson velvets, pink and yellow satins. Never have textures been so closely reproduced on a screen; one can almost see the nap of the velvets and feel the sheen of the silks and satins; and in the breathtaking long-shots during the dancing one feels one remembers this scene hanging on the wall of some forgotten European art gallery. Zeffirelli makes the scene a lengthy series of images in which Romeo and Juliet, after having seen one another, seek one another for some time before they exchange their first words (at face value, the bare printed text would suggest a more immediate exchange of words).

Zeffirelli had demonstrated this visual technique in a somewhat cruder form in *The Taming of the Shrew*, an unrepresentative test, however, since the built-in interest provided by the participation of the Burtons, man and wife, was somewhat distracting. Nevertheless, the earlier film revealed that Zeffirelli knew how to make a play into a film, knew how to make use of the medium in such a way that the material became part of it. He absorbed the play into the film and broke the ground for his greater and more difficult achievement in *Romeo and Juliet* where he fuses his cinematic elements into a unified work of art which moves to an inexorable conclusion of overwhelming pathos that made capacity London audiences file out of the theater in stunned silence, in spite of the predictable mixed reactions of ultra-conservative film critics. He has worked carefully to produce this impression and the techniques are cause for admiration.

If, in *The Taming of the Shrew*, Zeffirelli cleverly merged the public personalities of his stars with the personalities of Katerina and Petruccio (Elizabeth Taylor and Richard Burton do, after all, fit nicely into the image of a flamboyant shrew tamed by the clever and virilely boisterous rowdy), we never really could forget that it *was* Elizabeth Taylor and Richard Burton, super-stars, up there on the screen. That is perhaps what we most enjoyed about the film—the implicit identification of one with the other. By choosing two complete unknowns for his Romeo and Juliet, however, Zeffirelli makes an even greater effect, for we view them with no outside associations, no image of public personalities whose Rabelaisian wanderings through the fashionable spas have provided picaresque reading in the tabloids. These actors have no existence until the film begins, when they *are* simply Romeo and Juliet, an illusion deliberately heightened by the suspension of the cast credits until the very end of a film which begins with a brooding shot of a bright-yellow, hazy Verona basking in the glare of an Italian summer sun. While the prologue is intoned by a solemn voice (which sounds suspiciously like Olivier's) we are given only the main credits, the title, the director, little else.

There is another significant fact about these actors: their youth, their approximation to the ages of the characters they play; and that is one of their principal virtues in spite of the controversy this has provoked among British film critics. It allows Zeffirelli to carry through his conception with perfect logic and plausibility, and it allows him to approach it afresh, without the standard, rigid Shakespearean style, almost completely eschewed here. By Shakespearean style I mean not that there is really a definitive, set way of acting Shakespeare, but what we have been conditioned to accept as proper Shakespearean acting by years of stifling reverence which has tended to make the plays monuments of stone. We have, for example, been so accustomed to seeing Romeo and Juliet played by mature, if accomplished, actors who make the recitation of the poetry an end in itself that the image of two actual teen-agers who have been directed to act naturally, to bring something of their own feelings and experience to the text and discard the customary rhetorical, golden-toned articulation, makes us a bit uncomfortable at first. They seem so young, like such children. But, then, this is the point. Romeo and Juliet are young; they are adolescents on the brink of experience, on the brink of consequences which their own guilelessness and innocence lead them to; we ought to have some awareness of this as it unfolds. The fact that we are moved, that we do laugh, that we are brought to the brink of tears, should demonstrate how right this conception is.

We are not just listening to the poetry; we are also seeing it, feeling it. One wants the *meaning* made relevant to a dramatic situation — here that of *youthful*, impetuous love — to a specific dramatic context, not solitary, virtuoso arias in which sheer sound hypnotizes us. Naturally the sonority of the poetry suffers somewhat, but it suffers in the interest of verisimilitude, particularly important in the close proximity and intimacy of a film. This means that actors whose voices and speech patterns, as well as whose appearance, suggest youth rather than maturity can be more convincing and moving than the tried and true Shakespearean veterans. Restoring the roles of Romeo and Juliet to the young—the very young—gives us actors who can not only bring the immediacy of their own experience and youth to the roles, but actors with still unformed voices which themselves become instruments to wring all of the youthful pathos out of the lines and scenes. These are actors who have a kind of intuitive understanding of the situation; who have not yet acquired the overly melodious voice, the mannered diction and approach that afflicted Renato Castellani's visually beautiful but badly miscast and misdirected film version of a few years ago.

Given his youthful protagonists Zeffirelli *can* make a film which shows, without embarrassment, what he has said he intended to show, the life and love of a young couple sacrificed to the outdated values of an older generation. In the overall framework of the film he accomplishes this in two general ways. First, he so structures the film that it falls into two natural, complementary halves. The first half, up to and including the wedding sequence, is youthfully exuberant, almost humorous and light in tone. It ends on a note of serene tranquility as the two are married in the golden hues of a quiet old church. The second half of the film, which begins immediately after the wedding, brings the lovers face to face with those factors in their environment which are working against their happiness from the beginning, factors personified in the neurotic (as portrayed in the film) Mercutio, whose restlessness is symbolized by his constant fiddling with his handkerchief, an object associated with him from his first scene where he uses it dramatically in the Queen Mab speech, and continues to use it in various ways, ultimately shielding his fatal wound with it until Romeo makes his challenge to Tybalt by rubbing this bloody object in his face. The headstrong Tybalt, and the willfulness of the older generation, particularly as seen in Lord Capulet, are other aspects of the lovers' environment which, though potential in the first half of the film, now become intrusive, and force the lovers to their tragic end.

This half of the film suddenly becomes serious when the brilliantly staged duel between Tybalt and Mercutio, which had begun (as Zeffirelli conceives it) as a playful joust, becomes fatal simply because Romeo, with the best of intentions, gets in the way. The fortunes of Romeo and Juliet which up to this point seemed in the ascendant are now suddenly reversed by a chance encounter for which Romeo himself is partially responsible, lending considerable force to his pitiful cry that he is fortune's fool. Certainly, the "interaction of ill-doing and ill-luck" which is the essence of this scene is "basic in the design of the play as a whole," as Harbage has said; but Zeffirelli's handling of the scene makes this potently clear in performance. The tragic seriousness of this half of the film is all the more effective because it is superimposed on our consciousness of the lighter tone of the first half with its indelible sense of youth.

On this point, I must say that the film was made to be shown with an intermission after the wedding scene. It was so shown in London where I first saw it some months ago, the lead-in to the second half, with the erratic Mercutio wandering aimlessly about the church square during the afternoon, being a gradual one, prepared for by introductory music and a slow fading into focus on the scene from the image of a broken circle which had also been projected on the screen at the beginning of the intermission, just after the fade-out on the wedding scene. In the American screening, this has been vitiated by the elimination of the intermission and a quick, rather jarring cut from the fade-out on the wedding scene to Mercutio's wandering, eliminating the projected image of the broken circle which I take to have some import. The intermission gave a respite at the best possible moment, providing a period of calm to prepare the audience psychologically for the second half of the film with its change and development of tone.

The second general way in which Zeffirelli underlines his contrast between the values of the young lovers and those of the older generation is implicit in the former's less accomplished articulation. All of the older characters in the film are more adept at handling language and verse than the young protagonists; they *are* more articulate: the Prince, who very majestically makes his first judgment from his white horse and, in the final scene, movingly pronounces against the two families; the mature, rich voice of the unseen narrator who speaks the prologue and the epilogue; the Montagues and the Capulets; and even Paris. Their means of communication is essentially verbal and articulate in accordance with the old rhetorical values. Yet, they achieve no real communication or relationship, Zeffirelli's direction suggests. Juliet's parents are, ever so subtly, shown as unhappily married. When we first see Lady Capulet, it is as Lord Capulet looks at her sourly through a window, across the distance of a courtyard (the image of separation and distance here is telling), warning Paris that women too early wed are too soon marred. Discordant chords sound as Lady Capulet returns his sour look, closing her window haughtily.

In her first full scene, shortly after, she is shown as a vain, impatient woman who barely has time for or interest in her daughter even to discuss something so important as a possible marriage. With its color and quality of a Flemish painting this scene, accompanied by gentle lute and recorder music, is only one of many such scenes of exceptional beauty in the film. Lady Capulet repeatedly primps herself, looks in the mirror, and seems nervous about, and virtually incapable of, talking to her daughter. Referring to her own early marriage (we have already learned that she was marred by it), she is the image of a mature, yet still attractive woman (she is cast younger than the customary Lady Capulet), early and unhappily married to an older man, just ready for a young lover. The suggestion that she is having an affair with her nephew, Tybalt, is quite clearly made in the intimacy with which she can calm him down at the ball (Zeffirelli helps this by giving her a line or two here that belong to Lord Capulet in the text), in the incredibly aggressive stance of her grief at his death, with her vehement cries for vengeance on Romeo. *She* is always quite articulate — except with her young daughter — even musical in her speech. So, too, is Lord Capulet, whose only interest, in the final analysis, is shown not to be the happiness of his daughter, but the "I'll not be forsworn" attitude which he expresses in his anger at Juliet's refusal to marry Paris, an attitude which seems to be part of the code of his generation. He has given his word in promising Juliet to Paris and that is what is important. Thus, we see Juliet in a familial circle which is not a harmonious one and with which she has no real communication.

The Montagues, who have less to say in this film, say it well; but we never see Romeo with them. In contrast to Juliet, he does not seem to exist in a family. Like most Italian males he aimlessly wanders the streets, either alone or with his friends (both Tybalt and Mercutio, too, generally move about the streets with a group of young friends); and Zeffirelli's management of the scene in which the nurse comes to learn of Romeo's arrangements for the wedding is the epitome of this Italianate vision. Romeo and his friends seem to haunt the central square, passing remarks at itinerant females of every age. Here, the nurse, with her elaborate regalia and haughty stance, is the focus of attention as Romeo and his friends greet her, in unison, with "A sail, a sail!" deflating her obvious pretensions to grandeur, particularly in the bawdy exchange which follows. Romeo has no home, no family, it would seem, except these companions — and Friar Laurence with whom his relationship, as Zeffirelli's direction shows, bridges the age gap between them.

There is some significance in the fact that the Friar has been both tutor and companion to Romeo since the latter's childhood (he refers to Romeo as "pupil mine"); Friar Laurence thus seemingly combines youth and age. He is at once Romeo's brother and father — both the younger and the older generations. His whole relationship to Romeo, Zeffirelli shows as that short of camaraderie which exists between young men who are close friends. It is an intimate relationship expressed in gesture and action rather than words. Friar Laurence playfully pulls Romeo's hair, lovingly and gently slaps him, shakes his head several times. Romeo can giggle, the way one can at one with whom one is close, when the Friar trips after telling the impatient Romeo, "They stumble that run fast."

All of this suggests an intimate bond of instinctive communication between friends and companions. Yet, Romeo's courtly gesture in bowing to let the nurse precede him from the church after he has told her of his plan to marry Juliet, as if to make amends for her rough treatment by him and his friends earlier; his impulsive throwing of a kiss to the crucifix when he realizes that he and Juliet will be wed, show that he has learned what the Friar had to communicate as a superior—manners, and the kind of religious background that would make an ardent young man throw a kiss to the crucifix when his love is about to be sanctified by the church. Even later, when the Friar chides him severely, striking him hard for his suicidal gesture after learning of his banishment, it is the kind of action that communicates love rather than disaffection. That Romeo understands this is vividly suggested by his impulsive kissing of the Friar's hand, through his tears, as he leaves to ascend to Juliet's chamber on the Friar's orders. These gestures are of Zeffirelli's devising and consistent with an interpretation which emphasizes a gap between the young and the old which cannot be mediated by words. The kind of relationship Romeo has with the elder Friar Laurence simply does not exist between Romeo and his family, nor between Juliet and hers.

What Zeffirelli suggests is that the means of communication between the young, or those who understand the young, is not essentially words, as it is for the older generation, but gesture and action. Romeo and Mercutio, for example, seem to establish their rapport not through the words they speak to one another, but through action and gesture. During his dynamically staged and spoken Queen Mab speech (which makes that speech indicative of Mercutio's restlessness rather than a static recitation) Mercutio shakes Romeo understandingly; and when Mercutio fades off in seemingly vacant ravings, Romeo touches and embraces him; their heads meet in understanding and communication. As Mercutio is propelled to the Capulet ball by their companions, leaving Romeo behind, the two extend their hands out to one another.

The epitome of this kind of communication is seen in Romeo's relationship with Juliet. The beautiful, lengthy sequence by which they come together at the ball is done with looks and gestures long before they exchange a single word; they see one another; they touch one another while dancing; they look at one another across a closed circle of their elders, make their way around the circumference of that circle to make their first contact through the touching of their hands as Romeo grabs Juliet's left hand from behind a pillar. The playful little flirtatious sequence which follows, in which Shakespeare is flaunting his wings in youthful wit-writing, is essentially oblique in its language. The two speak indirectly of pilgrims and shrines—all of the time touching hands in rather ceremonious fashion—one of Zeffirelli's most inspired pieces

of business in the film; for when Romeo first sees Juliet she is using her
hands, palms held up, in the dance. Romeo can hardly refrain from
touching her, and this is visible. In spite of their seeming inarticulateness, their inability to speak well—at least as well as traditional Shakespearean actors would—one has probably never had so complete a sense
of their immediate, almost intuitive contact with one another. They really
do not need the words, as young lovers seldom do. Zeffirelli has his
Romeo almost literally *breathe*, in a tone of hushed ecstasy, the final
words of his lines to Juliet as he kisses her hand:

> If I profane with my unworthiest hand
> This holy shrine, the gentle sin is this,
> My lips two blushing pilgrims ready stand
> To smooth that rough touch with a tender *kiss*.
>
> (my italics)

Kiss is the important word here: gesture, action are the effective
expressions of one's feelings and thoughts. And it is the kiss on the lips,
later, that seals this rapport. This touching of hands is one of the most
repeated gestures in the film; it recurs, with the vows of their love, in
the balcony scene; and as they part at the end of that scene, the camera
focuses on their hands extended towards one another until they sub-
sequently back away from one another with their hands raised in a thrown
kiss. At their last parting, as Romeo descends the balcony to go into
exile, they again stretch their hands out to one another.

The young can achieve through gesture and action what the old
have been unable to achieve through words roundly uttered. This is
what makes the balcony scene one of the highlights of the film, and
probably one of the most refreshing balcony scenes ever staged, for it
fits in with the overall production; it does not stand in isolation as the
purple passage everyone waits for. It is played between two very young
people obviously eager to touch one another, eager for one another even
in the hazardous circumstances of the meeting, not as a scene between
two accomplished actors self-conscious of their facility in handling iambic
pentameter; and it is not played as a piece before which we must genu-
flect as before a sacred, and ever so distant, religious scene. For once
Romeo is really young enough to climb balconies, to swing from trees,
so that these actions seem genuine projections of his youthfulness.
All of the customary "dignity," the "high seriousness" is gone, because
it does not belong there.

As Romeo enters the garden to escape his tipsy companions, the
sound-track is silent. Suddenly, he sees a light, and with the famous
"What light through yonder window breaks?" the camera begins to pan

Romeo and Juliet (1968) "Gesture, action are the effective expressions of one's feelings and thoughts. . . . This touching of hands is one of the most repeated gestures in the film." (Still courtesy Paramount Pictures Corporation)

through the trees just as we hear the barking of a dog in the distance. The effect of the distant barking in the silent orchard is almost magical — like the whistle of a train or a ship in the night — a remote, lonely sound, followed by the beginning, very softly, of a rather rapturous musical theme that develops while the camera moves through the trees to the spot of light. To the ringing of a distant church bell the foliage parts, revealing Juliet bathed in white light against the dark blue background of the night. Now the ringing of church bells occurs in six scenes of the film (four of which are significant here), each time with specific dynamics to dictate a specific effect. The bell is first heard when Romeo, on his way to crash the Capulet ball, has misgivings about the outcome. In one of the most haunting passages in the play, he says:

. . . . . . my mind misgives
Some consequence, yet hanging in the stars,
Shall bitterly begin his fearful date
With this night's revels, and expire the term
Of a despised life closed in my breast,
By some vile forfeit of untimely death.
But he that hath the steerage of my course
Direct my sail.

He is in the church square; the bell begins to toll as he utters the
word "death," causing him to look in the direction of the church when
he speaks his last line and a half. The ringing of the bell in the immediate
vicinity gives a heavy foreboding quality which underlines his sense of
dread. Each of the other times (except the balcony scene) the church bell
rings, it is in the immediate vicinity of the action and conveys the same
scene of foreboding: when Romeo is banished, and when the two lovers
are laid to rest at the end of the film. Only in the balcony scene is the
ringing distant; and that distance softens both its sound and its effect,
making it one of promissory ecstasy; it becomes evocative and romantic,
sweetly melancholy. When the foliage opens on the bright radiance of
Juliet to the romantic notes of distant bells, a few hundred years of
romantic symbolism *do* have an effect whether we are aware of the
progeny or not. These are the same bells which rang, and this is the
same light which shone, when Beatrice appeared to Dante, when Laura
appeared to Petrarch, when a whole series of apparently divine beauties
who became petrified in literary convention appeared to ardent young
lovers who just happened to be poets. Romeo's subsequent reference
to her as a "bright angel" places her in this line; and the omission of
the overfamiliar passage beginning with "It is the East, and Juliet is the
sun" (already trite when Shakespeare wrote it, as his audience would
probably have recognized) is not really felt because we have seen it
projected on the screen.

As played here the balcony scene assumes all of the exuberance
and passion one would associate with two young people in love. Obviously, in Zeffirelli's conception, Romeo is anxious to touch Juliet.
With Romeo's sign, "It is my lady; O it is my love," it becomes clear
that he has all he can do to keep from making himself known. Later, he
is all motion, leaps, and gestures; he climbs a tree, leaps onto the edge
of the balcony towards Juliet with a deep sign when she tells him she
is indeed "too fond." Zeffirelli suggests, with engaging subtlety, that
Juliet is the more articulate one here, is really in command of the situation, as she should be, as the lady in these romantic situations really
always was. Even as she—with studied coyness—tells Romeo that she

should have been more strange, looking down demurely, yet furtively glancing at his reaction, she is clearly controlling his response. At the nurse's interruption of their embraces with her repeated calling from within, Juliet's command of things is concretely, humorously, suggested by the way in which she grabs Romeo's sleeves to move him along the rim of the balcony, tantalizingly pulling herself back just as he is about to complete another kiss; yet she commands him to "be true," to "stay but a little," she will come again. For all of her obvious girlishness this Juliet is in charge of a properly boyish, ardent Romeo. His inarticulateness—he can finish his oath, "If my heart's dear love . . ." only by grabbing Juliet and smothering her with kisses at which she repeats her delightful giggle—his awkwardness when he bumbles out of the bushes, earlier in the scene, to reveal his presence while blurting an uncalled-for

Romeo and Juliet (1968) Flirtatiousness, youth, charm, and girlish vitality contrast with the sobriety of the older people. (Still courtesy Paramount Pictures Corporation)

response to her musings, suggest perfectly the adolescent in a passionate situation which probably has no real precedent for him, for his previous infatuation with another has undoubtedly been much less close and intense than this.

Important in this scene, as it is throughout the film, is Juliet's deep-throated but girlish giggle. Zeffirelli uses it to suggest her youth and charm, to evoke in an instant that girlish vitality which would enrapture a Romeo. In fact, this giggle had been established as a kind of *leitmotif* for her in our first distant glimpse of Juliet when her father and Paris glanced at her through a window across the courtyard of the Capulet home. There she was playing with the nurse, and her giggle drifted across the courtyard to enrapture the watching Paris. It contrasted with the immediately subsequent image, through another window, of her mother, whose sour expression was underlined by discordant, flatting chords in the background. Juliet's giggle, on the other hand, becomes a kind of charming harmony that surrounds her even at the ball when the giggle accompanies her raising of her arms to shake the tiny bells she has put on for the Moresque dance. All of this exuberance, all of this charming bumbling, can only be effective because the actors are young enough not to seem ridiculous. With such actors it works, so that Romeo's question when Juliet takes her first good night, "Wilt thou leave me so unsatisfied?" becomes the impatient question of an impetuous young lover at the height of passion, as it should be, rather than, as it so often appears, a call for more mellifluous poetry.

II

Let me now try to suggest, in rather broad strokes, the kind of pattern Zeffirelli develops in the film through a synthesis of sound, color, and music, by recalling three particular scenes: the wedding scene, the crypt scene, and the final funeral, in order to show how he relates one to the other so as to build towards his final catharsis. The wedding scene, as I pointed out earlier, really ends the first half of the film. It would seem to be the culmination of the lovers' romantic dreams, for in spite of the split in the adult world around them, they have, with the help of two members of that world — the nurse and Friar Laurence — managed to form their own circle of love. The image of the circle takes on special importance in this scene as the culmination of a series of circle images established earlier. During their first meeting at the ball, Romeo and Juliet had danced in concentric circles whirling in opposite directions. Shortly after, one of the principal musical motifs of the film is established when

Romeo and Juliet (1968) The lovers have formed their own circle of love, and the image of the circle takes on special importance. (Still courtesy Paramount Pictures Corporation.)

a young man stands at the center of a circular design on the floor surrounded by a circle of guests, the circle around which Romeo and Juliet
move to come together. The song which the young man sings is about
youth and love. As Romeo moves around the circle the camera lingers
briefly on various older faces listening with nostalgic expressions to
this song of youth and its fading. The series of patterns suggests that
the young exist either at the center of a circle to which elders look
longingly from a distance, or outside the circumference of that circle
where they must meet to form their own circle. In the wedding scene,
where they will actually be united, where the whirling concentric circles
in which they passed one another will become one, the floor of the
church is covered with mosaics which form circular patterns.

   In this scene Zeffirelli has calculated every detail to emphasize the
childlike quality, the youth, and innocence of the two lovers. The cos-
tuming of the two — Romeo is again wearing blue tones, and Juliet is in
a pale, very simple costume that makes her look exceptionally tiny and
childlike — is one factor. Romeo's hair is carefully, noticeably, trimmed
and shaped, very neatly and boyishly combed. The importance of this
otherwise negligible detail may be measured by his appearance in the
following scene in which he appears in the church square immediately
after his wedding. His hair is then longer, very unkempt, and ragged.
An ordinary director, with an obvious emphasis on false realism, would
have taken pains to have Romeo's appearances match in the two scenes
(which were obviously filmed at two very different periods). But this
is not what is important to Zeffirelli, a director who so consistently
emphasizes visual communication for its symbolic qualities. What
is important is that Romeo, as well as Juliet, in this climactic scene
of the first half, be made to seem as childlike and innocent as possible.
This is why their impulsive "smooching" when they run to meet one
another in the church, with Friar Laurence trying to hold them apart, is
so charming. They *are* children — at least symbolically — hardly aware of
the implications of what they are about to do; they *are* innocent. In the
second half of the film, where they are forced into maturity, their appearance becomes somewhat older — Romeo has ragged hair, even a
distinct beard when Balthazar comes to inform him of Juliet's death.
The final effect in the wedding scene is achieved by camera angles and
lighting as well as atmospheric music. As the two kneel, *within* one of
those mosaic circles, bathed in the radiant white and gold tones of the
church, unable to be really serious even at this solemn moment (Romeo
knowingly pokes Juliet with his elbow), the voice of a single choir-boy
is heard in the echoing tones of a haunting theme in sacred measures.
As Friar Laurence begins the cermony the camera takes and *holds* a
medium shot as if to impress this image on our memories. What we see —

in one of the most unforgettable moments of the entire film — is two tiny, innocent children, radiantly happy, surrounded by an aura of peace. As originally shown (with an intermission at this point) this shot was held, like a still-life, for a few brief minutes until it faded into the image of the broken circle, mentioned earlier, while the curtains slowly closed. This emphasis on their youth and innocence increases the pathos of the second half where that circle of love is immediately penetrated (the broken circle was flashed on the screen again at the beginning of the second half) by the adult world, and the young lovers are suddenly, visibly, forced into maturity.

In the crypt scene, where the lovers take their last farewell of one another, Zeffirelli weaves his pattern more closely. When Romeo, looking at the drugged Juliet whom he believes to be dead, says "Why art thou yet so fair?" we realize how right Zeffirelli was to cast a very young actor in the part. For the effect here depends on the nature of the youthful male voice, still unformed, still uncertain. It breaks on this question; it wavers, falters with the naturalness of youth that brings home to the audience with heartbreaking immediacy the sense of a very young love, a youthful passion, about to be *unnecessarily* thwarted; *we* know why Juliet is still so fair: she is not really dead, and we wish we could tell Romeo that and avoid what is about to happen. With the beginning of Romeo's famous passage over Juliet's body ("Eyes look your last./Arms take your last embrace. And lips, O you/The doors of breath, seal with a righteous kiss/A dateless bargain to engrossing death.") the music that swells in the background is the same music heard at the wedding, now in a different tempo, and, of course, orchestrated. As Romeo dies with the words "Thus, with a kiss I die," instead of kissing her lips, as is customary (he has, in any case, just kissed them at the conclusion of the phrase "seal with a righteous kiss . . ."), he grabs and kisses the same hand he had kissed at the ball when he first met her. Just as at the ball, he has to wrench that hand loose (it is clasped on her breast in the attitude of the dead).

Later, after Romeo has expired, the camera focuses on that hand as it hangs over the bier until it suddenly begins to pulsate with life. The camera follows its movement up Juliet's body which its touch seems to bring to life. Only when that hand touches her eyes do they open — this awakening accompanied, one should notice, by the rapturous musical theme from the balcony scene. It is as if the force of Romeo's kiss, flowing from her hand through her body, brings her back to life. The kissing of the same hand that he had kissed when first they met connects the beginning of love (life) with the end of love (death), and perhaps new life.

The colors of the final funereal scene are stark blues, grays, and blacks. A mournfully howling wind, the solemn tolling of the church bell, torch flames spitting in the wind, underscoring the echoing footsteps of the mourners, are the only sounds. Only at the very end, after the Prince has made his solemn castigation of himself and the two families, when the voice of the narrator begins the epilogue (". . . never was a story of more woe . . .") does the music resume, softly and slowly, as the camera lingers on the two young bodies. The theme is the one heard at the wedding and again in the crypt scene to Romeo's last embrace. The second half of the film is thus balanced with the first: a death with a wedding, an end with a beginning. In fact, there is some suggestion that the lovers' death is a new beginning, that their sacrifice initiates a new era of peace, in the final image of the two families embracing and looking at one another understandingly during the final procession.

Having a musical theme, established in earlier, happier contexts, recur in a different tempo and orchestration at a tragic moment moves the audience profoundly in the way described by Dante's Francesca da Rimini: "Nessun maggior dolore/Che ricordarsi del tempo felice/Nella miseria" — "There is no greater sorrow than to recall happy times in times of sadness." With the recurrence of the musical theme, one scene, one moment, is filtered through another in our consciousness; one scene is infused with the emotional color of another. The effect depends on the integration of all of the elements of the film; but Zeffirelli has one final touch of the same order as the repetition of musical themes: the two lovers are buried in the same costumes they wore at their wedding. The solemnity of the Prince's final statement, the picture of the two very young, attractive bodies displayed, in death, in their wedding garments, all underscored emotionally by the sounds of silence modulated into a musical theme with earlier, happier associations, make the pathos of the final moments almost unbearable.

One could discuss other aspects. The beautifully paced bedroom scene, for example, is so carefully cut into after the highly charged scene in Friar Laurence's cell by having the sacred sounds of organ music modulate into the aubade of the lovers' awakening, the melody played on the organ being that of the Gregorian chant sung earlier by the monks in the church when Friar Laurence agreed to marry them. The whole scene is bathed in a soft, bluish tone which seems to radiate from the triptych of the madonna hanging opposite the bed: a tone which lends a soft, almost sacred quality to the scene, surely among the least sensual nude scenes ever put on film. Its purpose seems simply to make these very young, trapped lovers look like innocent babes asleep. Nino Rota's memorable score delicately, almost poetically, punctuates the dialogue and its pauses here (notice the effect of this "pacing" and the effect of the music as Romeo pauses to bend down to kiss Juliet after saying "night's candles are burnt out," to resume with "And jocund day/Stands tiptoe on the misty mountain tops" after the kiss).

Some of Zeffirelli's other touches are the highly original handling and development of the character of Mercutio; and most of all, the direction of Juliet's final moments with her faint little whimpers when she comes to the full realization that Romeo is dead, her "Thy lips are warm" after she kisses Romeo's mouth, just before showering his body with kisses, said so as to bring home the full force of her knowledge that he has only *just* died. Every aspect of the film is extraordinarily enriched by Nino Rota's musical score, which contributes to the effect by providing a kind of sonic coloring and punctuation that are complemented by the color photography itself.

All of these are details of sight and sound which, of course, do not impress themselves on one's consciousness at a single viewing. They are the elements which, together, make the unified impression. But, just as an intelligent reader of a good poem, wanting to know what makes the poem effective, rereads it, isolating those details that have contributed to the poem's power, so the intelligent viewer of a good film becomes aware of those techniques, those directorial touches, which have brought the film to life. Invariably, they will be details, seemingly inconsequential in isolation, which when wedded into a consistent, unified pattern provide the film's life force. Perhaps nowhere but in a film can so many details, so many effects, be so closely meshed when a director knows what he is about; and though I hate to use current, fashionable cant terms, I think that in this film Zeffirelli has certainly made the medium at least part of the message. And this, in essence, is all I have meant to suggest: that an inspired director can so make a work part of his medium that one becomes the other in a meaningful way. He can take what is today's most popular, perhaps even most significant, medium and make it a life-giving force for a work which has long been merely embalmed. For one of those rare times in the history of the cinema a man has so succeeded in harmonizing the means available to him that the result is a film which brings us closer to an immediate sense of the tragic pathos of this play than most stage versions could.

What, then, is Zeffirelli's art in this *Romeo and Juliet* — aside from his obvious ability to make a play into a real film? Quite simply, he has taken an old story, a story not only old in the sense of familiar, happening again and again throughout time, but a story old in the sense that, by our over-reverent attitude towards it, we have petrified it into an Elgin marble; he has taken this story and restored it to youth in every conceivable way. I mean, not that he has simply cast young actors in the leads (although it is the genuine youthfulness of his cast that

Romeo and Juliet (1968) (Still courtesy Paramount Pictures Corporation.)

makes all of the rest convincing and workable), but that he has *made* it young again, restored it to life and freshness. He has done what only the rarest scholars and teachers could do, brought to the story the ability to paint in the colors, in the music and sound of a modern medium, its meaning in the chiaroscuro light of the present and shade of the past simultaneously. Just as he has made almost every frame a Renaissance painting come to life, he has made the play live for us here and now as a kind of life we see around us every day. This is an art which makes the past present in terms of the past in such a way that both become one; an art by which he utilizes all of the techniques, the tools of his medium — sight, sound (not simply music, but sound-effects: bells, barking dogs, the hooting of an owl), color, photography, pictorial composition — in the way that a poet uses rhythm, rhyme, and recurrent imagery, to move us as most of us, perhaps, have never been moved by this play before.

Much of this is admittedly spectacle or pageantry, but it is spectacle or pageantry inspired by, indeed which proceeds from, the text, the kind of spectacle or pageantry by which a real director fills out the *implications* of the text.

All has been done in a series of images so intensely — almost painfully — beautiful that, even in this era of overlong, overblown movies, one wishes the all too short two and one quarter hours of this film had been longer; that, as one London viewer stated it, it would never end. Not the least of Zeffirelli's achievements is that he has shown us, in what Philip Sidney would have called "pregnant images of life," that Shakespeare's attitude towards romance is not stuffy tradition hardened into literary attitudes, but a truth of life that we all know or remember, a cycle that renews itself every day in the life that surrounds us, grows old and dies, only to renew itself again.

This will not be a *Romeo and Juliet* for the purest of the purists. If you are among those who must have your Shakespeare syllable perfect and line complete, who must visit *Romeo and Juliet* in a museum or library rather than in the streets around you, who must have it transferred *to* rather than recreated *in* a new medium; if what you want is a document, not a movie, then this is not for you. But when, and if, the time ever comes to decide who gave us the *Romeo and Juliet* Shakespeare wrote, and felt, as a young man feels the first real pangs of love, I do not think it will be the man who did the definitive edition, or the man who corrected that edition to give us the definitive-definitive edition, and so on down through the last cycle of scholarly time; it will be the man who gave the play life and vigor *even* in a new medium, who made it meaningful here and now; the man who gave it something of the immediacy it had when it was lived in the Verona of long ago, and reenacted in the London of some four hundred years ago. I think his name will be Zeffirelli, and perhaps it is he, after all, who has done one braver thing than all the Worthies did.

18

Donald P. Costello

PYGMALION

In *The Serpent's Eye: Shaw and the Cinema*
his study of George Bernard Shaw's relationships to film, Professor Costello
reveals the weaknesses of Shaw's film
theory. In this selection he details the
major concessions made by Shaw that
led to *Pygmalion* becoming a financial
and artistic movie success. One wonders
what Shaw's reaction would have been
to *My Fair Lady*, an even more romantic
treatment of the Pygmalion theme.

In 1937 a statement signed by Bernard Shaw appeared in a motion-
picture trade journal: "We are to have a British *Pygmalion* film presently.
Pascal Films have announced it. Wait and see. At all events, this time it
will be an authentic Shaw screen version." Behind that "authentic Shaw
screen version" lies a tale, a tale of a three-year tug of war between two
mighty wills and two mighty egos. Shaw and Pascal worked with one
another and against one another, but they were united in purpose in
one mighty crusade: to the cinema. . . .

    Only an examination of the changes which *Pygmalion* underwent
in its journey from stage to screen will show just how startling were the
concessions that Pascal was able to wring from Shaw. Shaw's partnership
with Gabriel Pascal moved him in his cinema practice far from his stated

cinema theory. Pascal knew that if the motion picture *could* depart from the restrictions of the stage, the audience would demand that it do so. A work of art is expected to move about freely within its own limitations, not to assume the limitations of another medium. Pascal was out to adapt *Pygmalion* to the motion picture medium, not to repeat the filmed-play disasters of *How He Lied to Her Husband* and *Arms and the Man.* The medium of the motion picture itself controlled the demands which Pascal, Anthony Asquith, and Leslie Howard made upon Shaw.

The most obvious difference between the screen version and the play version of *Pygmalion* is the large amount of new material written especially for the screen. Shaw himself admitted that Pascal talked him into writing "all the new scenes that the screen makes possible and that are impossible in the theatre." These new scenes numbered fourteen, plus a written prologue. Seven of these new scenes were retained in some form by Shaw when, in 1941, he published a new Penguin edition of *Pygmalion* "technically possible only on the cinema screen or on stages furnished with exceptionally elaborate machinery." But, contrary to the contention of several commentators, the actual sound track version of *Pygmalion* is very different in dialogue and picturization from that published screen version. Indeed, the published screen version is closer to the text of the play than it is to what is presented in the actual movie. Only an examination of the movie itself shows just how extensive, and how in keeping with the demands of the movie medium, were the changes which Shaw made, or at least allowed, in the filming of his play.

The film begins with this message flashed upon the screen:

> Pygmalion was a mythological character who dabbled in sculpture. He made a statue of his ideal woman, Galatea. It was so beautiful that he prayed the gods to give it life. His wish was granted. Bernard Shaw, in his famous play, gives a modern inter-pretation of this theme.

This prologue not only explains the significance of the film's title for the benefit of the unsophisticated movie audience, but, introducing the romantic music which occurs again and again throughout the film, and speaking as it does of a "beautiful" and "ideal woman," it establishes the emphasis on the Higgins-Eliza relationship, a romanticization which continues throughout the film and which climaxes — in the most startling Shaw concession of all — in the romantic ending.

After this prologue, the film opens with a new, visual scene, which lasts for a full four minutes without significant dialogue, and which succeeds in establishing — in purely visual terms — the feeling of the locale. The first shot is a close-up of a violet. The camera pulls back to reveal

Eliza holding her basket of flowers amid the hustle-bustle of a typical
Covent Garden scene; she is surrounded by a colorful crowd engaged in
inarticulate cockney chatter. Pickering approaches and listens, fascinated
and amused, to the conversation about him. Then Professor Higgins is
revealed, also listening interestedly. Suddenly thunder and lightning
begin, and the scene cuts to a shot of milling opera-goers seeking shelter
on the porch of a church next to the opera house down the street. The
dialogue then proceeds with Freddy calling for a taxi, as in the play.

At the end of what was Act I, the movie adds a second new visual
scene, this one lasting only twenty seconds. Yet in this short time the
scene succeeds in communicating—again in purely visual terms—the
atmosphere of Eliza's home neighborhood, just as the previous new
scene established the atmosphere of her working locale. While Eliza
and the taximan who has taken her home to Angel Court dispute over
the fare (the dialogue of this new scene was included in the published
screen version), the camera wanders about the narrow, dark court,
probing up and down the street and alley, showing an obvious slum, with
shots of garbage, dreary buildings, and an alley cat.

The third new sound track scene is, again, wholly visual. It is a
forty-five-second pantomime scene of Eliza in her room, but it is entirely different from the pantomime scene which Shaw included in the
printed movie version. That printed pantomime scene described, in
stage directions, states of mind which would have been almost impossible to convey visually:

> Eliza, chronically weary, but too excited to go to bed, sits,
> counting her new riches and dreaming and planning what to do
> with them. . . . This prodigal mood does not extinguish her
> gnawing sense of the need for economy sufficiently to prevent
> her from calculating that she can dream and plan in bed more
> cheaply and warmly than sitting up without a fire.

Instead, the sound track version shows Eliza dancing into her
room, and then, to the accompaniment of charming lilting music, waltzing
about, light and gay. She bustles about happily, stops to talk to her bird.
She goes over to her mirror, stares at herself reflectively, then piles her
hair on top of her head, duchess fashion, and makes aristocratic faces at
herself in her mirror.

Act II of the play began just after Higgins has shown his elaborate
phonetic equipment to Pickering. The movie creates a fourth new highly
visual scene to let us in on the show. This thirty-five-second scene fades
in on an extreme close-up of a lighted match. To the accompaniment of
busy, buzzing music, the screen shows, in montage, a gas flame being lit,

a flickering lamp spinning, a close-up of something that looks like radar to modern eyes. Higgins is seen in the foreground, pointing, explaining. Quick cuts throughout, then the camera moves to an extreme close shot of a human ear; the camera pulls back slowly to reveal that the ear is a cast model. Several quick shots of recording apparatus are then shown, making confusing chattering noises. Higgins speaks: "So you see, my dear Pickering, a perfect recording, amplified!" He then adds, "Well, tired of listening to sounds?" and the conversation continues as in the play.

The movie shows the preparations for Eliza's bath which took place off-stage in the play. The movie scene, which contains only nineteen lines of dialogue, is much more visual and much less verbal than the scene Shaw included in the published movie version, which includes sixty-five lines of dialogue. This fifth new movie scene lasts two minutes and is connected with the previous and subsequent scenes by cinematic continuity. After being told that she has to take a bath, Eliza, screaming and protesting inarticulately all the while, is pushed out of Higgins's drawing room by Mrs. Pearce. Higgins interrupts Eliza's shouts, and the camera zooms in for an extreme close-up of his face as he says to her, almost threateningly: "I will make a duchess out of you!" Her screams and protests continue on the sound track as the scene is wiped off the screen like a bulls-eye shrinking into a dot, which then quickly opens up again as Eliza, now out in the hallway, pleads with Mrs. Pearce for mercy and insists upon the unnaturalness of bathing. The camera follows Mrs. Pearce as she goes to the bathroom, where in a quick montage sequence, we see shots of water faucets, of steaming water, a big jar being emptied into the tub, all accompanied by ominous music. Eliza appears at the door of the bathroom in a big bathrobe, obviously Higgins's. Mrs. Pearce says, "Now come along. Take that thing off." Eliza replies, "Oh I couldn't, Mrs. Pearce: I reely couldn't. I never done such a thing." Mrs. Pearce bares Eliza's shoulders, as Eliza lets out still another whoop, and the camera pans quickly to a shot of the mirror, covered with steam. Eliza screams harder than ever, evidently having just seen herself in the mirror. A towel quickly covers the mirror just as the camera settles on it. Eliza's screams are deafening as a quick montage sequence shows shots of Eliza covered with soap, a close-shot of the shower head, then the water suddenly bursting out, steaming, right into the camera. At this, Eliza lets out the worst screech of all and then several long screams, as the sound dissolves into the sound of piano music taking up the rhythm of the screams, and at the same time the visual scene dissolves into a shot of Pickering and Higgins, talking, as in the play, of Higgins's character with respect to women.

At the very end of Act II, just before the tea-party scene in Mrs. Higgins's drawing room, the printed movie version creates a scene which begins with narration: "There seems to be some curiosity as to what Higgins's lessons to Eliza were like. Well, here is a sample." The sample given, a conventional stage conversation scene, was not the one used in the actual film. Instead, an entirely new visual scene, the sixth sound track addition, was created as an example of the lessons; and it was moved to a place immediately *after* instead of immediately *before* Eliza's tea-party failure. The highly impressionistic scene drastically telescopes time, and uses some extreme technical tricks — motion, music, editing, light — to heighten tension, to break the ordinary tone of reality, to make us believe that Eliza's ordeal is an unusual one and might well produce unusual results. Here is that scene, which lasts for four minutes and fifty seconds, but which has only a few lines of dialogue:

> *Fade-in to close-shot of the back of Eliza's head, throbbing, as if she is crying. The camera pulls back and reveals Eliza lying on a sofa with her face buried, her whole body wracked with sobs. In the background we hear, and then see, Higgins and Pickering shouting at one another:*
>
> PICKERING. Let's call the whole thing off.
>
> HIGGINS. Nonsense! I said I'd pass this gutter-snipe off as a duchess and pass her off as a duchess I will! [*Taking out a card*]. You see that? It's an invitation from the Transylvanian Embassy. I'm going to take her there!
>
> PICKERING. You're mad!
>
> HIGGINS. I tell you, Pick, that girl can do anything. [*Turning to Eliza*] Eliza! Eliza! Stop snivelling, girl! Eliza, I'll give you another chance. Will you work? [*Close-shot of Eliza, who looks up and smiles*].
>
> HIGGINS. Good! [*Close-shot of both their faces, framed together, slightly smiling, with a slight but unmistakable romantic suggestion*].

The scene dissolves into a long montage sequence, with Higgins's voice growing louder and sharper, accompanied by plodding and insistent music, as he demands, "NO! NO! NO!" He repeats, "NO! NO! NO!" and then, "Do it again! I've told you five hundred times! Once more!" Quick fades and cuts, showing much passage of time, and servants and teachers coming and going, coming and going. A tilted, dizzy camera cuts to Eliza, repeating Higgins's words to the accompaniment of a plunking xylophone, "How kind of you to let me come." Higgins pops several marbles into Eliza's mouth. Cut to Eliza in bed, reading *Etiquette*. Higgins comes in and orders her out of bed. Cut. Higgins and Eliza curtsy and then waltz. Pickering and Higgins dance with each other to instruct

Eliza. Quick cuts and fades throughout this entire scene, much of it in shadow and in silhouette. Eliza responds to Higgins's questions with a string of honorary titles: She says, "Your holiness." He shouts, "An Archbishop, not the Pope!" She whines and cries. In several quick cuts, Eliza practices more titles. Several more quick cuts of Eliza talking and studying furiously. Higgins cries, "If I can do it with a splitting headache, you can do it." The cuts and fades grow quicker and quicker until all is unintelligible and spinning; the music screeches, faster and faster, until SMASH. The camera suddenly stops and Eliza conks Higgins on the head with an icebag. Dissolve. Higgins says: "Send for dressmakers, hair-dressers, make-up artists, manicurists, and all the rest of those parasites." And the pace begins again, as the "parasites" come and go, in innumerable quick shots, at one place the shots succeeding one another in a star-flash fade. Then a close-shot of a foot being pedicured; the camera moves up the leg to a full view of Eliza—miserable, in a mud pack; the camera keeps moving into a shot of Higgins, eating placidly. Fade-out.

Immediately after this highly visual, cinematic lesson scene, the elaborate Embassy Ball scene, which was merely an off-stage garden party in the play, begins. The actual movie scene, as we would expect, is much more visual than the scene Shaw included in the printed movie version. In this long ten-minute, forty-second scene, the seventh new sound track scene, Eliza's triumph is communicated to the viewer in visual terms, with the sparse dialogue always secondary. The arrival of the elegantly dressed Eliza and Pickering and Higgins at the Embassy, in the rain, and the awed reaction of the crowd, is much as described in the printed movie version. As the Duchess arrives at the Embassy, the crowd bows. Next, Higgins, Pickering, and Eliza enter the Embassy, and the movie exploits its possibilities for spectacle: beautiful costumes, lovely music, dancing, the camera moving in waltzing motion, mirror scenes, lovely rooms. Higgins is accosted by his Hungarian pupil, called Aristid Karpathy in the sound track version, Nepommuck in the printed movie version, and referred to as Nepean—although he doesn't actually appear—in the play version. After Karpathy moves off, Eliza joins Higgins and Pickering. She looks frightened; she mutters "Ready" under her breath, and they are announced. The three walk up the stairs amid crowds of people: then Higgins hides behind a post, watching the crowd surround Eliza. As Eliza wanders about, and is introduced to the elegant crowd, everyone gazes at her admiringly. Much social chit-chat is heard, and much questioning about the identity of Eliza. Quick cutting throughout indicates the passage of time. In the background, a woman says, "She has such a proud look. As though she belongs at Covent Garden." An imposing woman asks, "My child, my son would very much like to dance with you." The son adds, "If I may be allowed the honor." Higgins and

Karpathy are seen separately taking in Eliza's triumph. Then Karpathy moves over to Eliza, and Higgins watches as they talk together. The camera shoots Eliza from a very low angle, thus making her look very imposing and regal. Eliza moves off, says to the hostess, perfectly, with the xylophone rhythm practiced in the lesson scene: "How kind of you to let me come." And the hostess responds with a gasp, overcome: "O my soul!" As Eliza turns to bow before the Duchess, the Duchess is heard to murmur, "Charming!" Higgins and Karpathy and the hostess then speculate about the identity of Eliza. Karpathy exults, as he did in the printed movie version, about her "air of divine right," and "those resolute eyes"; but in the film he adds the phrase, "those high cheek bones," especially appropriate to the very lovely Wendy Hiller. Finally Karpathy decides that Eliza must be a Hungarian princess. Pickering smiles happily. Higgins nods, satisfied. After several more elegant views and dynamic cuts, dazzling the viewer with all the spectacle, Eliza dances with a gentleman, and everyone backs up and makes room for them. The camera moves back from Eliza and the crowd, giving a spectacular panoramic view of the whole lovely ballroom, with Eliza in triumph at the center, as the lilting waltz music swells. The scene fades out.

The eighth and the ninth new scenes were included in the printed movie version (but in a more verbal form) as well as in the actual film. In the movie they are both short (twenty-five seconds; and one minute, fifteen seconds) transitional scenes establishing continuity between the play's Act IV and Act V. Act IV of the play version of *Pygmalion* ended with Eliza down on her hands and knees on the hearthrug looking for the ring which Higgins has violently dashed into the fireplace. In the movie, Eliza finds the ring, then flings it down on the dessert stand, and goes upstairs in a tearing rage. We then see a mooning Freddy, in montage, hopelessly waiting at the closed door to the Wimpole Street home. Suddenly Eliza comes out of the house, and, startled, shouts at Freddy, "What are you doing here?" "Nothing," he answers. "As a matter of fact, I spend most of my nights here. It's the only place I feel really happy." After a little dialogue, as in the printed movie version, about her plans to jump into the river, Freddy tells Eliza: "I think you're the most wonderful, the loveliest . . ." and he kisses her on the cheek, sighing. He says sheepishly, "You let me kiss you!?" "Well, why not?" demands Eliza. "Why shouldn't I let you? Why shouldn't you be good enough for me? Kiss me again! Kiss me again!!" Freddy answers pleasantly, "All right." And he does. Their street scene is interrupted by a disapproving constable, who remarks, "This isn't Paris, you know!" Eliza walks away haughtily, as the scene fades out.

The next new movie scene, the tenth, is also a transitional scene. It lasts one minute, thirty seconds. It shows Eliza walking alone in Covent

Garden, surrounded by a moody early morning haze. Nostalgic music from the ballroom is heard. A flower girl walks up to the fine lady Eliza and asks, in precisely the cockney dialect that Eliza had once used, "Buy a flower from a poor girl?" Eliza smiles, then, in a close-up, turns sad, and then turns angry. The play had narrated this scene in dramatic exposition much later in the story: In the play, Eliza told Pickering, "Last night, when I was wandering about, a girl spoke to me; and I tried to get back into the old way with her, but it was no use."

The scene cuts to Higgins and Mrs. Pearce in the Wimpole Street apartment. This is the eleventh new scene; this one, fifty seconds long. When Mrs. Pearce gives Higgins his morning coffee, he asks tartly, "Didn't Eliza tell you to bring tea?" "She didn't wait to tell me," replies Mrs. Pearce matter-of-factly, "she's gone." "Gone!" Higgins explodes, as he tumbles out of bed. He paces over to the table and around and around it at increasing speed. Suddenly he shouts, "Where the devil is my engagement book? What are my appointments?" He throws the papers from the table all about the room. Calmly, Mrs. Pearce replies, "I don't know." Threateningly, Higgins mutters, "If she isn't here, confound her. . . ." And Mrs. Pearce interrupts rationally, "Then you'd better *find* her." Higgins bellows, inspired: "We'll put an ad in the newspaper!" After a cut to show the passage of a few moments, Higgins yells into the telephone, "What! You can't help us find her? What are the police for, in heaven's name?" He slams the telephone down and then turns savagely to Mrs. Pearce: "Oh I don't care *what* becomes of her. . . . Where the devil could she be?" The scene fades out.

The twelfth new scene, only twenty seconds long, follows immediately. It shows Higgins and Pickering running frantically across a busy street in Covent Garden, searching. A succession of quick, short shots shows the desperation of their pursuit as the staccato camera cuts alternately to a fountain, bustle on the street, flower girls, more bustle. Higgins goes up to one of the flower girls and demands, "Have you seen Eliza Doolittle?" "Nyo," she replies haughtily. Fade-out. The scene then fades in to Higgins and Pickering running up a flight of stairs. The camera follows them as they burst into Mrs. Higgins's drawing room, and the movie continues with Act V of the play.

The thirteenth new movie scene is a one-minute interlude showing Higgins furiously stalking down the street after Eliza's departure from his mother's home.

The final new scene is the most famous and most startling of all the changes which Pascal wrung from Shaw. This two-minute scene, gives the film a romantic ending, in keeping with the increased romantic tone of the whole film. The play had ended ambiguously, with Higgins fully expecting Eliza to come back. But Shaw told us in an epilogue to the play that Eliza married Freddy. In the printed screen version, Higgins declares that Eliza will marry Freddy, and the epilogue confirms this. In the actual movie, Eliza and Higgins are reunited, although still somewhat ambiguously, when Eliza appears at the Wimpole Street apartment and Higgins asks her, incurably Higgins-like, "Where the devil are my slippers, Eliza?" There is no epilogue to the actual film. The movie's new final scene, like most of the cinematic additions, was used, incidentally, by Alan Jay Lerner in *My Fair Lady*. The many similarities of text explain why that fabulously successful musical play and, later, musical film, were presented "in association with Gabriel Pascal" and why the Pascal Estate, like the Shaw Estate, receives one per cent of the *My Fair Lady* profits. Shaw certainly did not intend all along to imply in his film that Higgins and Eliza are to be permanently united. In the early stages of the filming, Shaw, as we have already seen, was fearful that a romantic ending might be imposed upon him. Instead, he intended to show on the screen scenes from the play's epilogue where Eliza and Freddy, now married, are described in their flower shop. . . .

These fourteen new scenes represent a considerable total quantity of new material. Shaw's insistence that a movie could simply reproduce a play as it had appeared on the stage had been modified by his later admission that events which for practical reasons had to take place offstage could effectively be represented on the screen. Indeed, this admission brought into the film of *Pygmalion* new visual scenes which occupied thirty-one and a half minutes, out of a total playing time of eighty-five minutes. These new visualizations in the screen version of *Pygmalion* thus account for 37 per cent of the film's entire playing time.

The professional film makers who created the actual film of *Pygmalion* from a script which Shaw worked on and approved saw to it that this was not a mere recorded play. Shaw's theory of the cinema was simply not followed. In addition to the fact that over one third of the film consisted of new material, many other changes prove the fact that this *Pygmalion* exploited many filmic possibilities which the stage, of course, could not offer.

The film contains a good deal of visual material accompanying the dialogue, the filmic counterpart to "stage business." The film exploits the visual possibilities of this "stage business," however, for many effects which the stage, far-away, at a constant distance, without visual dynamism, could never duplicate. The film combines elements of spectacle and movement, speed and surprise, and musical and lighting virtuosity to create a visual excitement which parallels the emotional and intellectual excitement at such climactic scenes as Eliza's lessons and Eliza's triumph at the Ball; but the film also creates a visual excitement throughout, at less climactic moments, as the camera races about, often blurring in its speed, as it tries to keep up with a restless Higgins who is often chasing after a fearful Eliza, a restless Higgins who is always pacing, always playing with objects in his hands, paper-weights, apples, vases. This motion is compounded over stage motion, for when Higgins moves, the camera moves to keep up with him, and the observer has the illusion that he himself is moving. Motion is even more dramatically felt through the technique of cutting, as the observer constantly changes the distance and angle of his vantage point.

The cinema's increased powers of visualization accompanying the dialogue are used in *Pygmalion* for increased humor as well as for increased dynamism. This use of visual humor is shown most obviously in the famous tea-party scene at the home of Mrs. Higgins, the scene which provides Eliza with her first test. The wonderfully prim artificiality of the situation is established at the very beginning, with a lingering close-up of Clara Eynsford Hill and Eliza shaking hands by daintily rubbing two of their fingers together. Throughout the scene, all of Eliza's remarks are greeted with close-shots of varying facial reactions to her shocking sentences, subtle reactions which the stage could not force us to see. The scene is filled with long silent pauses while everyone frantically stirs his tea and we watch their faces. Thus, when the subject of weather comes up and Eliza adds two *new* lines — "The rain in Spain, they say, stays mainly in the plain," and "In Hampshire, Hereford, and Hartford, hurricanes hardly ever happen" — the camera slowly pans from face to bewildered face during an excruciatingly long pause, longer certainly than could have been maintained with interest on the stage. Similarly, when Eliza says, ". . . but my father he kept ladling gin down her throat till she came to so sudden that she bit the bowl off the spoon" we are treated to close-shots of both the exasperated Pickering and the shocked Vicar. Eliza's own later discomfiture is communicated by the close-shot of her puzzled face as she finds herself crippled with a cup in one hand and a plate in the other. After she finally gets rid of her plate, her frantic effort to succeed is shown by her imitating the whirlwind tea-stirring of the other guests, and by her holding out *all* her fingers, instead of just the little one, as she tries to drink. Finally, when Higgins signals Eliza that it is time to leave, she coolly replaces on the serving tray her half-eaten sandwich, as the camera catches the bulging eyes of Mrs. Eynsford Hill.

Much of the close-up visual humor is more fleeting than in the tea-party scene. Throughout the scene of Doolittle's first appearance, for example, he continually wheezes, as the others back away reeling from the smell, with expressions of utter asphyxiation on their faces. Mrs. Pearce at one time snatches a box of chocolates away from Higgins with the disapproving look of a den mother.

A third function is served by visual additions acting as an accompaniment to the dialogue: subtle editorial comments can be made by the position of the camera. It is an old cinematic trick to shoot a character from a high angle when he is dominated, to shoot him from a low angle when he is dominating. Thus, a very low camera and some dark shadows — a good exploitation of creative lighting as well as creative camera angle — make Doolittle very imposing, even frightening, when he says at his first appearance, "I come about a very serious matter, Governor." The most interesting camera-angle editorial comments are those which silently comment on the changing Higgins-Eliza relationship. When Higgins decides, "I shall make a duchess of this draggletailed guttersnipe," he stands over Eliza, as the camera shoots him from her angle, Higgins towering majestically high. When he tells her the conditions of her stay, "If you're naughty and idle you will sleep in the back kitchen among the black beetles . . .," he not only is shot from a low angle, but he even walks partway up the stairs so as to get still higher. And the ultimate step in camera angle as editorial commentator comes when Higgins says to Eliza, "If you refuse this offer you will be a most ungrateful and wicked girl," and he walks in front of her, blotting her completely out of view. The worm turns when finally, toward the end of the movie, Eliza asserts her newly found independence from Higgins. Then *she* is shot from a low angle, and she becomes the towering figure.

The framing power of the camera can make editorial comments as well as can its angle. Thus, early in the movie, as Higgins and Eliza haggle over the price of lessons, the camera suddenly shoots a close-up of the two of them, very close together, obviously framed into the shot. They are held there, framed together, with an unmistakable romantic suggestion.

Visual accompaniment in *Pygmalion* adds subtleties of character development, as well as visual excitement, humor, and editorial comment. The camera, of course, more efficiently and surely than any stage techniques, concentrates our minute attention on the character speaking, revealing subtleties in face or body as well as in word. But the camera can also concentrate our attention on the reaction of the character listening. Thus we are able to watch social experimenter Higgins becoming interested as Doolittle expounds his social philosophy regarding middle-class morality. And thus, in a more extended manner, during the whole of the scene in which Higgins ignores Eliza after her triumph at the Ball, the attention of the film viewer is concentrated on Eliza's reaction to the conversation, for *that* is what is essential to the theme, preparatory as it is to her rebellion and, consequently, to her finally coming to life as an independent soul. The scene begins with a shot of the inside of a door, which Eliza opens. She walks toward the camera very slowly, very dejectedly. The camera follows her as she turns on the lights. Higgins tells Pickering about his boredom with the whole affair, but the camera remains quite steadily focused on Eliza, as she listens and reacts to their conversation. The camera frames her face in a close-shot as Higgins says, "Thank God, it's all over," and we watch her shudder. The camera follows her as she gets Higgins's slippers and places them in front of him. We see her shudder again, and start to get angry, as Higgins says, "Now I can go to bed without dreading tomorrow." After Higgins leaves the room, the camera remains on Eliza during a long pantomime: she sits in the dark, the ball music swells in the background. The camera shoots Eliza's back, shaking with sobs; then it shoots a close-up of her face, weeping, and of her clenched fists. All of this is in place of the play version's and printed movie version's more obvious and exaggerated direction, which perhaps would have been necessary for communication of her reaction on the far-away stage: "Finally she gives way and flings herself furiously on the floor, raging."

Throughout the film version of *Pygmalion*, music, of course, as well as visuals, accompanies the dialogue. The cinema achieves a much greater unity of sound and sight than is possible in the theatre, not just because there are fewer sound limitations imposed upon the film maker, and because the music can be better regulated to enhance rather than drown out the dialogue, but because *all* of the sound is mechanically reproduced through the microphone and there is thus no jarring—as there is in the theatre—between real sound and mechanical sound. The music of Arthur Honegger throughout *Pygmalion* helps to set the background mood and to guide the emotional reaction of the viewer, whether romantic in the ballroom, or exciting in the laboratory scenes, or nostalgic in the repetition of the ballroom waltz when Eliza returns to Higgins.

The film version of *Pygmalion* departed from Shaw's theory of the cinema, and obeyed some of the demands of the motion picture medium, not only in the *addition* of visual material but in the economy that results from *omission* and by *replacement* of the verbal by the visual. Under the economy of the cinema, things which are shown do not have to be said. Thus, for example, the parlormaid does not have to tell Mrs. Higgins that Henry is sending the police after Eliza because we saw and heard it for ourselves. Dramatic exposition can thus be replaced by direct representation.

Economy also results from the fact that the motion picture, unlike the stage, does not have to preserve conversational continuity. Where the stage has to move conversation from one topic to another, connected by some logical coherence, the motion picture can simply cut into that part of a conversation which it wants and then cut away. This cinematic economy is especially obvious near the beginning of the film *Pygmalion*, where much nonessential subject matter is cut out of the dialogue. Almost all of the Eynsford Hill family chatter is cut out of the film, because conversation does not have to be continuous while Eliza's presence and Higgins's eavesdropping are being established for the audience. In the crowd scenes, too, continuous but nonessential conversation is replaced by occasional remarks and a good deal of visualization.

The technical freedoms of the movie medium allow a similar economy in exits and entrances. Characters appear or disappear simply by a cut of the film: dialogue does not have to prepare for their entrance onto the stage or their exit from it. Thus all the printed movie version dialogue preparing for the exit of Eliza, Higgins, and Pickering from the Embassy Ball is omitted from the actual film version of *Pygmalion*. Pickering does not have to say to Eliza, as a kind of summary, final statement, as he did in the printed movie version, "You have won it ten times over," because we have *seen* her unmistakable triumph. Higgins does not have to say, "Let us get out of this. I have had enough of chattering to these fools," and Pickering does not have to add, "Eliza is tired; and I am hungry. Let us clear out and have supper somewhere." Instead of all this, with the economy of the cinema, when enough has been shown, the scene simply fades out — and, very dramatically, at a point of visual and musical climax.

The technique of the cinema allows other kinds of economical replacement, too. Because the time continuity of reality and of the stage can be broken by the editor's shears, series of actions can be telescoped in time and consequently increased in excitement, as in the highly cinematic lesson scene and ballroom scene, which, through editing, take up much less time and much less dialogue on the screen than they would in reality or on the stage. This economy is shown more simply in hundreds of places throughout the film, as when Higgins goes to the telephone to call the police, and the editor cuts away all the time-consuming details of the placing of the call.

The cinema's ability to destroy, similarly, the continuity of space also caused changes in *Pygmalion*'s stage-to-screen journey. During the tea-party scene, Higgins does not have to exclaim out loud "Covent Garden!" when he realizes where Eliza and the Eynsford Hill's had previously met. Instead — and more naturally — in a close-shot which instantly bridges the space gap between Higgins and us, he whispers it to himself on top of the others' lines, while only we are watching him. Similarly, while Higgins and Pickering are talking about their profession in the first scene, all of Eliza's muttered complaints ("Let him mind his own business and leave a poor girl . . .") are spoken over their lines, with the camera moving us closest to those characters whom we are to hear most clearly at the moment.

Many of the minor omissions and replacements in the screen version of *Pygmalion* were due not to the intrinsic nature of the film medium but were due to external circumstances of the cinema industry. Lines and situations were changed because somewhere on the globe someone might have been offended: the film, as Shaw had pointed out, had to, for profit reasons, "go around the world unchallenged." Thus, for example, the language of *Pygmalion* on the screen is less explosive than the language of *Pygmalion* on the stage. All of Higgins's frequent damnings are deleted, and Freddy's "Damnation!" is changed to "O blast!" Mrs. Pearce's comment about Eliza not wanting to be a "dirty slut" is changed to "dirty girl," and Higgins does not call Eliza a "damned impudent little slut." Eliza does still use her "scarlet expletive," which had caused a major scandal when the play was first produced in London in 1914. But by 1938 the impact of "Not bloody likely" had so weakened that it no longer created a sensation, not even in the sensitive movies. *My Fair Lady,* incidentally, to get the desired impact from Eliza's social gaucherie found it necessary to substitute Eliza's "move your bloomin' arse," spoken at the Ascot races. . . .

Some of the most significant differences between the play and the film are caused by cinematic tendency toward simplification. Several hundred lines of dialogue are cut, whole pages are lost, in an effort to narrow the story, to concentrate on the Eliza-Higgins relationship. Just as the additions tended to emphasize the Eliza-Higgins theme, so do the omissions. Doolittle's lines are the ones which are most severely cut. Not only details about Doolittle's background are lost, but also much of his Shavian philosophy about middle-class morality. As Doolittle's class consciousness is weakened, so is Higgins's. He does not say, for example, "Don't you know that a woman of that class looks a worn out drudge of fifty a year after she's married?" nor does he tell Eliza that as a common girl she has no possible future.

Light chatter that is nonessential to the basic Eliza-Higgins relationship, no matter how filled this dialogue is with Shavian paradox, is eliminated from the severely cut tea-party scene. And the subtleties of the Eliza-Higgins debate in the last act, again filled with Shavian paradox, are freely cut.

As the social dimension of *Pygmalion* is weakened, the romantic Cinderella-like story is correspondingly strengthened. Even certain characteristics of both Higgins and Eliza are altered so as to make them more immediately attractive, more fitting as a romantic pair. Higgins is made less violent and harsh than he was in the play. He simply says to

Eliza, "A woman who utters such depressing and disgusting sounds has no right to be anywhere"; he does not add, as he did in the play, "no right to live." He does not shout, "Give her orders: that's enough for her." His antiwoman and antimarriage speeches are omitted, and so is his devotion to his mother. Eliza, as a flower girl, is not quite so crude as in the play. The lines about her not knowing what to do with her handkerchief are cut, and so are those in which Mrs. Pearce makes clear the necessity of burning Eliza's hat. And Eliza, as a lady, is made even more attractive in the film because we have *seen* Freddy's devotion to her and, most significantly, her great triumph at the Ball. Later, Eliza's snobbery about attending her father's wedding is conveniently eliminated, as all reference to Doolittle's nonmarried state are cut. What remains, after a great deal of omission, is the clear and simple situation of a Galatea finally being fully created by her Pygmalion, finally asserting her own individual soul, and, becoming independent, being free to choose. She chooses Higgins.

In transferring *Pygmalion* to the screen, then, Shaw allowed, as he had earlier forbidden, "transpositions, interpolations, omissions, and alterations." The finished film, with much added and much left out and much changed from the play, opened at the Leicester Square Theatre in London on October 6, 1938. Ignoring the changes, Shaw wrote to Pascal: "You have had a tremendous triumph, on which I congratulate you and myself." Shaw was as happy with his new Eliza as he was with the triumphant new film. He told Wendy Hiller: "You've nearly wiped my old play off the map."

19 Pauline Kael

THE CONCEALED ART
OF CAROL REED

Pauline Kael, one of the major film
critics writing today, has written for such
magazines as *Partisan Review, The At-
lantic, Holiday, Life, Sight and Sound,
Film Quarterly,* and *The New Yorker.*
She has lectured on film at universities
from UCLA to CUNY. In her analysis of
Oliver! (from her book *Going Steady*) she
ranges from Dickens' novel *Oliver Twist*
to the New York and London performances
of the musical *Oliver!* to the film version.
As usual, she is provocative, provoking,
and very perceptive.

Carol Reed has just made the kind of movie they don't make anymore,
and it's as good as ever—maybe better, coming when it's more difficult
to do. Maybe the most revolutionary thing that can be done in movies
at the moment is to make them decently again. "Oliver!" has been made
by people who know how; it's a civilized motion picture, not only
emotionally satisfying but so satisfyingly crafted that we can sit back
and enjoy what is going on, secure in the knowledge that the camera
isn't going to attack us and the editor isn't going to give us an electric

shock. It's not an innovative work or a disturbing work, it does not advance the art of the film, but if we don't admire the real thing in fine big-studio methods, then we probably can't perceive what is *new* in movie art, either. Carol Reed is in the tradition of the older movie artists who conceal their art, and don't try to dazzle us with breathtaking shots and razor-sharp cuts. They are there, all right, but we hardly notice them, because there is always a reason for the camera to be where it is; the camera and the complex, unobtrusive editing serve the story. "Oliver!" is not put together like TV commercials and it doesn't have a psychedelic look or a rock beat, but neither is it rotting on the screen, like "My Fair Lady." Reed uses tact and skill to tell a story that can be enjoyed by "everyone," and it's a very great pleasure to see a movie that can be enjoyed by everyone that one really does enjoy. There's something restorative about a movie that is made for a mass audience and that respects that audience.

Though "Oliver!" is not presented realistically, we become involved in the material—more consciously involved than we do in realistic movies. The tone of the picture is set in the opening sequence, in the children's workhouse, when Oliver's "Please, sir, I want some more" leads into a choreographed children's riot. The stylization encourages us to notice the conventions of the story as we are enjoying the story. It seems to put quotation marks around everything Dickensian, yet not in a cloying way—rather, in a way that makes us more aware of some of the qualities of Dickens' art. It's as if the movie set out to be a tribute to Dickens and a comment on his melodramatic art as well as to tell the story of Oliver Twist. The set designs—a remarkable blend of realism and stylization, by John Box—are an enormous aid in this. Similarly, Reed has got from little Mark Lester, as Oliver, what in an adult would be called Brechtian acting. We can sit there and enjoy the beauty and wit of the child's performance, because we are never pushed over into realism and pathos. Music is the most painless of all alienating devices; the songs provide the distancing that enables us to appreciate Dickens' pathos intellectually. Reed sustains the tone that tells us it's all theatre, and he's a gentleman: he doesn't urge an audience to tears, he always leaves us our pride. He offers his gifts modestly. Typically, the best moment is a quiet one. Oliver, who has been listening to "Who Will Buy?," the lovely early-morning song of the tradespeople in Bloomsbury, walks along singing a few bars to himself, and it is probably the most delicately beautiful reprise in movie-musical history.

No one who sees this movie is likely to say, "But you should have seen 'Oliver!' on the stage!" On the stage, it was the kind of undistinguished musical that people took their children to, dutifully. Though not on a level with "The Sound of Music," it had that detestable kind of

Oliver! (1968) Oliver Twist is about to ask for more—a request that in Carol Reed's movie leads into "a choreographed children's riot." (from Lionel Bart's *Oliver!*, a Romulus Production from Columbia Pictures. Copyright © 1968 Columbia Pictures Corporation.)

mediocre respectability; it was an English version of Broadway Americana, and I walked out on it. The material in "Oliver!" has been more than a little transformed. I hate to describe the Lionel Bart score as adequate—which always really means inadequate to one's hopes—but, at least, it's well sung. And though there is a Broadway-London sound and an awful kind of commercial thinking in numbers like "You've Got to Pick a Pocket or Two," the good voices and the playful performing spirit often suggest Gilbert and Sullivan. Ron Moody, as Fagin the fence, is a controlled singer-actor, and his performance grows and becomes very impressive. As Nancy, Shani Wallis is an unexpected pleasure — hearty (as Dickens described her), with a tough vitality that brings poignancy to the role, though her solo "As Long As He Needs Me" has that designed-to-stop-the-show vulgarity which is not redeemable when the song is as poor as this one. I never thought I'd have cause to praise Oliver Reed, but as Bill Sikes he has found the right outlet for his peculiar talents. The choreographer, Onna White, can take a banal song and a banal conception of a routine and build them up until the number

---

Oliver! (1968) "It's as if the movie set out to be a tribute to Dickens and a comment on his melodramatic art as well as to tell the story of Oliver Twist. The set designs — a remarkable blend of realism and stylization — are an enormous aid in this." (from Lionel Bart's *Oliver!*, a Romulus production from Columbia Pictures. Copyright © 1968 Columbia Pictures Corporation.)

becomes so effective it's just about irresistible; you can hardly help feeling elated, even though you're aware of the whole synthetic process. Her talent is not one I respect, but she succeeds where many others fail. The musical numbers emerge from the story with a grace that has been rarely seen since the musicals of René Clair. It isn't really surprising that Carol Reed, a master of planned montage, should be so adroit. Still, he was a young man when he made his last musical (thirty years ago), and we tend to think of him as the director of suspense films ("Night Train," "The Fallen Idol," "The Third Man," "The Man Between," "Our Man in Havana"), social dramas, and stories of outcasts ("The Stars Look Down," "Odd Man Out," and the brilliant commercial failure "An Outcast of the Islands"). He has always had a gift for handling children; the last example was in his generally underrated "A Kid for Two Farthings" — a realistic fantasy with a number of resemblances to "Oliver!" Like the boy in "A Kid for Two Farthings," Mark Lester and Jack Wild (the Artful Dodger) suggest that childhood is a period of fable, a period in our lives that we look back on as if we had dreamed it all. They are bemused in the midst of activity. The movie of "Oliver!" is much more than the stage production could be; it's not only a musical entertainment but a fine, imaginative version of "Oliver Twist" that treats the novel as a lyrical, macabre fable.

Dickens wrote "Oliver Twist" to counter seductive stories of criminal life — specifically, "The Beggar's Opera," with its gallant thief-hero. "To draw a knot of such associates in crime as really did exist; to paint them in all their deformity, in all their wretchedness, in all the squalid misery of their lives; to show them as they really were, forever skulking uneasily through the dirtiest paths of life, with the great black ghastly gallows closing up their prospect, turn them where they might; it appeared to me that to do this, would be to attempt a something which was needed, and which would be a service to society." And so it may seem ironic that "Oliver!" turns his book into what it was supposed to be against; Bart's libretto for "Oliver!" resembles "The Beggar's Opera," though it is much inferior to it. But perhaps it's not really so ironic; Dickens, only twenty-five when he wrote the novel, had already made low life commercially acceptable with the first of those great, silly, rhyming plots of his, and, later in life, he gave lurid public readings of the murder of Nancy. (Well pleased with one performance, he wrote, "We had a contagion of fainting. . . . I should think we had from a dozen to twenty ladies taken out stiff and rigid at various times!") And it's clear in reading "Oliver Twist" that, despite his cautionary purpose, Dickens fell in love with his scoundrels and couldn't do anything with his proper characters. (The movies have done better by them, and much better than Cruikshank, whose drawings of Oliver made him

Oliver! (1968) A dancing and singing Fagin: the film stylizes his villainy and makes him an appealing character — "an extension not of what Dickens thought he was doing but of what Dickens the emotional artist did." (from Lionel Bart's *Oliver!*, a Romulus Production from Columbia Pictures. Copyright © 1968 Columbia Pictures Corporation.)

so bleakly virtuous he looked malformed.) Bart has taken the next step — an extension not of what Dickens the pamphleteer thought he was doing but of what Dickens the emotional artist did. Bart has left only one unlovable villain — Bill Sikes. It's scarcely the first time in the history of the arts that a work written to break with a tradition has seemed in subsequent years to be much closer to that tradition than the rebel realized. This is almost a résumé of the development of any art.

"Oliver!" is much easier to take than the very fine non-musical film version of "Oliver Twist" produced in 1948, and I don't think the softening of this particular material is to be lamented. There were scenes in

Oliver! (1968) From a choreographed riot in the workhouse to a choreographed London street scene. (from Lionel Bart's *Oliver!*, a Romulus Production from Columbia Pictures. Copyright © 1968 Columbia Pictures Corporation.)

the David Lean film that were simply too painful, and the trumpery of the Dickensian plotting was too stylized and conventional to go with the pain of the child's suffering and the horrible murder of Nancy. (I know in my bones why those women turned rigid). In this new version, in which the whole story is stylized and the suffering and murder become conventions in themselves (as in an opera), the plot is entertainingly functional. When men sing about what rogues they are, when children sing about how hungry they are, they are domesticated. (This is probably why the villain Bill Sikes does not sing, though in an opera, as opposed to this musical-theatre form, he would doubtless have had an aria to express his anguish over his foul deeds.) One villain is enough, really; we simply cannot take the melodramatics of wickedness and virtue the way nineteenth-century readers did, and the omission of the mechanism of the mistreatment of Oliver (that whole apparatus of the half brother and the will) is a blessing—and not only because it's too much freight for a musical to carry. Closer fidelity to Dickens' text and his warnings about the perils of a sinful life would make the work not more realistic but quite absurd; it would turn into Camp.

I admire the artist who can make something good for the art-house audience, but I also applaud the commercial heroism of a director who can steer a huge production and keep his sanity and perspective and decent human feelings as beautifully intact as they are in "Oliver!" I'm not being facetious when I suggest that the quiet, concealed art of good craftsmanship may be revolutionary now. It's more difficult than ever before for a director to trust his accumulated knowledge and experience, because on big commercial projects there's so much pressure on movie-makers to imitate the techniques of the latest hit, to be "up to date," which means always to be out of date. The camera pranks and the flamboyant scissorwork that seem so creative to young film-makers are easy, and because they express nothing much deeper than Mod alienation and fragmentation, they're consumed by TV specials—if the commercials don't get them first. Artists like Carl Dreyer and Robert Bresson have pointed the way to a pure, austere style, and Jean-Luc Godard, the major new influence, has been evolving a technique that depends on long takes. The period of the cutups may be over—among movie artists, that is: the hacks are just beginning to call for scissors and strobes. In this context of a search for new ways of *integrating* material on the screen, the unostentatious work of a man like Carol Reed may be both behind and ahead of what is now exhaustingly fashionable.

20

Ambrose Bierce

AN OCCURRENCE AT OWL CREEK BRIDGE

Ambrose Bierce wrote many highly realistic and cynical stories dealing with the Civil War, in which he was a soldier. "An Occurrence at Owl Creek Bridge" is his best-known story and *The Devil's Dictionary* his best-known book. Born in 1842, he disappeared in Mexico in 1913, and the mystery of his death remains unsolved.

I

A man stood upon a railroad bridge in northern Alabama, looking down into the swift water twenty feet below. The man's hands were behind his back, the wrists bound with a cord. A rope closely encircled his neck. It was attached to a stout cross-timber above his head and the slack fell to the level of his knees. Some loose boards laid upon the sleepers supporting the metals of the railway supplied a footing for him and his executioners — two private soldiers of the Federal army, directed by a sergeant who in civil life may have been a deputy sheriff. At a short remove upon the same temporary platform was an officer in the uniform of his rank, armed. He was a captain. A sentinel at each end of the bridge stood with his rifle in the position known as "support," that is to say, vertical in front of the left shoulder, the hammer resting on the forearm thrown straight across the chest—a formal and unnatural position, enforcing an erect carriage of the body. It did not appear to be the duty of these two men to know what was occurring at the center of the bridge; they merely blockaded the two ends of the foot planking that traversed it.

Beyond one of the sentinels nobody was in sight; the railroad ran straight away into a forest for a hundred yards, then, curving, was lost to view. Doubtless there was an outpost farther along. The other bank of the stream was open ground—a gentle acclivity topped with a stockade of vertical tree trunks, loopholed for rifles, with a single embrasure through which protruded the muzzle of a brass cannon commanding the bridge. Midway of the slope between the bridge and fort were the spectators—a single company of infantry in line, at "parade rest," the butts of the rifles on the ground, the barrels inclining slightly backward against the right shoulder, the hands crossed upon the stock. A lieutenant stood at the right of the line, the point of his sword upon the ground, his left hand resting upon his right. Excepting the group of four at the center of the bridge, not a man moved. The company faced the bridge, staring stonily, motionless. The sentinels, facing the banks of the stream, might have been statues to adorn the bridge. The captain stood with folded arms, silent, observing the work of his subordinates, but making no sign. Death is a dignitary who when he comes announced is to be received with formal manifestations of respect, even by those most familiar with him. In the code of military etiquette silence and fixity are forms of deference.

The man who was engaged in being hanged was apparently about thirty-five years of age. He was a civilian, if one might judge from his habit, which was that of a planter. His features were good—a straight nose, firm mouth, broad forehead, from which his long, dark hair was combed straight back, falling behind his ears to the collar of his well-fitting frock coat. He wore a mustache and pointed beard, but no whiskers; his eyes were large and dark gray, and had a kindly expression which one would hardly have expected in one whose neck was in the hemp. Evidently this was no vulgar assassin. The liberal military code makes provision for hanging many kinds of persons, and gentlemen are not excluded.

The preparations being complete, the two private soldiers stepped aside and each drew away the plank upon which he had been standing. The sergeant turned to the captain, saluted and placed himself immediately behind that officer, who in turn moved apart one pace. These movements left the condemned man and the sergeant standing on the two ends of the same plank, which spanned three of the crossties of the bridge. The end upon which the civilian stood almost, but not quite, reached a fourth. This plank had been held in place by the weight of the captain; it was now held by that of the sergeant. At a signal from the former the latter would step aside, the plank would tilt and the condemned man go down between two ties. The arrangement commended itself to his judgment as simple and effective. His face had not been covered nor his eyes bandaged. He looked a moment at his "unsteadfast footing," then let his gaze wander to the swirling water of the stream racing madly beneath his feet. A piece of dancing driftwood caught his attention and his eyes followed it down the current. How slowly it appeared to move! What a sluggish stream!

He closed his eyes in order to fix his last thoughts upon his wife and children. The water, touched to gold by the early sun, the brooding mists under the banks at some distance down the stream, the fort, the soldiers, the piece of drift—all had distracted him. And now he became conscious of a new disturbance. Striking through the thought of his dear ones was a sound which he could neither ignore nor understand, a sharp, distinct, metallic percussion like the stroke of a blacksmith's hammer upon the anvil; it had the same ringing quality. He wondered what it was, and whether immeasurably distant or near by—it seemed both. Its recurrence was regular, but as slow as the tolling of a death knell. He awaited each stroke with impatience and—he knew not why—apprehension. The intervals of silence grew progressively longer; the delays became maddening. With their greater infrequency the sounds increased in strength and sharpness. They hurt his ear like the thrust of a knife; he feared he would shriek. What he heard was the ticking of his watch.

He unclosed his eyes and saw again the water below him. "If I could free my hands," he thought, "I might throw off the noose and spring into the stream. By diving I could evade the bullets and, swimming vigorously, reach the bank, take to the woods and get away home. My home, thank God, is as yet outside their lines; my wife and little ones are still beyond the invader's farthest advance."

As these thoughts, which have here to be set down in words, were flashed into the doomed man's brain rather than evolved from it the captain nodded to the sergeant. The sergeant stepped aside.

II

Peyton Farquhar was a well-to-do planter, of an old and highly respected Alabama family. Being a slave owner and like other slave owners a politician, he was naturally an original secessionist and ardently devoted to the Southern cause. Circumstances of an imperious nature, which it is unnecessary to relate here, had prevented him from taking service with the gallant army that had fought the disastrous campaigns ending with the fall of Corinth, and he chafed under the inglorious restraint, longing for the release of his energies, the larger life of the soldier, the opportunity for distinction. That opportunity, he felt, would come, as it comes to all in war time. Meanwhile he did what he could. No service was too humble for him to perform in aid of the South, no adventure too perilous for him to undertake if consistent with the character of a civilian who was at heart a soldier, and who in good faith and without too much qualification assented to at least a part of the frankly villainous dictum that all is fair in love and war.

One evening while Farquhar and his wife were sitting on a rustic bench near the entrance to his grounds, a gray-clad soldier rode up to the gate and asked for a drink of water. Mrs. Farquhar was only too happy to serve him with her own white hands. While she was fetching the water her husband approached the dusty horseman and inquired eagerly for news from the front.

"The Yanks are repairing the railroads," said the man, "and are getting ready for another advance. They have reached the Owl Creek bridge, put it in order and built a stockade on the north bank. The commandant has issued an order, which is posted everywhere, declaring that any civilian caught interfering with the railroad, its bridges, tunnels or trains will be summarily hanged. I saw the order."

"How far is it to the Owl Creek bridge?" Farquhar asked.

"About thirty miles."

"Is there no force on this side of the creek?"

"Only a picket post half a mile out, on the railroad, and a single sentinel at this end of the bridge."

"Suppose a man — a civilian and student of hanging — should elude the picket post and perhaps get the better of the sentinel," said Farquhar, smiling, "what could he accomplish?"

The soldier reflected. "I was there a month ago," he replied. "I observed that the flood of last winter had lodged a great quantity of driftwood against the wooden pier at this end of the bridge. It is now dry and would burn like tow."

The lady had now brought the water, which the soldier drank. He thanked her ceremoniously, bowed to her husband and rode away. An hour later, after nightfall, he re-passed the plantation, going northward in the direction from which he had come. He was a Federal scout.

III

As Peyton Farquhar fell straight downward through the bridge he lost consciousness and was as one already dead. From this state he was awakened—ages later, it seemed to him—by the pain of a sharp pressure up his throat, followed by a sense of suffocation. Keen, poignant agonies seemed to shoot from his neck downward through every fiber of his body and limbs. These pains appeared to flash along well-defined lines of ramification and to beat with an inconceivably rapid periodicity. They seemed like streams of pulsating fire heating him to an intolerable temperature. As to his head, he was conscious of nothing but a feeling of fullness—of congestion. These sensations were unaccompanied by thought. The intellectual part of his nature was already effaced; he had power only to feel, and feeling was torment. He was conscious of motion. Encompassed in a luminous cloud, of which he was now merely the fiery heart, without material substance, he swung through unthinkable arcs of oscillation, like a vast pendulum. Then all at once, with terrible sud- denness, the light about him shot upward with the noise of a loud splash; a frightful roaring was in his ears, and all was cold and dark. The power of thought was restored; he knew that the rope had broken and he had fallen into the stream. There was no additional strangulation; the noose about his neck was already suffocating him and kept the water from his lungs. To die of hanging at the bottom of a river!—the idea seemed to him ludicrous. He opened his eyes in the darkness and saw above him a gleam of light, but how distant, how inaccessible! He was still sinking, for the light became fainter and fainter until it was a mere glimmer. Then it began to grow and brighten, and he knew that he was rising toward the surface—knew it with reluctance, for he was now very com- fortable. "To be hanged and drowned," he thought, "that is not so bad; but I do not wish to be shot. No; I will not be shot; that is not fair."

He was not conscious of an effort, but a sharp pain in his wrist apprised him that he was trying to free his hands. He gave the struggle his attention, as an idler might observe the feat of a juggler, without interest in the outcome. What splendid effort! What magnificent, what superhuman strength! Ah, that was a fine endeavor! Bravo! The cord fell away; his arms parted and floated upward, the hands dimly seen on each side in the growing light. He watched them with a new interest as first one and then the other pounced upon the noose at his neck. They tore it away and thrust it fiercely aside, its undulations resembling those of a water snake. "Put it back, put it back!" He thought he shouted these words to his hands, for the undoing of the noose had been succeeded by the direst pang that he had yet experienced. His neck ached horribly; his brain was on fire; his heart, which had been fluttering faintly, gave a great leap, trying to force itself out at his mouth. His whole body was racked and wrenched with an insupportable anguish! But his disobedient hands gave no heed to the command. They beat the water vigorously with quick, downward strokes, forcing him to the surface. He felt his head emerge; his eyes were blinded by the sunlight; his chest expanded convulsively, and with a supreme and crowning agony his lungs engulfed a great draught of air, which instantly he expelled in a shriek!

He was now in full possession of his physical senses. They were, indeed, preternaturally keen and alert. Something in the awful disturbance of his organic system had so exalted and refined them that they made record of things never before perceived. He felt the ripples upon his face and heard their separate sounds as they struck. He looked at the forest on the bank of the stream, saw the individual trees, the leaves and the veining of each leaf—saw the very insects upon them: the locusts, the brilliant-bodied flies, the gray spiders stretching their webs from twig to twig. He noted the prismatic colors in all the dew-drops upon a million blades of grass. The humming of the gnats that danced above the eddies of the stream, the beating of the dragonflies' wings, the strokes of the water spiders' legs, like oars which had lifted their boat—all these made audible music. A fish slid along beneath his eyes and he heard the rush of its body parting the water.

He had come to the surface facing down the stream; in a moment the visible world seemed to wheel slowly round, himself the pivotal point, and he saw the bridge, the fort, the soldiers upon the bridge, the captain, the sergeant, the two privates, his executioners. They were in silhouette against the blue sky. They shouted and gesticulated, pointing at him. The captain had drawn his pistol, but did not fire; the others were unarmed. Their movements were grotesque and horrible, their forms gigantic.

Suddenly he heard a sharp report and something struck the water smartly within a few inches of his head, spattering his face with spray. He heard a second report, and saw one of the sentinels with his rifle at his shoulder, a light cloud of blue smoke rising from the muzzle. The man in the water saw the eye of the man on the bridge gazing into his own through the sights of the rifle. He observed that it was a gray eye and remembered having read that gray eyes were keenest, and that all famous marksmen had them. Nevertheless, this one had missed.

A counter-swirl had caught Farquhar and turned him half round; he was again looking into the forest on the bank opposite the fort. The sound of a clear, high voice in a monotonous singsong now rang out behind him and came across the water with a distinctness that pierced and subdued all other sounds, even the beating of the ripples in his ears. Although no soldier, he had frequented camps enough to know the dread significance of that deliberate, drawling, aspirated chant, the lieutenant on shore was taking a part in the morning's work. How coldly and pitilessly—with what an even, calm intonation, presaging, and enforcing tranquility in the men—with what accurately measured intervals fell those cruel words:

"Attention, company! . . . Shoulder arms! . . . Ready! . . . Aim! . . . Fire!"

Farquhar dived—dived as deeply as he could. The water roared in his ears like the voice of Niagara, yet he heard the dulled thunder of the volley and, rising again toward the surface, met shining bits of metal, singularly flattened, oscillating slowly downward. Some of them touched him on the face and hands, then fell away, continuing their descent. One lodged between his collar and neck; it was uncomfortably warm and he snatched it out.

As he rose to the surface, gasping for breath, he saw that he had been a long time under water; he was perceptibly farther down stream—nearer to safety. The soldiers had almost finished reloading; the metal ramrods flashed all at once in the sunshine as they were drawn from the barrels, turned in the air, and thrust into their sockets. The two sentinels fired again, independently and ineffectually.

The hunted man saw all this over his shoulder; he was now swimming vigorously with the current. His brain was as energetic as his arms and legs; he thought with the rapidity of lightning.

"The officer," he reasoned, "will not make that martinet's error a second time. It is as easy to dodge a volley as a single shot. He has probably already given the command to fire at will. God help me, I cannot dodge them all!"

An appalling splash within two yards of him was followed by a loud, rushing sound, *diminuendo*, which seemed to travel back through the air to the fort and died in an explosion which stirred the very river to its deeps! A rising sheet of water curved over him, fell down upon him, blinded him, strangled him! The cannon had taken a hand in the game. As he shook his head free from the commotion of the smitten water he heard the deflected shot humming through the air ahead, and in an instant it was cracking and smashing the branches in the forest beyond.

"They will not do that again," he thought; "the next time they will use a charge of grape. I must keep my eye upon the gun; the smoke will apprise me—the report arrives too late; it lags behind the missile. That is a good gun."

Suddenly he felt himself whirled round and round—spinning like a top. The water, the banks, the forests, the now distant bridge, fort and men—all were commingled and blurred. Objects were represented by their colors only; circular horizontal streaks of color—that was all he saw. He had been caught in a vortex and was being whirled on with a velocity of advance and gyration that made him giddy and sick. In a few moments he was flung upon the gravel at the foot of the left bank of the stream—the southern bank—and behind a projecting point which concealed him from his enemies. The sudden arrest of his motion, the abrasion of one of his hands on the gravel, restored him, and he wept with delight. He dug his fingers into the sand, threw it over himself in handfuls and audibly blessed it. It looked like diamonds, rubies, emeralds; he could think of nothing beautiful which it did not resemble. The trees upon the bank were giant garden plants; he noted a definite order in their arrangement, inhaled the fragrance of their blooms. A strange, roseate light shone through the spaces among their trunks and the wind made in their branches the music of Aeolian harps. He had no wish to perfect his escape—was content to remain in that enchanting spot until retaken.

A whiz and rattle of grapeshot among the branches high above his head roused him from his dream. The baffled cannoneer had fired him a random farewell. He sprang to his feet, rushed up the sloping bank, and plunged into the forest.

All that day he traveled, laying his course by the rounding sun. The forest seemed interminable; nowhere did he discover a break in it, not even a woodsman's road. He had not known that he lived in so wild a region. There was something uncanny in the revelation.

By nightfall he was fatigued, footsore, famishing. The thought of his wife and children urged him on. At last he found a road which led him in what he knew to be the right direction. It was as wide and straight as a city street, yet it seemed untraveled. No fields bordered it, no dwelling anywhere. Not so much as the barking of a dog suggested human habitation. The black bodies of the trees forced a straight wall on both sides, terminating on the horizon in a point, like a diagram in a lesson in perspective. Overhead, as he looked up through this rift in the wood, shone great golden stars looking unfamiliar and grouped in strange constellations. He was sure they were arranged in some order which had a secret and malign significance. The wood on either side was full of singular noises, among which—once, twice, and again—he distinctly heard whispers in an unknown tongue.

His neck was in pain and lifting his hand to it he found it horribly swollen. He knew that it had a circle of black where the rope had bruised it. His eyes felt congested; he could no longer close them. His tongue was swollen with thirst; he relieved its fever by thrusting it forward from between his teeth into the cold air. How softly the turf had carpeted the untraveled avenue—he could no longer feel the roadway beneath his feet!

Doubtless, despite his suffering, he had fallen asleep while walking, for now he sees another scene—perhaps he has merely recovered from a delirium. He stands at the gate of his own home. All is as he left it, and all bright and beautiful in the morning sunshine. He must have traveled the entire night. As he pushes open the gate and passes up the wide white walk, he sees a flutter of female garments; his wife, looking fresh and cool and sweet, steps down from the veranda to meet him. At the bottom of the steps she stands waiting, with a smile of ineffable joy, an attitude of matchless grace and dignity. Ah, how beautiful she is! He springs forward with extended arms. As he is about to clasp her he feels a stunning blow upon the back of the neck; a blinding white light blazes all about him with a sound like the shock of a cannon—then all is darkness and silence!

Peyton Farquhar was dead; his body, with a broken neck, swung gently from side to side beneath the timbers of the Owl Creek bridge.

Fred H. Marcus

21

FILM AND FICTION:
AN OCCURRENCE
AT OWL CREEK BRIDGE

Robert Enrico, a French filmmaker, directed the film based on the Ambrose Bierce story about Owl Creek Bridge. The movie won the Grand Prize at the 1962 Cannes Film Festival. It also won an Academy Award in 1963. Professor Marcus has shown the movie in high-school and college film classes; it fascinates viewers and is a fine example of how great pictures can be adapted from literary sources.

Without a wasted word, Ambrose Bierce plunges into a Civil War story filled with Gothic horror and spiced by authorial intrusions of sardonic observation. Precise details frame the tale. The opening three sentences picture Peyton Farquhar positioned for hanging. The closing sentence focuses upon his body swinging beneath the timbers of Owl Creek Bridge.

Bierce violates normal time sequence to enhance the horrors of his story. Between the end of section I and the story's concluding line,

First published in this book

no more than a few seconds elapse. Yet the bulk of the narrative occurs during these seconds. All of section II, a fairly short expository segment, occurs prior to the story's opening sentence. The last and longest segment, section III, is made *unreal* by the closing sentence. Within this complex time structure, the story is told by an omniscient author; even Peyton Farquhar's first person thoughts are narrated by the author, who tells his readers what Farquhar thinks, feels, says, and does. With the exception of a descriptive adjective or two for other characters, we do not enter into their perceptions, thoughts, or feelings.

Bierce's tools are narration and description. Plot dominates "An Occurrence at Owl Creek Bridge." Details make up the bulk of the story; however, strategically placed short, terse sentences underscore Bierce's artful orchestration of mounting horror.

The plot of the narrative can be stated simply. Peyton Farquhar, a loyal southern civilian during the Civil War, is tricked by a Federal agent into an attempted act of sabotage aimed at the Union-held Owl Creek Bridge, an act punishable by hanging. Captured, sentenced to hang at sunup, he spends the short minutes before execution observing the preparations for his death and thinking about escape and family. Farquhar escapes — an illusion treated realistically until the final revealing sentence of the story. In the full context of the opening and closing lines, the reader recognizes the wishful thinking of the dead man's last few moments alive.

"An Occurrence at Owl Creek Bridge" is, however, more than just a tale of terror with a macabre ending. Several themes enhance the plot's prominence. Man's inhumanity to man; the role of status even at the time of death's supposed impartiality; nature's beautiful, but usually unobserved details: these are all facets of the story. Poe's injunction to create a single unified effect is apparent in the descriptive and narrative details, but themes of importance to Bierce extend a narrowly homogenized Gothic tale of horror. Many of the story's details would delight Poe; they strike notes leading to a crescendo of terror. For example, the sound effects of "metallic strokes of a blacksmith's hammer upon the anvil" remind one of a "tolling of a death knell." Meanwhile, the "intervals of silence grew progressively longer; the delays became maddening. With their greater infrequency, the sounds increased in strength and sharpness. They hurt his [Farquhar's] ear like the thrust of a knife; he feared he would shriek. What he heard was *the ticking of his watch.*" [Italics mine.] No reader could possibly fail to be reminded of Poe's story of "The Tell-Tale Heart." Stylistically, it is important to note the recurring device used by Bierce. The horror reaches its apogee in the terse closing phrase which flares like luminous evil over the preceding lines.

Bierce follows one climactic moment of terror with subdued hope as Farquhar thinks about freeing his hands, casting off the noose encircling his throat, springing into the stream below, evading the bullets, and escaping. Having established this flicker of hope, Bierce concludes section I of the story by completing the earlier military preparations; ". . . the captain nodded to the sergeant. The sergeant stepped aside." With the stepping aside, the reader visualizes Farquhar hurtling off his plank toward the water, the noose around his neck fastened to a beam above Owl Creek Bridge. The abrupt closing words, short and terse, are like the shriek and thrust of death. Indeed, the closing sentence of section I could logically be followed by the closing lines of the story: "Peyton Farquhar was dead; his body, with a broken neck, swung gently from side to side beneath the timbers of the Owl Creek Bridge." But the verbal detail separating the two sentences, sequential in time, contains the bulk of Bierce's narrative.

Section II of the story clarifies the desperate plight of Peyton Farquhar and his imminent execution. Among the many events of the narrative tale, it is sequentially first in real time. Briefly, the reader learns that Farquhar is a well-to-do planter eager for military involvement. Enter a "gray-clad" soldier who tells him about the importance and vulnerability of Owl Creek Bridge. Farquhar is encouraged to sabotage the bridge despite the danger of hanging if caught. When the soldier leaves, Bierce uses the same stylistic technique to conclude section II. The closing line is abrupt. "He [the gray-clad soldier] was a Federal scout." The eerie light illuminates section I and maintains the chill mood of Bierce's horror tale. While section II uses description, narration, and dialogue, it serves primarily as exposition. Because it violates real-time sequence, it subtly foreshadows the later violation of real-time order. Finally, it establishes that "things are not only what they seem to be," so crucial to the horror of section III.

The universal concept of man's inhumanity to man, particularly during a period of war, meshes naturally with the Gothic horror tale. However, Bierce's intrusions into the story in his own *persona* both adds to and detracts from his art. Two sardonic observations illustrate this point. The author says, after describing the military preparations in considerable concrete detail, "Death is a dignitary who when he comes announced is to be received with formal manifestations of respect, even by those most familiar with him. In the code of military etiquette silence and fixity are forms of deference." While Bierce s observation is entirely accurate, he has also hinted at the necessity for formal procedures so men will not look too closely at the enormity of their inhumanity. Bierce's social consciousness of caste is reflected by another *obiter dictum.* Having noted that Farquhar is ". . . no vulgar assassin," he adds, "The liberal military code makes provisions for hanging many kinds of persons, and gentlemen are not excluded." Again, the sentence is linked to the excessive breadth of military formal preparation for Farquhar's execution. The author's words *tell* us these things.

In section II, when Bierce continues his earlier descriptions of Farquhar, he uses authorial omniscience to let the reader know the protagonist's view that "all is fair in love and war." But the author himself has colored this statement with his own view by describing the planter's notion as a "frankly villainous dictum. . . ." The irony is that Farquhar is hoist with his own petard, that he is destroyed by a value system in which he himself believes.

The author's intrusions are contrary to Poe's dictum that everything in a story should aim at the single focal point of emotion desired. Bierce's observations are more intellectual than emotional. They add a dimension to the story; they detract from emotional power gained by an unswerving focus.

One final critical point merits attention. When Farquhar apparently escapes from execution and emerges from below the surface of the river, he is both physically battered and exultant. Quickly, he regains his senses. Bierce describes his sensory perceptions as "preternaturally keen and alert. Something in the awful disturbance of his organic system had so exalted and refined them (his senses) that they made record of things never before perceived." The lines are frankly didactic. Bierce follows immediately with brilliant concrete observations: "the veining of each leaf," "prismatic colors in all the dewdrops," "gnats that danced above the eddies of the stream," and "the strokes of the water-spiders' legs, like oars. . . ." The observations suffice without any need to preface them with explanatory statements. The details reveal man's usual insensitivity to the vibrant, throbbing life pulsating about him.

II

Robert Enrico's film, *An Occurrence at Owl Creek Bridge*, seizes the viewer with sounds of violence. Even as the opening credits appear and eyes scan the screen for action and information, our sensory impressions are assaulted by the insistent drum roll of military fervor. Smoke drifts across the screen; free association screams war and the din of war. Caught by the immediacy and reality, we observe a charred tree stump to which a military order has been posted. In a close-up, the camera permits the viewer to read the words: ORDER in large capitals captures immediate attention; the smaller print warns against civilian interference with the railroad, Owl Creek Bridge, etc., and in smaller capitals at the base of the poster, the words SUMMARILY HANGED stand out. Thus, the opening moments of the film warn against sabotage, establish the military situation, and substitute for the exposition in Bierce's section II. When the camera cuts away from the poster and pans through the black trees and branches silhouetted against the sky, sounds enhance the life and death symbolism of black etched against white; we hear birds' calls, many of them ominous in tone, appropriately reinforcing such dire symbols as the poster, charred trees, drifting smoke, and the lack of visible humanity.

The first clue to any human presence comes from the military sounds accompanying reveille in the predawn gray light. The Civil War background becomes apparent in shots of sentries rigidly fixed; the shots are angled, allowing the viewer a glimpse upward toward an unmoving sentry high on a rock, formidable but distant enough to keep him detached and uninvolved with the evolving action. A squad of soldiers marches in the gray and white pre-dawn to an army cadence; they are mechanical. A close-up reveals a Federal officer. He bawls out, "At ease," and the troop moves into position, expressionless. The visual shots create the mood: cold, unemotional, impersonal. The viewer feels a faint unease, possibly even a slight tremor of apprehension. The camera cuts to a soldier carrying a hangman's noose; he marches to the center of the bridge. His heavy tramping cadence is appropriate to his purpose: sights and sounds converge.

The initial shot of Peyton Farquhar is a close-up; he resembles the physical description in the Ambrose Bierce short story. Enrico, however, modifies one important story detail. Farquhar's neck is not already "in the hemp." Instead, the camera concentrates, using a series of quick shots, on Farquhar being readied for the hanging. The coldly efficient camera shots of the hangman preparing the noose contrast with shots seen through Farquhar's eyes. Peyton is marched to the far end of a board plank projecting out over the river. He looks down. An angle shot from above focuses on his feet at the very edge of the plank, the river moving sluggishly below.

At this point, the director reverses a standard shot sequence. Usually, movies increase dramatic intensity and tension by a) a shot of the character's face, a close-up, as he focuses upon something the audience has not yet seen. His emotion is reflected by his expression. Then, b) the camera cuts to the character's eye view of the object, person, or event. Enrico, however, focuses on a squad of soldiers followed by a shot of Farquhar observing what we have already seen. The reversal lessens the dramatic intensity. Enrico repeats his reversal technique by

An Occurrence at Owl Creek Bridge (1962) The visual images compress the narrative and enhance the symbolic dimensions of the story.

letting the viewer see the sentry atop the boulder followed by Farquhar's similar observation. By slowing down the dramatic intensity, the director can establish tension at a more tempered and deliberate pace. He does not emphasize the horror of the preparations; instead, he emphasizes the greater horror of what is *not* occurring: the detachment of the humans present toward the forthcoming execution, the importance during war of concentrating upon petty official activities, thereby more easily ignoring the substantive event—the imminent destruction of a fellow human.

Enrico shoots a log slowly floating downstream; Farquhar sees it after we do. The feel of fear looms larger in the film when the camera cuts to Farquhar closing his eyes followed by a quick cut to the onset of sunup. Sunrise traditionally symbolizes hope. In the film, the shot forces us to squint; our discomfort increases with the recognition that sunup is the moment of execution. The glare of sunrise not only assaults the viewer but jolts the Union soldiers into official ritual. A soldier replaces the officer on the balancing end of Farquhar's plank. Using his film medium perfectly, Enrico shoots the scene at leg level. Quick cut back to Farquhar; his eyes are still closed while the noose frames the left side of the screen. When he calls out his wife's name in agony, the slow motion shots that follow reveal his thoughts of wife, home, and family. We recognize the "unrealistic" slow motion shots as Peyton's thoughts.

An Occurrence at Owl Creek Bridge (1962) Farquhar awaits his death and dreams of home. The camera visualizes his thoughts.

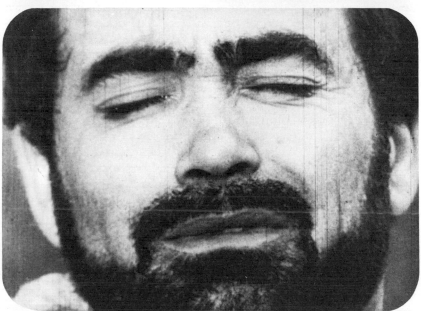

The director introduces onto the sound track a thumping sound. The beat pulsates more loudly; off screen, we hear the officer's voice asking for Farquhar's watch. The viewer is quickly returned to filmic reality. In a waist-high close-up without any faces, we see his watch removed. Unlike Bierce's story in which watch ticking enhances the horror, Enrico invents a marvelously ironic scene. The officer's hands open the watch face and we hear a music box tune, gentle and melodic, in the context of onrushing death. The officer places the watch in a waist container attached to his belt, an action that suggests the immoral looting that accompanies war.

As smoke drifts across the setting (a continuation of the war symbolism) the director cuts to a close-up of Farquhar's teeth and mouth
quivering. We see and almost feel his sweat. Enrico cuts to Peyton's
wrists bound behind his back while Farquhar fumbles in his efforts to
free his hands. The shot foreshadows action yet to come.

The sun rises. An officer—his expression ranges somewhere between set and immobile—glances from the sunrise to the soldier balancing the deadly plank. He nods tersely. The action is accompanied by
a deadly silent sound track. The viewer suddenly sees and hears. The
camera captures, at boot level, the stiff, ritualistic movements as the
soldier steps militarily from the plank; the sound track erupts into
abrupt sound. The shot angle emphasizes the action of the military movements; we see no human faces. The camera angle shifts to a looking down
shot as the plank tilts and we observe Farquhar rocket down into the
river. The director avoids the cliché of a broken noose, but Peyton
Farquhar's rapid and noisy plunge into the stream shows us the failure
of the anticipated hanging and strangulation. We observe Peyton's
descent into deep water and watch his thrashing efforts to free himself
while gurgling sounds fill the sound track.

Enrico shows us contrasting shots of Farquhar freeing himself and
rising toward the surface with shots of the sun's rays dazzling on the
water. One cut shows the rope about his neck being torn free and flowing,
almost snakelike, in the river. The detail reflects one of Bierce's descriptive sentences. Enrico exploits the allusion later when he inter-
polates a shot of an actual water snake yet avoids any melodramatic
confrontation between man and snake.

While Bierce links the horrible irony of a man both drowning and
strangling under water, then escaping both only to be shot at, the film-
maker wisely avoids this abstract notion. The omniscient writer uses
verbal techniques to place the bitter irony in the very thought processes
of Farquhar. Enrico, employing the film art of *showing* concrete images,
uses his sound track to suggest drowning while we watch Peyton Farquhar
free himself by tugging successfully at his ties. When Farquhar breaks
through the water surface and gasps audibly for air, a new phase of
action begins. Escape for the planter momentarily brings a near smile
to his close-up face. The film's ominous music shifts to a more melodic
mood. We hear the song "I'm a living man" accompany Peyton's "preternaturally" alert observation. This *livingness* is literal; we see more
vitally through his eyes as the camera focuses on minute details. The
song's words, "He looks around" blend with a swivelling set of observations. "I see each tree" leads into fine filmic close-ups: the veins of a
leaf, a black centipede walking across the face of another leaf, the
diamond-like droplets of water on a different leaf. Enrico utilizes

Bierce's details and links "living" to a more intensive perceiving and visual appreciation of nature's tiniest phenomena. The close-up of a spider spinning its web bridges the gap from beauty to the possibility of death as description is replaced by narrative action. A sharpshooter fires at Farquhar. The file of soldiers, rifles moving in unison, fire in response to their officer's command. The "living man" music yields to army commands on the bridge and we hear these as Farquhar hears them, ugly and distorted and dangerous. The sound track leads the viewer/listener. We hear Farquhar's labored breathing and the intercut command, "Fire at will" while observing his frantic swimming away from Owl Creek Bridge. The director uses quick cuts to further the tension: the sentry firing, the water snake, Farquhar's frantic strokes, the world whirling about. The sound track adds an ominous note of increasing violence as a shot from above shows Farquhar in a new perspective—a puny human speck caught up in swirling rapids of threatening whitewater. Sound both leads and accompanies action, thereby increasing tension. For a few moments, as the sound track reaches a crescendo of violence and is most ominous, we lose sight of Farquhar in the rapids until he re-emerges in a pool of calm water, temporarily safe.

Robert Enrico uses the Griffith shot alternation pattern to maintain suspense. A cannon shot reminds Farquhar and the audience that the irony of distant death hovers in the air after the close escape. Peyton swims for the shore; reaching a sand beach, he clutches handfuls of sand in delight. Enrico subtly adds the sounds of birds, hopeful and tuneful, to the soundtrack. Farquhar's hands, bloodied from knuckles to wrists, are intercut with his near hysterical laughter and abandon. He rolls on the sand, ecstatic, until he lies exhausted on his back—with the camera peering down at him from above. The music of "I'm a living man" recurs as he responds to trees and sky, as he crawls toward and smells a flower. The visuals reveal the "living" man. A cannon shot recalls the recent harsh reality; Farquhar leaps to his feet and races toward safety through sparse countryside. A last cannon shot propels him; the director jump-cuts to a heavy woods while Farquhar's labored breathing fills the sound track. A drum and cymbal crescendo accompany distance shots as he races toward safety. His pace finally slows; ominous bird sounds are replaced by songbirds' sounds. As the sounds cease entirely, we realize that he is running *to*, not away from, something. With Farquhar, we see the plantation gates. When sound resumes, Enrico uses the "living man" theme.

Farquhar sees his wife and home; she moves toward him in slow motion. Because slow motion often connotes "dream," the escape suddenly becomes ambiguous. A "reunion" looms but audience apprehension mounts, too. Is Farquhar's escape *real*? Reluctantly, the audience recalls the earlier slow motion sequence. Farquhar races toward his wife; she approaches him, still in slow motion. His action carries him out of the dense black woods to a landscape of trees flecked with white leaves. He calls her name; as he nears her, the director slows her approach to a near freeze. She raises her arms lovingly to embrace him. Her fingers touch his neck, the very spot where the noose had been. A sinister musical track, a shriek, and a visual jump-cut to Farquhar hanging from the beams of Owl Creek Bridge coalesce.

While Bierce concludes his story on this note of horror, Enrico's film does *not* cease with the melodramatic leap from "dream" to reality. The viewer sees the hanging body of Peyton Farquhar for about fifteen interminably long seconds while the camera slowly backs away to enlarge the field of vision. We see the immobile soldiers and the whole of Owl Creek Bridge. The file of soldiers moves off in military cadence, ignoring the dangling corpse. As the soldiers move off screen, we continue to hear the ritual cadence until it fades away. The camera pans to trees and stream as human voices cease. The screen credits are paralleled by the sound track, which picks up the musical sound of songbirds counterpointed against the stark freeze of Farquhar's body hanging motionless as the film ends.

Enrico's adaptation emphasizes man's inhumanity to man as well as the naturalistic indifference in nature to human catastrophe. Bierce's sardonic view of man yields to an emphasis on plot and the shock of horrifying action. His exposition is dropped by the director, whose single poster close-up visually conveys the information. A superb sound track enriched by visual shots permits the director to use virtually no speech while communicating the experience of horror to his audience. Where Bierce employed an omniscient author technique to communicate Farquhar's thoughts and feelings, Enrico uses the resources of the film medium (angle shots, symbolic details, sound, jump-cuts, slow motion, and close-ups) to render the experiences of Peyton Farquhar. Like the story, the film expands real time. The jump-cut from love (the wife's embrace) to death (Farquhar's hanging body) emphasizes the irony as well as maintaining the element of shock. In fact, the concrete image of her fingers tenderly touching the exact place where the noose had been is an invention of the director, and stems from film's necessity to be concrete. An embrace is abstract; the details of an embrace are necessarily more specific

The symbolic use of bird sounds enhances the film. Sound and picture, emotion and narrative, coexist. Bierce is forced by the nature of his medium to narrate or describe. The linearity of words in sequence does not permit coexistence.

By using his medium so effectively, Enrico endows his film with universality. Even the film title, unchanged from the original story title, assists. The tonal quality of "an occurrence" suggests the merely trivial. In the director's structure, the "occurrence" is not framed as it is in the story. Details both precede and succeed Bierce's opening and closing lines. The added details underscore the ritualistic behavior toward Farquhar and minimize his human significance. The trivializing of death suggests contemporary events only too clearly. Thus, the late nineteenth-century story becomes highly relevant to our time and place.

DISTRIBUTORS
OF 16mm FILMS

Names and addresses of some major distributors of 16mm films. Many of these companies have catalogs available. [Addresses are current as of November, 1970.]

Audio Film Center/Ideal Pictures
    34 MacQuesten Parkway S., Mt. Vernon, NY 10550
    406 Clement St., San Francisco, CA 94118
    1619 N. Cherokee Ave., Los Angeles, CA 90028
    512 Burlington Ave., La Grange, IL 60525
    8615 Directors Row, Dallas, TX 75247
AVCO Embassy Pictures
    1301 Ave. of the Americas, New York, NY 10019
Brandon Films, Inc./Western Cinema Guild, Inc./Film Center, Inc.
    Dept AV, 221 W. 57 St., New York, NY 10019
    406 Clement St., San Francisco, CA 95118
    20 E. Huron St., Chicago, IL 60611
Carousel Films, Inc.
    1501 Broadway, New York, NY 10036
Cinema 16
    Grove Press, Inc., Film Division, 80 University Place, New York, NY 10003
Columbia Cinemathèque
    711 Fifth Ave., New York, NY 10022

Contemporary Films/McGraw-Hill
  330 W. 42 St., New York, NY 10036
  828 Custer Ave., Evanston, IL 60202
  1714 Stockton St., San Francisco, CA 94133
Continental 16
  241 E. 34 St., New York, NY 10016
Creative Film Society
  14558 Valerio St., Van Nuys, CA 91405
Embassy Films
  1301 Avenue of the Americas, New York, NY 10019
Film Classics Exchange
  1926 S. Vermont Ave., Los Angeles, CA 90007
Films, Incorporated
  Main office: 1144 Wilmette Ave., Wilmette, IL 60091
  Local offices: 5625 Hollywood Blvd., Hollywood, CA 90028
  Kerr Film Exchange, 3034 Canon St., San Diego, CA 92106
  2494 Tea Garden St., San Leandro, CA 94577
  277 Pharr Rd. N. E., Atlanta, GA 30305
  4420 Oakton St., Skokie, IL 60076
  161 Massachusetts Ave., Boston MA 02115
  38 W. 32 St. New York, NY 10001
  2129 N.E. Broadway, Portland, OR 97232
  1414 Dragon St., Dallas TX 75207
  Deseret Book Co.—Film Division, 44 E. South Temple, Salt Lake
  City, UT 84110
International Film Bureau Inc.
  332 S. Michigan Ave., Chicago, IL 60604
Janus Films
  745 Fifth Ave., New York, NY 10022
Modern Sound Pictures
  1410 Howard St., Omaha, NB 68102
Museum of Modern Art Film Circulating Programs
  11 W. 53 St., New York, NY 10019
Royal 16 Films International
  711 Fifth Ave., New York, NY 10022
Sterling Educational Films
  241 E. 34 St., New York, NY 10022
Swank Motion Pictures, Inc.
  201 S. Jefferson Ave., St. Louis, MO 63166
  1257 Russ Building, 235 Montgomery St., San Francisco, CA 94104
Teaching Film Custodians, Inc., 25 W. 43 St., New York, NY 10036
Trans-World Films
  332 S. Michigan Ave., Chicago, IL 60604

Twyman Films, Inc.
329 Salem Ave., Dayton, OH 45401
United World Films, Inc.
221 Park Ave. S., New York, NY 10003
1025 N. Highland Ave., Los Angeles, CA 90038
287 Techwood Dr., Atlanta, GA 30313
425 N. Michigan Ave., Chicago, IL 60611
5023 Sandy Blvd., Portland, OR 97213
6434 Maple Ave., Dallas, TX 75235
United Artists 16
729 Seventh Ave., New York, NY 10036
Universal 16
221 Park Ave. S., New York, NY 10003
1025 N. Highland Ave., Los Angeles, CA 90038
205 Walton St. N.W., Atlanta, GA 30303
425 N. Michigan Ave., Chicago IL 60611
5023 Sandy Blvd., Portland, OR 97213
810 S. St. Paul St., Dallas, TX 75201
Walter Reade 16
241 E. 34 St., New York, NY 10016
Warner Bros. Inc.
Non-Theatrical Division
666 Fifth Ave., New York, NY 10019

B

SOURCES FOR FILMS MENTIONED IN TEXT

A selective list of films referred to in the text and the sources from which 16mm prints can be obtained. Films treated in detail in the text are in **boldface.**

All Quiet on the Western Front (United World, Contemporary)
All the King's Men (Audio, Brandon, Contemporary, Trans-World, Twyman)
The Birth of a Nation (Audio)
Becket (Films, Inc.)
Blow-up (Films, Inc.)
Bonnie and Clyde (Warner Bros., Non-Theatrical Division)
The Bridge on the River Kwai (Audio, Brandon, Modern Sound, Trans-World, Twyman)
Catch-22 (not yet available in 16mm)
Citizen Kane (Brandon, Contemporary, Modern Sound, Trans-World)
Death of a Salesman (Brandon, Contemporary, Modern Sound, Trans-World)
$8\frac{1}{2}$ (Audio)
The Fallen Idol (Continental 16)
The Graduate (AVCO)
The Grapes of Wrath (Brandon, Contemporary, Films, Inc.)

Great Expectations (United World)
Hamlet (Olivier's 1948 version) (Twyman)
Henry V (Contemporary, United World)
High Noon (Brandon, Contemporary, Audio, Modern Sound, Trans-
    World, Twyman)
Hiroshima, Mon Amour (Audio)
Hud (Films, Inc.)
The Hustler (Brandon, Films, Inc.)
Ikiru (Brandon)
The Informer (Brandon, Contemporary, Films, Inc)
Julius Caesar (1953 MGM version) (Films, Inc)
A Kind of Loving (Audio)
La Dolce Vita (Audio)
Last Year at Marienbad (Audio)
L'Avventura (Janus)
A Long Day's Journey Into Night (AVCO Embassy, Audio)
The Loneliness of the Long Distance Runner (Continental 16)
Lord of the Flies (Continental 16)
The Maltese Falcon (Brandon, Contemporary, Films, Inc., Trans-World)
A Man for All Seasons (Columbia Cinemathéque)
Midnight Cowboy (not yet available in 16mm)
An Occurrence at Owl Creek Bridge (Contemporary)
Odd Man Out (Contemporary, United World)
Oliver! (not yet available in 16mm)
A Place in the Sun (Films, Inc.)
Potemkin (Brandon, Museum of Modern Art)
Pygmalion (a 45-minute version of this film is available from Teaching
    Film Custodians, Inc.)
Rashomon (Janus)
Romeo and Juliet (The Zeffirelli version is not yet available in 16mm)
Room at the Top (Continental 16)
Rosemary's Baby (Films, Inc)
The Seventh Seal (Janus)
This Sporting Life (Contemporary, United World)
Tom Jones (United Artists 16)
A View From the Bridge (Continental 16)
The Virgin Spring (Janus)
Viridiana (Audio)
Wild Strawberries (Janus)
Zorba the Greek (Films, Inc.)

APPENDIX

C

NOTABLE NOVELS, STORIES, AND PLAYS ON FILM

A selected list of notable novels, stories, and plays that have been adapted for the screen. Where titles differ, the film title is given in parentheses.

NOVELS AND SHORT STORIES

Author
  Title
    Film Director

Akutagawa, Ryunosuke
  Rashomon and In a Grove (Rashomon)
    Akira Kurosawa (1950)
Austen, Jane
  Pride and Prejudice
    Robert Z. Leonard (1940)
Braine, John
  Room at the Top
    Jack Clayton (1959)
Brontë, Emily
  Wuthering Heights
    William Wyler (1939)

Author
　　Title
　　　　Film Director

Cervantes, Miguel de
　　Don Quixote
　　　　Gregori Kozentsev (1957)
Clark, Walter Van Tilburg
　　The Ox-Bow Incident
　　　　William Wellman (1943)
Conrad, Joseph
　　The Secret Agent (Sabotage)
　　　　Alfred Hitchcock (1936)
　　Lord Jim
　　　　Richard Brooks (1965)
Crane, Stephen
　　The Red Badge of Courage
　　　　John Huston (1951)
Defoe, Daniel
　　Robinson Crusoe
　　　　Luis Buñuel (1953)
Dickens, Charles
　　David Copperfield
　　　　George Cukor (1935)
　　Great Expectations
　　　　David Lean (1947)
　　The Pickwick Papers
　　　　Noel Langley (1952)
Dostoievsky, Feodor
　　The Brothers Karamazov
　　　　Richard Brooks (1958)
　　The Idiot
　　　　Georges Lampin (1946)
Dreiser, Theodore
　　An American Tragedy
　　　　Josef von Sternberg (1931)
　　(A Place in the Sun)
　　　　George Stevens (1951)
Faulkner, William
　　Intruder in the Dust
　　　　Clarence Brown (1949)
Gorky, Maxim
　　Mother
　　　　V. I. Pudovkin (1926)

Author
   Title
      Film Director

Greene, Graham
   The Basement Room (The Fallen Idol)
      Carol Reed (1948)
Hawthorne, Nathaniel
   The Scarlet Letter
      Victor Sjostrom (1926)
James, Henry
   The Turn of the Screw (The Innocents)
      Jack Clayton (1961)
   Washington Square (The Heiress)
      William Wyler (1949)
Joyce, James
   Ulysses
      Joseph Strick (1967)
Kazantzakis, Nikos
   Zorba the Greek
      Michael Cacoyannis (1964)
Lawrence, D. H.
   Sons and Lovers
      Jack Cardiff (1960)
   The Virgin and the Gypsy
      Christopher Miles (1970)
Lee, Harper
   To Kill a Mockingbird
      Robert Mulligan (1962)
McCullers, Carson
   The Heart is a Lonely Hunter
      Robert Ellis Miller (1969)
   The Member of the Wedding
      Fred Zinnemann (1953)
Melville, Herman
   Moby Dick
      John Huston (1956)
   Billy Budd
      Peter Ustinov (1962)
Moravia, Alberto
   The Conformist
      Bernardo Bertolucci (1970)

Author
   Title
      Film Director

Norris, Frank
   McTeague (Greed)
      Erich von Stroheim (1923)
O'Flaherty, Liam
   The Informer
      John Ford (1935)
Pasternak, Boris
   Doctor Zhivago
      David Lean (1965)
Remarque, Erich Maria
   All Quiet on the Western Front
      Lewis Milestone (1930)
Roth, Philip
   Goodbye, Columbus
      Larry Peerce (1969)
Sillitoe, Alan
   Saturday Night and Sunday Morning
      Karel Reisz (1960)
Stendahl, Henri
   The Red and the Black
      Claude Autant-Lara (1954)
Vassilikos, Vassilis
   Z
      Costa-Gavras (1969)
Warren, Robert Penn
   All the King's Men
      Robert Rossen (1949)

PLAYS AND TELEVISION DRAMAS

Albee, Edward
   Who's Afraid of Virginia Woolf?
      Mike Nichols (1966)
Anouilh, Jean
   Becket
      Peter Glenville (1964)

Author
    Title
        Film Director

Bolt, Robert
    A Man for All Seasons
        Fred Zinnemann (1966)
Chayefsky, Paddy
    Marty
        Delbert Mann (1955)
Delaney, Shelagh
    A Taste of Honey
        Tony Richardson (1962)
Gorky, Maxim
    The Lower Depths
        Jean Renoir (1936)
        Akira Kurosawa (1958)
Hansberry, Lorraine
    A Raisin in the Sun
        Daniel Petrie (1961)
Hellman, Lillian
    The Little Foxes
        William Wyler (1941)
Miller, Arthur
    Death of a Salesman
        Laslo Benedek (1951)
O'Casey, Sean
    Juno and the Paycock
        Alfred Hitchcock (1930)
O'Neill, Eugene
    The Long Voyage Home
        John Ford (1940)
Osborne, John
    Look Back in Anger
        Tony Richardson (1959)
Pinter, Harold
    The Caretaker
        Clive Donner (1963)
Rose, Reginald
    Twelve Angry Men
        Sidney Lumet (1957)

Author
> Title
>> Film Director

Shakespeare, William
> *Hamlet*
>> Laurence Olivier (1948)
>> Gregori Kozentzev (1963)
> *Henry V*
>> Laurence Olivier (1944)
> *Julius Caesar*
>> Joseph Mankiewicz (1953)
> *Macbeth (Throne of Blood)*
>> Akira Kurosawa (1957)
> *Othello*
>> Orson Welles (1953)

Shaw, George Bernard
> *Caesar and Cleopatra*
>> Gabriel Pascal (1945)
> *Major Barbara*
>> Gabriel Pascal (1941)

Strindberg, August
> *Miss Julie*
>> Alf Sjoberg (1951)

Wilde, Oscar
> *The Importance of Being Earnest*
>> Anthony Asquith (1952)

Williams, Tennessee
> *A Streetcar Named Desire*
>> Elia Kazan (1951)